LOOK ROUND FOR POETRY

Sara Guyer and Brian McGrath, series editors

Lit Z embraces models of criticism uncontained by
conventional notions of history, periodicity, and culture,
and committed to the work of reading. Books in the series
may seem untimely, anachronistic, or out of touch with
contemporary trends because they have arrived too early or too
late. Lit Z creates a space for books that exceed and challenge
the tendencies of our field and in doing so reflect on the
concerns of literary studies here and abroad.

At least since Friedrich Schlegel, thinking that affirms
literature's own untimeliness has been named romanticism.
Recalling this history, Lit Z exemplifies the survival of
romanticism as a mode of contemporary criticism, as well
as forms of contemporary criticism that demonstrate the
unfulfilled possibilities of romanticism. Whether or not they
focus on the romantic period, books in this series epitomize
romanticism as a way of thinking that compels another relation
to the present. Lit Z is the first book series to take seriously this
capacious sense of romanticism.

In 1977, Paul de Man and Geoffrey Hartman, two scholars
of romanticism, team-taught a course called Literature Z that
aimed to make an intervention into the fundamentals of literary
study. Hartman and de Man invited students to read a series of
increasingly difficult texts and through attention to language
and rhetoric compelled them to encounter "the bewildering
variety of ways such texts could be read." The series'
conceptual resonances with that class register the importance
of recollection, reinvention, and reading to contemporary
criticism. Its books explore the creative potential of reading's
untimeliness and history's enigmatic force.

LOOK ROUND FOR POETRY

Untimely Romanticisms

Brian McGrath

Fordham University Press

New York   2022

Fordham University Press gratefully acknowledges financial assistance and support provided for the publication of this book by Clemson University.

Cover art:

Elizabeth King, *Animation Study: Pose 7*, 2005, Chromogenic Print, 20 × 20 inches

Sculpture: Elizabeth King, *Pupil*, 1987–90; porcelain, glass eyes, carved wood, brass; half life-size, all joints movable; Collection of the Hirshhorn Museum and Sculpture Garden, Washington, D.C.

Pose and composition: Elizabeth King

Lighting and camera: Eric Beggs

Master printer: Lauren Kylie Wright

Fordham University Press has no responsibility for the persistence or accuracy of URLs for external or third-party Internet websites referred to in this publication and does not guarantee that any content on such websites is, or will remain, accurate or appropriate.

Fordham University Press also publishes its books in a variety of electronic formats. Some content that appears in print may not be available in electronic books.

Visit us online at www.fordhampress.com.

Library of Congress Cataloging-in-Publication Data available online at https://catalog .loc.gov.

Printed in the United States of America

24 23 22   5 4 3 2 1

First edition

Contents

LOOK ROUND FOR POETRY

Introduction

They will look round for poetry, and will be induced to
enquire . . .
    —William Wordsworth, advertisement to *Lyrical Ballads* (1798)

The longer I linger with the grammatical and rhetorical structures that give a poem shape the more I feel I see these same structures around me. Linguists and psychologists have various terms for this experience (or condition), as selective attention leads to confirmation bias: when one learns something new or studies something for a while, one tends to see it more often and even all around one. The idea that one who studies poetry might see poetry all around may surprise few, but in *Look Round for Poetry* I take this experience as a charge. I place in apposition select poems and various tropes and figures common in economic, technological, and political discourse and celebrate poetry's capacity to make the rhetoric of contemporary life differently legible.

This book started to emerge as various social media platforms, such as Facebook and Twitter, became increasingly ubiquitous. At the time I was leading a Theory colloquium for students in a PhD program called Rhetorics, Communication, and Information Design, during which we read a range of texts, from Aristotle to Wendy Hui Kyong Chun. The students were well prepared to think about rhetoric and interested in contemporary media and contemporary media theory. They were, generally speaking, less interested in poetry, but not because they disliked it. To many of them poetry just did not seem to fit the program's description. But the more we discussed the rhetoric of contemporary media, the more it felt, to me at least, like we were talking about poetry. As I only half-joked during one meeting, to me both Twitter and Facebook operationalize poetry for profit and so owe much to poetry. By happy chance, the *Oxford English Dictionary* (*OED*) offers Geoffrey Chaucer, author of *The Canterbury Tales*, as the originator of the word *twitter* around 1380, used as a verb meaning to give a call consisting of repeated light tremulous sounds. Twitter owes at least its name to poetry. But extending this argument a little, one might say that Twitter realizes, or at least works to allow users to realize, a long-standing and relatively common poetic dream. To participate in Twitter, to tweet, is to imagine oneself a bird; and as many introductory poetry textbooks show, poets often write about birds, imagine themselves as birds, ask readers to imagine themselves as birds. The topic is an old one, but one put to dramatic purpose when one dominant form of human communication in the twenty-first century subtly (or not so subtly) blurs the line between human and nonhuman tweets. This argument was only almost persuasive in the colloquium, among students trained in the available arts of persuasion; so I tried another example. Facebook's name has a literal referent, a book of faces, but it also recalls a dominant poetic trope, *prosopopoeia*, by which a poet grants a face (and so the possibility of voice) to a nonhuman entity or inanimate object. When the poet-speaker is a corpse or a cloud, the poet gives voice and life to the voiceless and lifeless. And while this trope might appear only every so often and only in select poems, especially elegies, the rhetorical structure has been immensely important to the study of poetry, especially when authors of poetry textbooks discuss and celebrate the poet's so-called voice.[1] To learn to read a poem well is to learn to hear the poet's voice. The poet's voice "lives" in the poem. Readers are taught to grant the poem a face so that it might speak, so that they might hear it.

But these common rhetorical tropes that determine the study of poetry, of "lyric," perhaps especially, also determine reading more generally. As Barbara Johnson explains in *Persons and Things*: poetry "convinces the reader that the poet speaks, that the poem gives access to his living voice—even though the individual author may have been buried for more than two hundred years. This is the immortality of literature brought about by reading—to bring alive the voice of the dead author. A text 'speaks.'"[2] For Johnson, one reads as a poet when one attempts to make the dead speak. One grants a book a face so that it might speak all the more powerfully. Facebook extends this rhetorical situation even to users who find poetry irrelevant to contemporary society, by recalling the trope of the speaking book. The name Facebook might lead one to ask: what is it about imagining faces that makes communication (and perhaps even affection) possible? Not by chance does Yohei Igarashi suggest in *The Connected Condition* that dreams of communication realized by advances in technology today begin with romanticism, with Romantic poetry.[3]

Even as poetry has seemed to become increasingly less important, the rhetorical and grammatical structures that give it shape have come to dominate many modes of communication, even though one might not think of them as "poetic." There is, I suggested to students in the colloquium, something deeply "lyrical" about Facebook and Twitter. Everywhere I look—especially as social media companies assert their presence in the culture and society of the United States—I see poems, or things that seem poetic by virtue of familiar, even commonly shared, tropes and figures.

If some of the thinking for this book began with that colloquium, the book has been finished as several important writers published counter-intuitive defenses of poetry, like Ben Lerner's *The Hatred of Poetry* and Stephanie Burt's *Don't Read Poetry*. *Look Round for Poetry* is likewise a defense, but like these recent titles also a perhaps counter-intuitive one. Burt begins: "I am here to say that anyone who tells you that they know how to read poetry, or what poetry really is, or what it is good for, or why you should read it, in general, is already getting it wrong."[4] Because *poetry*, the word, has many overlapping meanings, Burt suggests "don't read poetry"—don't assume *poetry* means only one thing. Don't read poetry. Read poems. To the extent to which *Look Round for Poetry* is a defense of poetry, it is a defense of poetic attention that emerges from encounters with specific poems.[5] My basic premise is relatively simple: in looking round for poetry one might discover the grammatical and rhetorical structures that give particular poems shape in sometimes surprising contexts. The chance for such discoveries is possible in part because the grammatical and rhetorical structures that give poems shape are not dissimilar from those that give shape to other sorts of objects, especially as one recognizes the ways other sorts of objects are likewise "made." In "Against National Poetry Month as Such," Charles Bernstein suggests that instead of celebrating poetry one month out of the year, we should try eliminating poetry for a month. In place of National Poetry Month, Bernstein offers International Anti-Poetry Month: "all verse in public places will be covered over.... Parents will be asked not to read Mother Goose.... Religious institutions will have to forgo reading verse passages from the liturgy.... *Cats* will be closed for the month by order of the Anti-Poetry Commission.... No vocal music will be played on the radio or TV.... Children will have to stop playing all slapping and counting and singing games and stick to board games and football."[6] As a result of poetry's absence, the public might be better prepared to celebrate all the various ways poetry challenges our received ideas of poetry and even the various ways poetry shapes and supports life. Instead of celebrating a particular idea of poetry, we might come to know poetry differently through its absence. Its absence might show us just how present it is.

My argument adopts a similar line, a line similar as well to the one Jonathan Culler charts in *The Literary in Theory*. Responding to various arguments over the "death" of theory, Culler suggests that theory is not dead; theory has, instead, become pervasive in literary study. The assumptions that governed theory, or what goes by the name Theory, as Theory emerged in the United States over the course of the twentieth century, have become foundational. "If theory is not so prominent as a vanguard movement, a set of texts or discourses that challenge insiders and outsiders," writes Culler in the first years of the twenty-first century, "it is perhaps because literary and cultural studies take place within a space articulated by theory, or theories, theoretical discourses, theoretical debates. . . . We are ineluctably in theory."[7] What has changed, argues Culler, is that theory is no longer literary. As theory became ubiquitous in literary and cultural studies, the importance of literature to theory was minimized. In *Look Round for Poetry* and in an attempt to prioritize attention to the literary, I begin by asking: despite arguments that discount the importance of poetry, if one looks round for it might one find it doing some sometimes surprising work all around one?

Let me tell a different but related origin story. This book would be very different without Barbara Johnson's *Persons and Things*. There, Johnson discovers the rhetorical figures that confer on things some properties of persons across a dynamic range of texts, from canonical poetry to pop culture, from advertisements to legal cases. One passage from "Toys R Us," the book's opening chapter, found its way into many early drafts of chapters from *Look Round for Poetry*. The passage is about Barbie Dolls, but Johnson's argument extends beyond Barbie to modern advertising, as she explores the frequent appearance in commercials of inanimate or inhuman entities that speak directly to consumers, selling themselves as products through the power of a literary trope, prosopopoeia, that same trope that gives shape to, that structures, *reading*. Johnson offers as one example of prosopopoeia a Barbie Doll box that proclaims "I say 100,000 different things! Try me!" When one presses the pink button at the back of the doll, which one can do even when the doll is still in the packaging, the doll chirps: "We should get a pizza after the game this weekend with Midge!" Here is the passage from "Toys R Us" from which *Look Round for Poetry* might be said to originate:

A speaking thing can sell itself: if the purchaser responds to the speech of the object, he or she feels uninfluenced by human manipulation and therefore somehow not duped. We are supposed not to notice how absurd it is to be addressed by the Maalox Max bottle, or Mr. Clean, or Mrs. Butterworth, or the Quaker Oats man, or Aunt Jemima, or the Elidel man, or the Aflac duck. . . . It is as though the relation between buyer and commodity were the entrance to a relationship—*res ipsa loquitar*. The beauties of the product are spoken about by that product, or by the animation and articulateness of a cat, a duck, a cow, a nose, a set of dentures. In one particularly daring use of prosopopoeia, talking weeds in a television ad express the pathos of being sprayed by weed killer as they die. It is not necessary that the speaking thing be the product itself: those that the product gets the better of are objects of identification too. The Juggernaut-like strength of the product is all the more believable if you are made to identify with its victims. . . . Alternatively the container or trademark person speaks for the commodity. Animation and voice give consumers a psychology and a humanness to identify with when buying heartburn remedies, cleaning fluids, pesticides, health drinks. It is as though the purchaser is seduced into feeling that buying the product is, in fact, carrying out the wishes of the product itself.[8]

Like much of Johnson's writing, this passage encapsulates for me the difference literature can make, especially a reading sensitive to the ways tropes and figures, grammatical and rhetorical structures, shape discourse, and, beyond discourse, whatever one might mean by the "world." Paying attention to the ways modern advertisers have embraced animating tropes common to the history of poetry, Johnson shows not only how present prosopopoeia has become but also how one might think differently about advertising, and by extension, modern capitalism, when one recognizes familiar poetic tropes in possibly unfamiliar contexts. The term I most want to use here is style: Johnson encapsulates a certain literary style of thinking. And given the importance of animating tropes such as prosopopoeia (but also apostrophe, personification, and anthropomorphism) to conceptualizations of poetry, maybe especially lyric poetry, I am tempted then to suggest that Johnson epitomizes a certain poetic style of thinking. If *Look Round for Poetry* is a defense of poetry, it is also, in its own way, a celebration of this style. In a late chapter from *Persons and Things*, "Anthropomorphism in Lyric and Law," Johnson asks about relations between the laws of genre, like those that define lyric, and the laws of the state and explores the question through a juxtaposition, placing together two sonnets and a legal case that put in play just what a "natural" or "literal" person might be. Many chapters of *Look Round for Poetry* attempt a similar juxtaposition, moving between literary and economic, technological, and political texts. My interest is less in how poets might have anticipated contemporary predicaments than in how individual poems may make possible a renewed critical vocabulary. When one looks round for poetry one might discover allusions to the contemporary rhetoric of economic downturns in William Wordsworth's frequent use of human figures with heads turned down toward the ground, which I discuss in chapter 2. When one looks round for poetry Apple's iCloud can seem an abbreviation of the first line of Wordsworth's "I wandered lonely as a cloud," which I discuss in chapter 3. Voters' frequent election of the dead (a not-uncommon occurrence in contemporary electoral politics) can itself recall familiar poetic acts, as lyric poets frequently throw their voice to the dead and thereby grant them new life, which I discuss in chapter 4, and with specific reference to a poem by Lucille Clifton. That poetry is all around us is a trite truism this book aims to exploit and, I hope, challenge. One can perhaps never be sure where the separation might lie.

"Its Materials Are to Be Found in Every Subject"

I lift my title from Wordsworth's advertisement to *Lyrical Ballads*, published anonymously in 1798. Arguing that poets find inspiration in a wider range of subjects than critics sometimes acknowledge or accept, Wordsworth begins the advertisement stating that the materials of poetry are "to be found in every subject which can interest the human mind."[9] In general Wordsworth means to defend his choices, as he offers experiments that challenge prevailing ideas of poetry, in both style and subject matter. But, and as my opening comments above suggest, I take Wordsworth to mean as well (or, reducing the pressure on Wordsworth's intentions, I discover in Wordsworth's language) that in every subject of interest to the human mind one finds poetic materials, the materials of poetry: one finds poetry. Not only can one take inspiration from a range of subjects: these subjects are already in some way made of poetic materials. Poetry's materials are *in* every subject. And it is with this subtle twist of Wordsworth's opening statement that I read the paragraph that follows in the Advertisement, as Wordsworth worries that readers, upon perusing *Lyrical Ballads*, will struggle with feelings of strangeness and awkwardness. They will look round for poetry:

> The majority of the following poems are to be considered as experiments. They were written chiefly with a view to ascertain how far the language of conversation in the middle and lower classes of society is adapted to the purposes of poetic pleasure. Readers accustomed to the gaudiness and inane phraseology of many modern writers, if they persist in reading this book to its conclusion, will perhaps frequently have to struggle with feelings of strangeness and awkwardness: they will look round for poetry, and will be induced to enquire by what species of courtesy these attempts can be permitted to assume that title.[10]

Wordsworth anticipates that readers accustomed to poetic norms of the day may, upon reading the book, "look round for poetry" because what they find there may not strike them at first, if ever at all, as poetry. He imagines a reader paging through the book in search of something that may not be there and hopes that *Lyrical Ballads* will provoke readers to question prevailing poetic norms. For Wordsworth, "looking round" is a sign of readerly dissatisfaction, as readers search elsewhere for poetry. But in taking Wordsworth's phrase as this book's title I transform Wordsworth's idiomatic expression into a charge, turning "look round for poetry" into a slogan and perhaps even a method: Look Round for Poetry![11] By placing tropes and figures, grammatical and rhetorical structures common to poems, especially those poems we sometimes label *Romantic*, even *lyric*, in conjunction with contemporary discourse, the chapters that follow open up both Romantic poems and contemporary discourse to the surprise of experiment. When taken as a charge, "look round for poetry" provokes readers to discover poetry's echoes in discourses not always read as poetry or not always read poetically. My point, following Wordsworth's language in the advertisement, is that poetry's materials are to be found in every subject if one, or when one, looks round for poetry. Poetry may be poetry even when it does not appear as such, and once one starts looking round for poetry one might discover it otherwise than one expected. Poets have perhaps always known that if poetry is to retain a vital, subversive power, one must become ignorant of what one thinks one means by the term (again and again); such may be one way to paraphrase Wordsworth's point. But here, "looking round" is not only a potential sign of readerly dissatisfaction with what is given (as when one reads something that one does not consider a poem and looks away from it) but also an opening to read what's around one as if it were a poem, as if poetically.

I borrow my title from Wordsworth but the phrase may also recall the title of Rei Terada's recent *Looking Away: Phenomenality and Dissatisfaction, Kant to Adorno*, in which Terada explores the relationship between feelings of dissatisfaction and acceptance of the world "as is" and discovers in Romantic texts, including the writing of Samuel Taylor Coleridge, the right to desire something else, something other, however fleeting and ephemeral.[12] Terada draws her title from Friedrich Nietzsche's *The Gay Science*, "Looking away shall be my only negation," which also forms her book's epigraph, where looking away is a sign neither of acceptance nor negation. For Terada, the one who looks away dwells with what remains at the margins of phenomenality. Similarly for me, looking round offers a chance to dwell with what might become differently legible, where looking and reading are not in any simple way opposed activities. Though Wordsworth uses the phrase "look round for poetry" in the advertisement to anticipate readerly dissatisfaction, he uses related phrases to name modes of lingering encounter that make slight, if any, demands. Elsewhere in Wordsworth's writing, *look round* is a multi-word verb, as is the case in the advertisement; at other times *round* functions as a preposition, as is the case in his "Ode": "The Moon doth with delight / Look round her when the heavens are bare."[13] But if "look round" signals dissatisfaction in the advertisement, in "Expostulation and Reply" it signals a manner of aesthetic, almost purposeless, relation. William, the speaker of "Expostulation and Reply," recalls how his good friend Matthew upbraided him, "You look round on your mother earth, / As if she for no purpose bore you," and turns Matthew's criticism into a mode of being, of looking, that is not purpose driven through-and-through.[14]

The poems one reads often challenge the ideas one brings to bear on them. Recently, scholars have lamented the rise to prominence of too narrow a concept of poetry after romanticism, one that collapses all poetry into lyric and makes lyric synonymous with poetry in general; this collapse, argue Virginia Jackson and Yopie Prins, impoverishes the experience of poetry in all its various forms and guises.[15] Jackson and Prins assert that we must historicize the conflation of poetry and lyric and that doing so will make the idea of poetry we have inherited from twentieth-century Anglo-American criticism less stable, and this effort, in turn, will allow us to imagine other ideas *of* poetry and other possibilities *for* poetry. Romanticism plays an integral role in this story, as Mary Poovey explains, for twentieth-century Anglo-American literary criticism organized itself around an idea of the Romantic lyric that became so powerful that it eclipsed other poetic forms, even forms poets of the period explicitly referred to in their titles (like "ode" and "sonnet").[16] In other words, one irony surrounding the critical reception of romanticism is that romanticism was used to promote an idea of poetry as lyric that Romantic poems more often than not question, if not directly challenge. Put too simply: Wordsworth does not offer a defense of the lyric as a privileged genre in the advertisement, and he does not offer poems that fit generic expectations in *Lyrical Ballads*. He offers the opposite: experiments that challenge generic expectations. On the one hand, then, the rise of the lyric is strongly associated with romanticism, with poems we commonly refer to as Romantic and with the critical and scholarly reception of these same poems, especially as literary criticism puts romanticism to work in the twentieth century. On the other hand, though, romanticism names a set of aesthetic practices and procedures that throw into question just what a poem is. Repeatedly, and in a structure that shows no sign of giving way any time soon, romanticism is both ideology and critique.

As Wordsworth mentions of *Lyrical Ballads*, the majority of the chapters in *Look Round for Poetry* are to be considered experiments.[17] Amusingly, Wordsworth does not say that all poems in *Lyrical Ballads* are to be considered experiments, leaving open which are experiments and which not. But in suggesting that the majority are to be considered thusly Wordsworth subtly shifts attention away from what the poems are to how they should be read (more precisely, how they should be considered). In drawing my method from Wordsworth's language, I consider reading an experiment in considering. The etymology of *consider* offered by editors of the *OED* is surprisingly speculative, as editors suggest that *consider* was, according to Festus, derived from "to observe the stars," from *sidus* (genitive *sideris*) "constellation": "The verb might thus," offers the *OED*, "be originally a term of astrology or augury, but such a use is not known in the Latin writers." The *OED* does not always allow itself such speculative fictions, but this one offers an opening. If we linger with Festus's imaginative etymology, then *to consider* means, in some way, "to observe the stars, to constellate."[18] This etymology extends my method: to look round for poetry is to consider it a constellation, to consider it as if in constellation. Challenging preestablished codes of decision, poetry need not name the thing encountered so much as the manner in which that something is encountered. Through the power of metalepsis Wordsworth reverses cause and effect: how one reads produces the thing one reads. One does not read poetry, one reads poetically; one does not read experiments, one reads experimentally. One experiments with considering poems as experiments. In this way my book is decidedly Wordsworthian and, indeed, the first three chapters take individual Wordsworth poems as points of departure. The majority of the chapters offer a test of experience, the experience of reading among poems, of reading the world as if it were a poem, of reading poetically by paying attention to the ways tropes and figures determine our reading as well as our experience of contemporary social life.

But more specifically, Wordsworth suggests that his poems are to be considered "as" experiments and so doubles-down on this figurative potential. Not wishing to evade the intricacies of *as*, to borrow a line from Wallace Stevens, Wordsworth does not consider his poems experiments (or simply experiments). He considers them *as* experiments, an analogy that is only sort of an analogy. The poems are to be considered *like* experiments, experiments of a sort.[19] It is as if the power of trope and figure were what Wordsworth were advertising, as trope and figure name the capacity of language to signify otherwise. What one reads in *Lyrical Ballads* are experiments in considering poems as (as if) experiments. I follow something of this method as I place into constellation various occurrences of specific grammatical and rhetorical structures. Reading is an experiment in considering, an experiment in constellating, as my fourth chapter, "On the Poetry of Posthumous Election," juxtaposes, or places into constellation, tropes common to Romantic lyric poetry and the election of the dead to public office in contemporary representative democracy.

In "Anthropomorphism in Lyric and Law," Johnson's preferred term is *jux-*

taposition, while Wordsworth moves us toward the not unrelated *constellation*. Placing different discourses beside or very near each other, looking round for poetry makes possible new rhetorical constellations. In describing her own method, one that depends on punctual conjuncture, Marjorie Levinson notes in *Thinking through Poetry* that "Like the concept of 'determination in the last instance,' 'conjuncture,' 'situation,' and 'constellation' (from Benjamin) are designed to ward off the kind of monocausal explanation sometimes associated with Marxist critique." The point of constellation, for Levinson, is not simply to explain the present by way of the past as if the relationship between past and present could be determined absolutely, but to encounter both past and present differently. Levinson quotes now famous lines from Walter Benjamin's *Arcades Project*: "It's not that what is past casts its light on what is present, or what is present its light on the past; rather, image is that wherein what has been comes together in a flash with the now to form a constellation."[20] In juxtaposing specific poetic tropes and figures and discourses not always read poetically, I try and bring the two momentarily together, reading poems as if among other sorts of poems. In my last chapter, "The Grammar of Romanticism: Shelley's Prepositions," I take Percy Bysshe Shelley's frequent use of the preposition *among* as an occasion to explore how parts of speech continue to inspire and challenge contemporary modes of assembly, and I use Shelley's poetic interrogation of prepositions to theorize assemblages as poems.

Romanticism Every Now and Again

In taking Wordsworth's "look round for poetry" as my title I foreground the importance of romanticism to the project, expanding the elasticity of a term like "poetry." As Maureen N. McLane summarizes in "Romanticism, or Now," "Romantic theorists strove to liberate poetry from a merely literary history and a merely literary criticism."[21] If the idea that when one looks round for poetry one sees poetry all around one is a Romantic idea, does this mean that when one looks round for poetry one sees romanticism all around one, over and over again? Is every now a Romantic now or is romanticism only every now and again? Indeed, a phrase like "every now and again" poses a methodological challenge central to this book. A literal reading of the phrase (one that puts great pressure on the word *every*) is undercut by the idiomatic understanding of the expression. If romanticism is *every* now and again then every now is romanticism, which makes of our present moment romanticism again. Like Wordsworth's egotistical sublime, romanticism is all that matters. As one looks round for poetry, one discovers not only the materials of poetry but also the continued persistence of romanticism, specifically the tropes and figures, the grammatical and rhetorical structures that give Romantic poems shape. One risks a presentism that downplays the differences between pasts and presents, as romanticism's untimeliness becomes all too timely, an extremely timely now. But if there is a strong claim about romanticism and its continued importance to contemporary discourse present in *Look Round for Poetry*, then the idiomatic understanding of a phrase like "romanticism every now and again" offers a counter, a different sort of untimeliness: an inconsequential romanticism or romanticism-as-inconsequential, a romanticism that embraces its own disappearing act. To look round for poetry is to discover romanticism every now and again: every now *and* never now. To look round for poetry is to discover something about the untimeliness of poetry.

Introducing their special issue of *New Literary History* titled "Romanticism, Now & Then," Bruce Holsinger and Andrew Stauffer set up a similar dynamic using a slightly different phrase and draw attention to the importance of Romantic texts to the development of historical analysis.[22] Holsinger and Stauffer frame the issue with attention to the ways Romanticist theory and criticism *now* works against the *then* of literary history. But as they note, citing the work of James Chandler, historicism finds its methodological posture and idiom, its "enabling framework," in the language of Romantic texts, in the discourse, for instance, of the "Spirit of the Age."[23] If the language of historicism, of literary historical periodization present in the "Spirit of the Age," is already Romantic, then romanticism names not one literary historical period among others but the very idea of literary historical periodization (constructed around a *now* and a *then*). "Romanticism resists being defined as a period or a set of qualities," writes Cynthia Chase, "that can be comfortably ascribed to others or assigned to the historical past."[24] Ted Underwood's *Why Literary Periods Mattered*—in which he outlines in broad conceptual terms the history of literary study—might productively be read as "What Was Romanticism For?"[25] If determining the difference between *now* and *then* enables historicist critical practice, and if this structure is already Romantic, then Romantic texts anticipate the critical practices meant to explain, or less dramatically, encounter, them. Reflecting on historicist arguments of the 1980s and 1990s that renounced romanticism as dehistoricizing, arguments that read Wordsworth as substituting Nature for history, Chandler suggests in *England in 1819* that "it is precisely by our work of situating Romantic writings historically that we share their blindness, their ideology. . . . Thus, our critical renunciations of Romanticism must be understood as a repetition of a certain kind."[26] Historicism, in other words, may not cure but perpetuate Romantic Ideology. The framework by which contemporary Romanticist criticism and theory understands itself *now* is already the result of "a certain kind" of Romantic work. Paul de Man makes a similar point in *The Rhetoric of Romanticism*, drawing out the interpretive dilemma with which Romantic poems confront readers. Because romanticism is our past, "we carry it within ourselves as the experience of an act in which, up to a certain point, we ourselves have participated."[27] Even if one does not include oneself in the "we" de Man imagines, when one turns to Romantic poems one frequently finds one's reading, one's search for understanding, powerfully anticipated and mirrored back. Reading is romanticism again and again.

In quoting work from Chandler, Chase, and de Man I cite texts published in the late twentieth century, but critical work of the twenty-first century has focused a little less on romanticism's anticipatory power and a little more on the occasional ephemerality of its inconsequential acts. The dramatic importance of romanticism to contemporary discourse and critical method has been thrown into relief not necessarily by downplaying the importance of Romantic texts but by exploring the ways Romantic texts challenge their own consequence. As Anahid Nersessian helpfully asks: "What if we thought of Romanticism . . . as a body of literature interested in reclaiming the value of *less*?"[28] In *Looking Away*, Rei Terada writes of the spectra's appeal for Samuel Taylor Coleridge, "casting a perception as mere appearance . . . allows the mind to entertain it without endorsing it, splitting the difference between delusion and the renunciation of enjoyment."[29] Similarly Anne-Lise François writes of the "lightness with which the protagonists of the lyric of inconsequence . . . pass over the crisis of modern subjectivity." "These indifferent heirs," continues François, "do not suffer a loss in committing their gain to inconsequence."[30] Such readings of romanticism discover other resources than consequential gain in the discourse of romanticism. Jacques Khalip in *Last Things* frames his reading of romanticism in the context of professional desires that mandate that the only way to participate in one's field is by asserting the importance of one's field.[31] Khalip begins with what it might mean to let romanticism go.[32] When staged against hyperbolic claims of romanticism's importance, more idiomatic readings of phrases like "now and then" or "every now and again" capture something of this critical turn, one that discovers in Romantic texts new forms of relation.

The idea that one might look round for poetry and discover the materials of poetry everywhere, in every subject that interests the mind, is a thoroughly Wordsworthian one. Even though I have taken Wordsworth's phrase out of context, borrowed a phrase he used to mark readerly dissatisfaction, I have, in a way, ended up back in a Romantic idea. But if Romantic poetry can come to feel important, what make of romanticism's simultaneous resistance to its own consequence? It may not be by chance that literary criticism and theory has turned from linguistic to material concerns at the same time that politicians have raised questions about whether literary criticism and theory, as well as the humanities more generally, have importance, as enrollments in various humanities departments decrease and resources are cut. Humanities scholars have turned to matter (things, objects, ontologies) as if responding to a perceived irrelevance. Romantic writing plays a complicated role in this story. At least since Immanuel Kant's *Critique of the Power of Judgment*, the aesthetic has named an inconsequential judgment that is in fact of tremendous consequence to the subject and even the state, especially as Friedrich Schiller reads Kant in his *Letters on Aesthetic Education*. Aesthetic philosophy works to explain the significance of judgments that may at first appear insignificant. If Romantic poems owe much to Kantian critical philosophy, they also challenge the easy reversibility Schiller imagines. I explore some of the implications in my first chapter, "Understating Poetry," where I read poems that foreground understatement over hyperbole, where poets settle for the little there is and resist, however minimally, making more and more of it. M. H. Abrams's celebration of the Greater Romantic Lyric in *The Correspondent Breeze* focuses on ways poets make something great of a relatively minor event, the climbing of a hill, for instance, where the act of describing the landscape occasions reminiscence and meditation, the more that becomes the poem.[33] Something minor becomes something major. In "Understating Poetry" I explore what I call, foregrounding litotes, the Not Lesser Romantic Lyric, as poets like Coleridge and Wordsworth frequently employ the trope. Indeed, my first two chapters begin with tropes commonly associated with the lyric: hyperbole and apostrophe. In these opening chapters I work to show not only how lyric tropes resonate across other discourses but also how they resist being put to work.

If to look round for poetry is to discover romanticism every now and again, *every now and again* means, on the one hand, "every" now but also, idiomatically, only intermittently, and, taking the idiom seriously, almost never: romanticism every *now and again* suggests the opposite of romanticism *every* now and again. Following these competing interpretations: romanticism is everywhere and keeps happening; it matters intensely because it continues to shape our contemporary discourse, our contemporary life, as the tropes and figures, the grammatical and rhetorical structures that define romanticism define us now. And yet, what is described and minimally captured floats free, disappears. Anahid Nersessian describes *The Calamity Form* as a book about, but not in praise of, vanishing, as the Romantic poems she discusses neither teach readers "what is to be done" nor "let us off the hook for doing it."[34]

Karen Swann describes Romantic poetry along similar lines, as "movements of thought that gain their impetus and power from an abstruse pressing away from function, aim, and end."[35] If romanticism is every now and again then it is also hardly ever *now*, hardly ever knowingly useful. With *Look Round for Poetry* I attempt to capture something of romanticism's untimeliness, which, as I have already intimated, poses readability as a question. For if untimeliness is just another word for timeliness, then something important about untimeliness is lost. The presence in various Romantic poems of what Holsinger and Stauffer call "fitful arrivals and sudden fadings," for instance, suggests that Romantic poems throw into question any easy translation of untimeliness into an ideal timeliness.[36] Over and over again, Romantic poems warn that such dialectical reversals run counter to the force of poetry and the difficulty of reading.

Look Round for Poetry offers a charge, as the phrase challenges readers to juxtapose, conjugate, and place into constellation sometimes competing discourses and discover, in the process, the resonance of poetry and representative grammatical and rhetorical structures across one's fields of vision; but I want the book to serve as well as a reminder that such juxtapositions, conjugations, and constellations themselves depend on the power of literary language. Romanticism is to some degree a theory of articulations, but to articulate is both to connect and separate, as when one articulates one's speech by distinguishing one's syllables.[37] My point is that Romantic poems stage questions about the sorts of constellations my book aims to provoke, and this at a time when contemporary criticism appears quite interested in assuming the self-evident stability of various connections and articulations. My book hopes to inspire readers to look round for poetry—admittedly, a Romantic project—but the book's individual chapters linger with grammatical and rhetorical unreadability. Each chapter stages as a question the possibility (and corresponding impossibility) of distinguishing articulation from disarticulation. As Jacques Khalip and Forest Pyle note in the introduction to *Constellations of a Contemporary Romanticism*, when one considers a constellation one depends on darkness (without which the stars are not visible) and one considers something that is not, strictly speaking, there. Some darkness is required for the constellation to appear, for the figure to emerge: "As a trope, romanticism allows us to read what is and is not there, the difference being . . . the urgency of figure to force an experience out of what might passively be relegated to the closed-off archives of historical time." Like them I work to develop an "untimely model of romantic contemporaneity" that foregrounds the necessary disarticulations that make articulation possible across temporal and discursive division.[38]

Stumbling Blocks

Highlighting the untimeliness of romanticism, of Romantic poems, of poetry perhaps more generally, *Look Round for Poetry* foregrounds the difficulty of reading. In her manifesto-like *The Limits of Critique*, Rita Felski argues for a shift in literary critical attention, from critical practices that rely on the *de-* prefix to practices that foreground the *re-* prefix, from versions of literary criticism and theory that privilege terms like *destabilize* and *denaturalize* to versions that privilege terms like *recontextualize* and *reconfigure*. In opposition to past literary critical practices that focused on moments of blockage (between aesthetics and politics, sign and signification, meaning and the conditions of meaning), Felski asserts, "No more separate spheres!" "Works of art, by default," she continues, "are linked to other texts, objects, people, and institutions in relations of dependency, involvement, and interaction. They are enlisted, entangled, engaged, embattled, embroiled, and embedded."[39] Because works of art are entangled and embedded, the critic has the chance to recontextualize and reconfigure them. She calls for a different affective relationship to the work of literary criticism and theory. As I have suggested, to look round for poetry is to discover momentary flashes of constellation between sometimes disparate discourses, to discover poetry (and the grammatical and rhetorical structures that give poems shape) in sometimes surprising contexts. My own sloganeering ("Look Round for Poetry!") recalls Felski's "No more separate spheres!"[40]

But if the flash of constellation (present, for instance, when one considers cloud computing alongside Wordsworth's "I wandered lonely as a cloud") always is at least a little untimely, then it is always also figural and so subject to the demands of reading and rereading. "By default" in the quote from Felski above poses interpretive challenges. The phrase assumes the absence of any alternative options. The links are necessary and natural. It could not be otherwise, suggests Felski.[41] But like articulation, which, indistinguishable from disarticulation, poses its own interpretive difficulties, "by default" introduces the possibility that such links are transgressive, even offensive, where "default" refers to an instance of doing something incorrectly or badly, an inadvertent error or mistake. Works of art may be linked to other texts, and so enlisted, entangled, engaged, embattled, embroiled, and embedded with other objects, people, and institutions, as Felski asserts; but if these links are by default, then they are not *only* natural. Such an understanding of *by default* makes legible an alternative that *by default* means to prevent. The language of natural articulation performs a possible disarticulation. In *Look Round for Poetry* I remain committed to the untimeliness of poetry, of romanticism, as the constellations across poems and technological, political, economic discourse remain stubbornly literary, figural, and possibly mistaken, even if it may not be possible to do without such fictions.

As contemporary critics assert the necessity of interconnection, they disclose the working power of trope and figure. To look round for poetry is to discover chance conjunctions. To look round for poetry is also to be reminded of the figuring and disfiguring power of such chance conjunctions. In the wake of the so-called linguistic turn and as recent literary criticism has attempted to assert itself in opposition to prior practices, critics have asserted the importance of overcoming differences that mattered more in past decades, like the difference between art and politics that Felski puts to test in *The Limits of Critique*. Caroline Levine begins *Forms: Whole, Rhythm, Hierarchy, Network* with a similar call, as she imagines a literary critic performing a formalist reading of *Jane Eyre* and contrasts this imagined formalist reading with her own version of formalism:

> This book makes a case for expanding our usual definition of form in literary studies to include patterns of sociopolitical experience. . . . Broadening our definition of form to include social arrangements has, as we will see, immediate methodological consequences. The traditionally troubling gap between the form of the literary text and its content and context dissolves. Formalist analysis turns out to be as valuable to understanding sociopolitical institutions as it is to reading literature. Forms are at work everywhere.[42]

As Levine suggests, literary scholars have shown an interest in literary form but have resisted describing politics in "formalist" terms. If one understands politics as also a series of forms, then analysis of literary forms makes possible analysis of political forms, as forms lead one to forms. My book owes much to the new critical directions Levine's book makes possible, though my key terms are more often words like *poem* and *trope*. When Wordsworth suggests that the materials of poetry are to be found in every subject, he may be suggesting that poems are at work everywhere, but what interests me most are the chance conjunctions. I am interested in the ways readers might discover the grammatical and rhetorical structures that help give individual poems shape in sometimes surprising, but not entirely unrelated, contexts.

I remain a little wary of Wordsworth's "every" and Levine's "everywhere," which may explain why I begin this book with figures of understatement. If poetry makes various critical leaps possible it also throws them into relief. I am tempted to say that if poems are at work everywhere, they are at work only every now and again. *Forms* "is an attempt to think about how we might make our world more just."[43] And with moral clarity, Levine identifies as "troubling" the gap between form and content. Levine does not describe building a bridge over the gap, as Kant may have done. More strongly, she asserts that once one's definition of form is broadened sufficiently, the gap between form and content (and, by extension, the gap between art and politics and so much else) "dissolves." While *gap* implies an absence, *dissolve* assumes some presence. In rhetorical terms, Levine employs not a metaphor but a catachresis, an abuse of metaphor as she describes the dissolution of an absence. Levine must give the gap material existence in order to—subsequently and through the power of catachresis—do something about it. Though tropes make our various critical pronouncements possible they can still be stubborn, and they remain stubborn in *Look Round for Poetry* too.

Positing interconnection depends on the work of trope and figure. If romanticism and the entire history of the discourse of the aesthetic raises questions about possible connections between meaning and the material conditions of meaning, as Wordsworth, for instance, hopes to connect the landscape and the "quiet of the sky" in "Lines Composed a Few Miles Above Tintern Abbey," increasingly contemporary versions of literary theory and criticism have asserted the importance of taking such connections for granted.[44] Dependent on the work of trope and figure, connections are untimely. They do not happen quite always at the right time. And they highlight both the importance and difficulty of reading. Tropes figure, refigure, and disfigure, and sometimes it can be hard to know the difference in advance.

My examples from literary criticism are meant to showcase the ways trope and figure can introduce surprise into literary criticism when one looks round for poetry. The self-evidence of inter-connection is subject to the work of reading, which can throw connection into some doubt. But the potential for surprise is also present in critical projects that assert the absence of connection. My examples from Felski and Levine are drawn from twenty-first-century texts that redirect critical and theoretical trends one might more commonly associate with the twentieth century's linguistic turn, perhaps with the work of Paul de Man. Indeed, de Man strongly suggests at the end of his essay "Shelley Disfigured," which prominently features one of the prefixes Felski plays down, "that nothing, whether deed, word, thought, or text, ever happens in relation, positive or negative, to anything that precedes, follows, or exists elsewhere, but only as a random event whose power, like the power of death, is due to the randomness of its occurrence."[45] In contrast to Felski and Levine, de Man asserts the absence of relation, the presence of gaps, and separate spheres.

But de Man's text is not immune to surprise. In the preface to *The Rhetoric of Romanticism*, in which "Shelley Disfigured" appears, de Man calls poetry the "obvious stumbling block" of his critical enterprise, and he explains how he was unable to pass through the language of poetry to something beyond it, to some historical totalization.[46] De Man describes the *Rhetoric of Romanticism* as a collection of essays, with each individual essay starting again as if from scratch. Poetry, suggests de Man through his choice trope, has the capacity to impede one's path, make one stumble or lose one's footing. De Man stumbled on poetry and his enterprise was blocked. But present in the language of the preface is a version of "stumbling block" rarely associated with de Man, a version of "stumbling block" nonetheless made legible by de Man's text. For at least in English "stumbling block" names both the cause of a fall (where block functions as a noun) and that which prevents one from stumbling (where block functions as a verb). Poetry, specifically Friedrich Hölderlin's poetry, causes de Man to stumble repeatedly but it also prevents him from stumbling. Hölderlin's poetry is an obvious stumbling block; that is, poetry, however paradoxically, also (always?) prevents or blocks stumbling. One hears in "stumbling block," in other words, both the cause of a fall and its opposite, as poetry props de Man up. Hölderlin's poetry is the obvious stumbling *block* of de Man's enterprise because, simply put, more chapters follow. Poetry compels. For my purposes here, one might say that poetry is not just a *stumbling* block but also a stumbling *block*. What's undecidable, in other words, is whether the difference is decidable.

De Man's suggestion that poetry is an obvious stumbling block is easily included in a thinking of reading that privileges the sort of suspicion Rita Felski rejects in *The Limits of Critique*. The reader "stumbles" because the text does not allow for any easy articulation of sign and meaning and so the poem demystifies (as it anticipates and mirrors back) one's reading strategies. In reading poetry, we stumble. Again and again. But if poetry is a stumbling block it is also a block to stumbling, a tool for the unmasking of ideological aberrations that also sustains and cannot help but sustain them. What is potentially surprising is the work of trope and figure in each of these passages. To look round for poetry (a Romantic project through and through, through and through?) is to discover the connections Romantic poems both inspire and challenge. Reading makes possible looking round for poetry. And looking round for poetry makes reading, I hope, a little surprising, a little difficult.

Chapter Narrative

The literary structures that give Romantic poems shape are not safely lodged in the past but return in sometimes surprising contexts. With my first two chapters, "Understating Poetry" and "The Poetics of Downturns," I take up the tradition of the lyric, a poetic form closely associated with hyperbole and apostrophe. In beginning with chapters on understatement (litotes in particular) and catastrophe, I turn around two tropes that have shaped discussion of poetry. Since at least Charles Baudelaire, poets have considered hyperbole central to their conceptions of poetry, lyric poetry in particular. Readers, similarly, have celebrated poetry's capacity to produce more from less, to produce excessively meaningful utterances using only a few words. In "Understating Poetry," I focus on some of the many ways poets employ tropes of understatement, like litotes, and I attempt to draw out a counter-narrative (one that includes Baudelaire too). The chapter concludes with attention to Wordsworth's common and repeated use of the double negative, with special focus on the use of litotes in "Tintern Abbey," where Wordsworth pursues a poetics of withholding.

The second chapter, "The Poetics of Downturns," extends the first chapter's interest in poetry and economics by drawing a line from Wordsworth's many "downturned" eyes and brows to the economic figure of the *downturn* (the term, a later nineteenth-century invention). Wordsworth's poetry features numerous figures described with eyes and brows turned down toward the ground. Beginning with passages from *The Prelude* and "A Night-Piece," where the poet's ability to look up conditions the possibility for poetic experience, I turn toward the Old Cumberland Beggar, whose eyes, by contrast, are always on the ground. I develop a reading of Wordsworth's downturned figures in the context of the economic downturn, itself already a figure for and a translation of catastrophe (from the Greek *cata*, "down," and *strophe*, "turn"). In looking round for poetry, I focus on these recurring figures in Wordsworth's poems to tease out some of the ways Wordsworth's figures touch on contemporary concerns, however briefly, as Wordsworth's downturned figures offer a language to think anew the rhetoric of the economic downturn. In *Romantic Sobriety*, Orrin N. C. Wang notes that for years scholars have situated romanticism in the context of the French Revolution, downplaying Marx's suggestion that democracy is unthinkable without the emergence of capitalism and commodity form.[47] In the opening chapters of this book I situate Wordsworth in the context of tropes and figures that recur in the rhetoric of capitalism today and use his writing to give shape to the book's motivating questions. Poetry—once one begins looking round for it—offers a chance for thinking the ways rhetorical tropes and figures encode violence.

The third and fourth chapters build on my initial investigations into lyric tropes to experiment more broadly and look round for poetry. The third chapter begins by embracing critical intuition and other accidents of

signification.[48] In "I Wandered Lonely as an iCloud" I explore how Wordsworth's poem "I wandered lonely as a cloud" anticipates—with the first
and last words of its opening line—Apple's "iCloud" (first launched in 2011,
though by now cloud computing extends far beyond Apple's products), as
Wordsworth's poem discovers itself today entangled within the rhetoric of
twenty-first-century cloud computing. Given these echoes, Wordsworth's
"I . . . cloud" resonates differently, but this difference is textual, an effect of
poetry and of the ways poems are simultaneously free from history and yet
always potentially, even aberrantly referential: untimely.[49] I take an interest in
the ways Wordsworth's speculations about clouds offer us a chance to think
the Romantic legacy of cloud metaphors as I situate Wordsworth's poem and
Romantic poems more generally in relationship to contemporary discussions
about materialism and labor, especially the labor practices of the knowledge
economy, an economy that increasingly demands worker mobility.

With the fourth chapter, I turn toward a poem by a twentieth-century
poet, Lucille Clifton, that extends earlier Romantic attempts to look round
for poetry. Building from early chapters centered on Wordsworth poems, this
chapter anticipates later chapters on Keats and Shelley, more traditionally
canonical Romantic poets, as the book looks to theorize the politics of
literary untimeliness. In "On the Poetry of Posthumous Election," I explore
how tropes common to poetry appear in contemporary democratic politics,
when voters vote for (and so throw their voice to) the dead. Election ballots
are closed prior to an election. When a candidate dies after the ballot has
been finalized, it cannot legally be changed. The dead candidate remains on
the ballot. And with surprising frequency, dead candidates win. In throwing
their voices to the dead, voters employ a trope common to lyric poetry,
prosopopoeia, when the absent, inanimate, or dead are given the ability to
speak as if from beyond the grave. In granting dead candidates the ability
to represent them, or "speak" for them, voters become Romantic poets.
With specific attention to Lucille Clifton's "jasper texas 1998," which situates racialized violence in the context of a posthumous election, I develop
a sense of poetry's function in contemporary democratic politics. Alongside
"I Wandered Lonely as an iCloud," this chapter explores some of the ways
poetry offers readers a chance to think again and anew the work of tropes
and figures in contemporary life.

Always with attention to the grammatical and rhetorical structures that
give poems shape, *Look Round for Poetry* moves from economic to political
considerations with my final two chapters, "Keats for Beginners" and "The
Grammar of Romanticism: Shelley's Prepositions." These chapters develop
what it might mean to live among poems. In the fifth chapter I read John

Keats on his own poetic beginnings to theorize the ways politics is unthinkable without the surprise of beginning. Though critics have alternatively celebrated and condemned Keats as the most apolitical of poets, Keats's poetry offers us a chance to think the importance of surprise at a critical moment when surprise is increasingly deemed risky. For Keats, there is no surprise without the presence of others. In his *Politics*, Aristotle studies the various and best forms of partnership—connection—between citizens. Grammarians, including Robert Lowth, define prepositions along similar lines: prepositions "serve to connect words with one another, and show the relation between them."[50] Politics describes connections between people; prepositions, connections between words. To constellate the political with the prepositional, I turn to the writing of Percy Shelley in my sixth chapter, "The Grammar of Romanticism," for lines from several of Shelley's most famous poems ("Hymn to Intellectual Beauty," "Ode to the West Wind," and *The Triumph of Life*) feature the prepositions "among" and "amongst" prominently, as the poems develop a series of related questions: What does it mean to be "among" others? What sort of political authority (if any) follows from this particular preposition? With attention to Shelley's interest in the preposition "among" I draw out some of Shelley's thinking about prepositions and situate Shelley's prepositional thinking in the context of political allegory, as politics names our various attempts to connect persons (and nonpersons).

In *Look Round for Poetry* my primary objects are poems and my commitment to literature. But if any act of reading is to retain a vital and subversive power, one must become ignorant, again and again, of the thoughts that have most changed one.[51] With that goal in mind I have placed in apposition poems and the rhetoric of contemporary life. As records of attempts at looking around for poetry, each chapter of this book labors not only to make accessible the surprise of poetry but also to make noticeable the tropes and figures that determine contemporary discourse. A poetry still capable of surprise is a poetry still capable of teaching one something about the language of one's current predicament.

1. Understating Poetry

> It's not untrue jobs were
> outsourced and it's not untrue an economic base
> was cut from under. It's not untrue.
> —Claudia Rankine, "Sound & Fury"

In *Look Round for Poetry* I pursue the resonant untimeliness of literary language, the grammatical and rhetorical structures that give poems shape; once one begins looking round for poetry one possibly discovers it in sometimes surprising contexts, as small moments in poems flash into constellation with contemporary and ongoing crises. But in attending to some of these small moments, in lingering over particular observations about poetic language, do I risk making too much of them? Is it possible to take an interest in poetry, perhaps even pursue a defense, without necessarily transforming poetry's perceived insignificance into its opposite, tremendous significance? This question betrays a hint of performed naivete. What does literary criticism do if not expound on and amplify the significance of seemingly minor observations about language, make much of the little that there is? In their *Lyric Theory Reader*, Virginia Jackson and Yopie Prins highlight the importance of the lyric to modern critical thought and discover in some techniques of close reading developed by Anglo-American New Criticism a theory of lyric reading that continues to shape critical discussion of poetry.[1] In calling attention to the importance of lyric to versions of critical reading, Jackson and Prins hope that other ideas of poetry and its possibilities may appear. Like Jackson and Prins I am interested in the ways poetry has shaped literary criticism, and here I pursue other ideas of critical reading, not by negating the importance of poetry, specifically the lyric, but by focusing on a trope theories of the lyric have downplayed.

In this opening chapter I focus on various uses of understatement in the history of poetry. When, in an essay on the poet Théodore de Banville, Charles Baudelaire declares that "hyperbole and apostrophe are the forms of language which are not only most agreeable but also most necessary" in lyric, he leaves little room for understatement.[2] Is understatement less necessary, less pleasing in lyric? What should one make of all the various moments in lyric poetry when poets moderate their language and say less than they mean? If Baudelaire aligns lyric with hyperbole—and if lyric comes to stand for all poetry, for better and for worse, after Baudelaire—how dependent on hyperbole is our understanding of poetry, specifically after romanticism? What would it mean to think poetry not through hyperbole or apostrophe but through litotes, a trope that prominently figures poetic restraint? In this chapter I track several uses of poetic understatement, specifically litotes, through to what M. H. Abrams names the Greater Romantic Lyric. Alongside a poetic tradition that embraces hyperbole, I show, is one that embraces understatement, where the poet's minimal affirmation is accomplished through the weak work of double negation. What possibilities for poetry emerge if one identifies poetry not with hyperbole but understatement? In the context of capitalism's rampant expansion, its expansive and expanding demands for more, how does poetry make legible the importance of less? How does poetry make more less legible?

Apostrophe, Hyperbole, Poetic Power

For Baudelaire, hyperbole and apostrophe figure poetic power. When poets apostrophize inanimate objects, for instance, they grant them new life, thus transforming objects into subjects through the power of poetic address. For this reason readers often associate apostrophe with Romantic and post-Romantic poetry, where poetic power rivals the divine. In *Theory of the Lyric*, Jonathan Culler draws on Baudelaire's definition of the lyric and offers his own version: "Lyric is characteristically extravagant, performing unusual speech acts of strange address."[3] Stressing the importance of apostrophe and building on his influential essay first published in *diacritics* in 1977, Culler devotes an entire chapter to "Lyric Address." Even though readers may sometimes feel a bit embarrassed by a poet's use of apostrophe (for who addresses an urn?) the language most necessary and pleasing to the lyric is not simply, or merely, descriptive. If it were, the poet's power would stem primarily from their ability to describe with precision. As Culler writes, "A primary force of apostrophe is to constitute the addressee as another subject, with which the visionary poet can hope to develop a relationship, harmonious or antagonistic; apostrophe treats that bringing together of subject and object as an act of will, something accomplished poetically in the act of address."[4] Through apostrophe poets grant themselves tremendous power, the power to make live, and in the process they remake the universe.

From the Greek for "throwing beyond," hyperbole overshoots the literal. In this way hyperbole results from and in turn inspires what is sometimes called the imagination, as poets stretch language beyond mere description. Culler glosses Baudelaire:"Lyrics hyperbolically risk animating the world, investing mundane objects or occurrence with meaning."[5] Through hyperbole poets animate the world and fill it with meaning and significance. Hyperbolic language reminds readers that the world is not simply given, as the poet fashions through poetic language a world that might be, that maybe should be, otherwise.

Hyperbole has not always been held in great esteem. In *On Rhetoric* Aristotle explicitly identifies hyperbole with immaturity and anger:"Hyperboles are adolescent, for they exhibit vehemence." In an effort to defend the importance of moderation in rhetoric, Aristotle continues:"It is inappropriate for an older man to speak [in hyperbole]."[6] Associating hyperbole with a loss of self-control, Aristotle warns speakers away from the trope. But just as Aristotle attempts to rescue rhetoric from Plato's criticisms in *On Rhetoric*, later rhetoricians attempt to rescue hyperbole from Aristotle's own. Quintilian, for instance, describes hyperbole as the boldest kind of ornament but resists maligning the trope:"I feel it distasteful to report the many faults arising from this Trope, especially as they are by no means unfamiliar or obscure. It is enough to remind the reader that Hyperbole is a liar, but does not lie to deceive."[7] While hyperbole lies, it lies transparently. In his defense of hyperbole, Quintilian explains that hyperbole has positive value "when the thing about which we have to speak transcends the ordinary limits of nature. We are then allowed to amplify, because the real size of the thing cannot be expressed, and it is better to go too far than not to go far enough."[8] Quintilian rescues hyperbole from Aristotle's criticism and embraces the timely use of overstatement, preferring going too far to not going far enough (at least when occasion demands it). In the English tradition George Puttenham defines hyperbole in *The Arte of English Poesie* as "immoderate excesse" and dubs it the "over-reacher."[9] Like Quintilian he believes there exist some occasions when hyperbole is acceptable, as when "we fall a-praising . . . of our mistress's virtue, beauty, or other good parts."[10] Against just this position Shakespeare crafts Sonnet 130, a poem suspicious of hyperbolic metaphors: "My mistress' eyes are nothing like the sun," he writes. Shakespeare rejects hyperbole for what seems like literal description: "My mistress, when she walks, treads on the ground."[11]

In claiming for hyperbole a central role in modern poetry, Baudelaire forcefully overturns Aristotle's position.[12] The effects of this overturning are wide-ranging. If one thinks that the point of poetry is not mimetically to represent the world but to make something happen, to surprise or startle a reader, to shake readers free from accepted uses of language or accepted norms of observation, then hyperbole is key to any theory of poetry that exceeds (mere) description. Poetry does something other than, something more than accept the world as it is. One might then trace from Aristotle to Baudelaire a story of shifting ideas of poetry, as hyperbole moves from something secondary (and adolescent) to something necessary, even primary, as a classical emphasis on language's mimetic function gives way to a more modern emphasis on poetic force.[13] Following Baudelaire, attention to hyperbole and apostrophe produces a theory of lyric language that tropes the power of the poet to shape and reshape the world.[14]

Poetic Restraint

By contrast, understatement figures poetic restraint. Instead of asserting more than one means, or even exactly what one means, one asserts less—in hopes that one's readers might supplement the thought. In rhetorical theory there are many types of understatement: *meiosis* and *litotes* (from Greek), *diminutio* and *extenuatio* (from Latin), just to name some of the more common.[15] Sometimes *meiosis* is considered the more general term. From the Greek for "lessening," meiosis involves calling something by a name that diminishes its importance, as when one calls a great mountain a molehill or refers to violence in Northern Ireland as "The Troubles."

From the Greek for "plain" or "meager," *litotes*, also sometimes the more general term, commonly refers to uses of language whereby one expresses a thought by denying its opposite: one tones down a too-bold statement by prominently figuring the work of negation, as when Quintilian suggests that the faults of hyperbole are not unfamiliar.

Litotes has a sort of odd history. Lee Hollander suggests that the Greek word is found for the first time in a Latin letter of Cicero's from 56 BC, where he uses it to mean "simplicity" or "frugality"; only later does the word come to refer to a rhetorical trope.[16] Puttenham calls litotes the moderator: "we temper our sense with words of such moderation, as in appearance it abateth it."[17] Puttenham's example features the work of negation: "I know you hate me not, nor wish me any ill," meaning "I know you love me very well and dearly." He likens litotes to paradiastole, which tends to flattery, as when one calls an "unthrift" a "liberal gentleman," and meiosis (which he names the Disabler). By the twentieth century litotes achieves a position of prominence in rhetorical theory. In *The New Rhetoric* Chaim Perelman and Lucie Olbrechts-Tyteca set litotes and hyperbole in explicit opposition: "Litotes is generally defined in contrast to hyperbole, as a manner of expression which seems to weaken the thought. . . . When it seeks to establish a value," they continue, "it relies on something that falls short of the value, instead of something beyond it."[18]

The trope features prominently in political and economic discourse, where one is not always rewarded for saying just what one means. In November of 2014 the then prime minister David Cameron made a speech on immigration as he attempted to navigate tensions in his own conservative party: "We should be clear," said Cameron: "It is not wrong to express concern about the scale of people coming into this country."[19] Here the use of litotes ("not wrong" in place of "right") allowed Cameron to introduce a political position while simultaneously diminishing it. Likely today, given the outcome of the Brexit vote and its sluggish but eventual consequence of a separate United Kingdom, Cameron knows he did not diminish it quite enough. J. R. Bergmann has recently explored the relative importance of litotes in the modern workplace: litotes "is one of those methods which are used to talk about an object in a discreet way. It clearly locates an object for the recipient, but it avoids naming it directly."[20] When marketing to consumers, one embraces hyperbole; when managing the workplace, litotes.

Arguably, the most conspicuous (and most reviled) form litotes can take features the use of double negation. One states less than one means by negating a negative, as when Sebastian says of Ferdinand in Shakespeare's *The Tempest*: "I have no hope that he's undrowned." Singling out the use of the double negative in litotes, George Orwell, writing in the twentieth century, argues that it should be possible to laugh litotes (and the *not un-* formation) out of existence once and for all: "One can cure oneself of the *not un-* formation by memorizing this sentence: A not unblack dog was chasing a not unsmall rabbit across a not ungreen field."[21] For Orwell, of course, the sentence "A black dog was chasing a small rabbit across a green field" is preferable because it is simpler. One should say what one means and mean what one says.

The use of double negation is conspicuously figurative, drawing unnecessary attention to itself and always possibly distracting the reader from the message conveyed. But Orwell's example of "self-translation" raises a general question about litotes: is double negation merely affirmation by other means? What lingers, persists, and remains even after the reader translates "not undrowned" into "drowned" or "not unblack" into "black"? If hyperbole is most necessary and most pleasing in the lyric, as Baudelaire suggests, litotes may seem conspicuously unpoetic. We may be better off ignoring it. But some uses of conspicuously unpoetic language are—perhaps—not entirely uninteresting.

Not . . . Unwept

However unnecessary or unpleasing, understatement is frequently employed by poets. Perhaps predictably enough, once one begins looking for a trope like litotes, one discovers it throughout literary history. Many examples are to be found in *Beowulf*, for example, as when the poet reports Grendel's descent from Cain, who "got no good [*ne gefeah*]" from killing Abel.[22] The poet does not say that only ill followed, but this decision highlights the poet's reliance upon (and simultaneous interest in establishing) a knowing community of readers. The poet uses litotes to stress the importance of shared opinion, as when the poet later reports that no one regretted Grendel's fatal departure (because all celebrated it). In this way poets use understatement for many of the same reasons speakers do in ordinary language, to set up a knowing persona and a shared community of readers. "The time is not remote," writes Jonathan Swift with a knowing nod in "Verses on the Death of Dr. Swift, D. S. P. D.," "when I / Must by the course of nature die."[23] I draw my examples from the *Norton Anthology of Poetry* to show the ways litotes appears in poems considered canonical. I turn now to a handful of examples to read in more detail. In what follows I am most interested in examples that employ the dreaded double negation in part because I wish to focus on examples Orwell might well have wanted to cull from the anthology.

Take Milton first. In one of the most powerful elegies in the English language, a poem that also announces the emergence of a new poet, John Milton writes of Lycidas: "He must not float upon his watery bier / Unwept, and welter to the parching wind, / Without the meed of some melodious tear."[24] Though Lycidas dies a young poet, having hardly proved himself worthy of an elegy, Milton presents Lycidas with a song of mourning. The poem transforms Lycidas into a proper subject of elegy. But at least at the close of the first verse paragraph, Milton is unwilling to declare straightforwardly that readers must weep for him. Here the double negative (not . . . unwept) invites several different interpretations. The enjambment that distances "He must not float" from "Unwept," which begins the next line, intensifies the poet-speaker's denial, as "He must not float upon his watery bier" feels for a moment like angry denial, a version of "He must not be dead" or "He is not dead." When "unwept" appears at the beginning of the next line, the trope is more plainly evident. Why does the poet-speaker not more simply write "we must weep for him"? Why elicit a call of mourning by negating a negative? Perhaps because "we must weep" forces one to acknowledge loss more directly; "he must not go unwept" softens the impact of an absence the speaker cannot yet bear, as if understatement were one way to defend oneself against the pain of loss. If poets employ apostrophe to build an image of themselves as sincere in the minds of readers, because it would be strange to lie to an absent or inanimate object, litotes here likewise gives shape to the poet-speaker through rhetorical effect; the poet-speaker is so powerfully affected by loss that he cannot directly name the weeping for which his poem calls.

At the same time, however, understatement communicates emotional control. The first verse paragraph's closing litotes stands in marked contrast to the poem's opening lines, which can seem overly violent:

> Yet once more, O ye laurels and once more
> Ye myrtles brown, with ivy never sere,
> I come to pluck your berries harsh and crude,
> And with forced fingers rude,
> Shatter your leaves before the mellowing year.[25]

The poem begins with the two figures Baudelaire privileges: apostrophe ("O ye laurels") and hyperbole ("with forced fingers rude, the poet comes to shatter leaves"). But when one focuses on the ways the poem foregrounds apostrophe and hyperbole, one also sees the ways the poem turns from apostrophe and hyperbole toward litotes by the end of the verse paragraph, as "shatter your leaves" gives way to "not . . . unwept." Milton's opening follows the advice of classical rhetoricians like Aristotle, as he moves from youthful exuberance toward mature restraint. Deliberate understatement, suggest Quintilian and the author of the *Rhetorica ad Herennium*, helps an orator express modesty in order to gain the audience's favor. To avoid arrogant display "we moderate and soften."[26] If the poem opens with hyperbole, it moves toward understatement before "beginning," as the second verse paragraph opens: "Begin then, sisters of the sacred well"—as if the poem could not begin properly until the poet had demonstrated restrained control, the ability to hold himself together even in the face of extreme emotion.[27]

To the extent to which the poem offers a new subject of elegy, as it becomes possible to elegize not only those who have already achieved fame and notoriety but also those who only might have, the use of litotes also signals the poet's hesitation, as the gesture acknowledges the ways the poet is boldly refashioning the subject of elegy. The poet will not be so bold as to say that we must weep for Lycidas, an unknown poet-to-be, from the start; he merely writes that Lycidas should not go unwept. As the opening paragraph sheds hyperbole for litotes, the poet searches for a language adequate to mourning the loss of a friend as well as language capable of announcing the arrival of a new, mature poet: here, not Lycidas but the poet of "Lycidas," the "uncouth swain" who touches "the tender stops of various quills" by poem's end. To the extent to which the poem thus announces the arrival of the "mature" poet of "Lycidas," a poet capable of uniting classical, pastoral and Christian traditions, the early use of litotes prepares the way for the poem's final declaration: "Weep no more, woeful shepherds, weep no more."[28] If hyperbole gives way to litotes, then the potential clumsiness of litotes (with its always possibly awkward double negative) gives way in turn to poetic command.

After passing through litotes, the poem returns to hyperbole and apostrophe. By the end of the poem, in other words, "Lycidas . . . is not dead," as litotes gives way to the reorganized hyperbole of Christian redemption.[29] And the poem prominently figures a return to apostrophe, as the poem closes by apostrophizing Lycidas himself: "Now, Lycidas, the shepherds weep no more: / Henceforth thou art the Genius of the shore."[30] The poet-speaker's willingness to call on Lycidas grants apparent life to the dead as the poem embraces the power of poetic language to animate. Lycidas is not dead because he can be called to. The early appearance of understatement in Milton's "Lycidas" signals two opposing feelings. The poet is overcome by loss even as he asserts poetic control, exhibiting the ability to restrain his emotions. The poet's use of understatement to perform self-de-possession also signals the poet's extreme self-possession, the mastery of emotion, where hyperbole, following Aristotle, would suggest the opposite. It is as if passing through various tropes of understatement allows the poet of "Lycidas" to return to the poem's opening tropes, hyperbole and apostrophe, in order to pass on to fresh woods and pastures new. In order to draw the poem to a close, Milton must move past litotes, as if understatement were a necessary stop along the way to poetic power but not a proper source.

Just as many poets found themselves blocked by Milton's *Paradise Lost*, struggling to find an appropriate topic for epic poetry, poets, sometimes in direct response to Milton, have variously attempted to find poetic power in understatement, associating understatement with something other than mature control. In "Ode on the Poetical Character," for instance, William Collins discovers "the inspiring bowers" overturned; the oak by which Milton lay can be seen but no longer approached.[31] In response, Collins celebrates poetic limitation and self-moderation. Richard Wendorf describes Collins's poetry thus: "It would be difficult to think of another poet who has been so successful in emphasizing his limitations."[32] Litotes is one form self-limitation might take, as the figure expresses the poet's ability to hold fast and not overreach. A poem like "Ode to Evening," for instance, begins with an apostrophe, but in apostrophizing evening, "chaste Eve," the poet personifies a transitional state, neither light nor dark, and asks for help discovering a softened strain of poetry opposed to hyperbole.[33] "Now teach me, maid composed," writes the poet,

> To breathe some softened strain,
> Whose numbers, stealing through the darkening vale,
> May not unseemly with its stillness suit,
> As, musing slow, I hail
> Thy genial loved return![34]

The poet conspicuously aligns this softened strain of poetry with litotes, as he searches for a strain that will suit "not unseemly." Litotes is one form this softened strain might take. The poet's use of litotes is a sign of his commitment to the softer strain for which he calls and, perhaps, a sign that he could use Eve's help, for this line is only rarely considered the poem's best. But Collins describes Evening as "composed" and so draws attention to the ways the poem too has been composed. Litotes gives the line a regular (perhaps softened) metrical pattern, and the poet discovers the proper "numbers." Philip Larkin achieves a similar effect in "Talking in Bed," which concludes: "It becomes still more difficult to find / Words at once true and kind, / Or not untrue and not unkind."[35] The final line's regularity, achieved in part by the double use of litotes (not untrue, not unkind) brings the poem to a close after the meter in the prior lines threatened to become irregular as the poet searched for words that fit truth and kindness. Like Collins, Larkin will settle for a softened strain.

Confronted by Milton's looming example, Collins turns to understatement as a source of poetic power and not, as with Milton's "Lycidas," one stop along the way; in apostrophizing "chaste Eve" Collins also draws on a conventional feminization of understatement. Alexander Pope, writing as Martinus Scriblerus, strongly associates litotes with "ladies, whisperers, and backbiters," for instance, and warns poets away from the figure with almost as much conviction as Aristotle warns poets away from hyperbole.[36] For Pope litotes stands for various forms of understatement that express one's unwillingness to say exactly what one means. But the association of understatement with women (and figures gendered female, like Collins's Evening) also conveys why understatement sometimes captures the political necessity of (apparent) reticence, especially in poems that announce the emergence of female poets.[37] One might connect Collins's emphasis on limitation to a poet like Elizabeth Bishop, of whom Marianne Moore wrote "Bishop is spectacular in being unspectacular," but sometimes poets turn to understatement to explode the limited options available to them.[38] In "The Author to Her Book," thought to have been written in 1666 while preparing a second edition of *The Tenth Muse*, Anne Bradstreet employs litotes to devastating effect. The poem begins with the poet's address to her book: "Though ill-formed offspring of my feeble brain."[39] The poet describes how her poems were snatched by friends and printed abroad. But with publication, suggests the poet, the book's "errors were not lessened (all may judge)."[40] And upon seeing the book in print, "my blushing was not small."[41] Bradstreet's use of litotes ("not lessened," "not small") closely aligns understatement with tropes of feminine modesty. Publication multiplied the book's errors and resulted in great blushing. The poem foregrounds apostrophe with its opening address, but then oscillates between hyperbole and litotes. By metaphorically describing the book as a child, one that must be "stretched," Bradstreet also calls attention to how such modesty tropes disguise and perpetuate forms of violence.[42] Here, litotes communicates appropriate levels of modesty, but in playing the part Bradstreet also shows up the ways "modesty" is always a performance, even if it is not understood to be one, even by those who perform it. If Milton's "Lycidas" moves from hyperbole to litotes to demonstrate poetic control, Bradstreet interrogates the ways women, and women writers specifically, are disciplined and moderated.[43]

Modesty can always have an edge to it. Jumping ahead in time, Phillis Wheatley's "A Farewell to America. To Mrs. S. W." (published in 1773) employs the now conspicuous double negation in the fifth stanza. On a ship bound for London, Wheatley, enslaved, waves adieu to New-England and S. W. (Susannah Wheatley, who purchased a seven-year-old Phillis Wheatley in 1761). Phillis Wheatley watches her cry: "Susannah mourns, nor can I bear / to see the crystal show'r, / Or mark the tender failing tear / At sad departure's hour."[44] But then the poet introduces litotes, one with bite: "Not unregarding can I see / Her soul with grief opprest."[45] Not unregarding, not without feeling: but not without feeling is not exactly the same as "with feeling." Sometimes litotes weakens a thought to make it more acceptable, at other times litotes expresses the poet's supreme emotional control, as if only those capable of maintaining poise in the face of powerful feeling are capable of understating the effect of feeling; at other times litotes disguises poetic force, as when understatement offers disguised critique.

Not Lesser Romantic Lyric

Few poets are as preoccupied with litotes as William Wordsworth. John Crowe Ransom recognizes Wordsworth's "relentless understatement," and compares Wordsworth with other poets who are "virtuosos [of] overstatement."[46] But despite Ransom's observation, readers still powerfully align Wordsworth in particular and romanticism more generally with figures of excess. Indeed,

Baudelaire's stress on hyperbole and apostrophe can be traced back in part to earlier Romantic rhetoric. Romantic poems are full of famous apostrophes ("O wild West Wind," "Thou still unravished bride of quietness") and often purported to overflow with powerful feelings. But attention to figures of understatement in what M. H. Abrams famously calls the Greater Romantic Lyric reveals many poetic examples of attenuated thought. I situate this chapter in the context of recent work in Romantic studies that runs counter to the still dominant general association of romanticism with excess, as if Wordsworth's statement that poetry is the overflow of powerful emotion were not so immediately followed by his statement that this overflow must be recollected in tranquility, where what is recollected is also collected, contained, formed and arranged. In *Utopia, Limited: Romanticism and Adjustment*, Anahid Nersessian focuses on the importance of limitation in Romantic writing and "reads the Romantic pursuit of limitation against the grain of a mass idealization of the unrestrained and inexhaustibly available."[47] Understatement is one form limitation might take. What would it mean to associate romanticism with pursuit of relentless understatement?

Abrams offers Coleridge's "The Aeolian Harp" as one early example of the genre of the Greater Romantic Lyric, and the poem features litotes repeatedly. The poem begins by foregrounding the work of negation: "Full many a thought uncalled and undetained, / And many idle flitting phantasies, / Traverse my indolent and passive brain, / As wild and various as the random gales / That swell and flutter on this subject Lute!"[48] Though not insisting on it, the poet figures the brain as almost too receptive. These opening negations call to mind not litotes but meiosis, the deliberate effort to minimize or make smaller, for it would seem that calling thoughts wild and free would go too far for the poet; instead, the thoughts are "undetained." The poet then asks his famous question:

> And what if all of animated nature
> Be but organic Harps diversely framed,
> That tremble into thought, as o'er them sweeps
> Plastic and vast, one intellectual breeze,
> At once the Soul of each and God of all?[49]

In response to this rhetorical question, the "beloved Woman" plays the unenviable role of metaphysical anchor. With her introduction the reader encounters the now familiar double negation of litotes: "But thy more serious eye a mild reproof / Darts, O beloved Woman! nor such thoughts / Dim and unhallowed dost thou not reject, / And biddest me walk humbly with my God."[50] If the opening of the poem gives negation minimal shape, the beloved's response, or at least the poet's description of it, intensifies the poem's preoccupation with negation. The beloved woman neither accepts nor rejects these dim and unhallowed thoughts. She does not not reject them: "nor . . . dost thou not reject." Coleridge complicates an already tangled syntax, and if this example seems a simple logical negation, the poem foregrounds the trope of litotes all the more explicitly a few lines later: "For never guiltless may I speak of him, / The Incomprehensible!"[51] The beloved's mild (or milded) reproof sends the poet back to God, toward a more conventional story of Christianity against which the poet (and the poem) strains. "Ever guilty" is perhaps too strong, so the poem offers "never guiltless" instead, thus weakening the thought.

If litotes is a recognizable feature of the Greater Romantic Lyric, then nowhere is it more so than in the classic example of the form: Wordsworth's "Lines Composed a Few Miles Above Tintern Abbey." Abrams suggests that Wordsworth's poem perfects the form he learns from Coleridge; and one aspect of this inherited form may be the preoccupation with understatement. Many of the most famous lines from "Tintern Abbey" feature litotes: the landscape has "not been to me / As is a landscape to a blind man's eye"; "feelings too / Of unremembered pleasure; such, perhaps, / As have no slight or trivial influence"; "a feeling and a love, / That had no need of a remoter charm"; "Nor wilt thou then forget."[52] Wordsworth's predilection for such formulations extends well beyond "Tintern Abbey." In "A Night-Piece," for instance, Wordsworth describes the mind as "not undisturbed" and in *The Prelude* he hopes that by pursuing his theme he will be "not uselessly employed."[53] John Jones writes of Wordsworth's style with evident frustration: "Wordsworth carries his delight in negatives to the point of tiresome mannerisms: there are too many double-negatives."[54] Complicating a still dominant reading of romanticism that aligns it with excess, an excess of feeling for instance, Wordsworth also participates in a literary tradition that embraces litotes (as one figure among many for moderation). If one wanted to, one might say that the not lesser Romantic lyric is excessively litotic.

Excessive use of litotes can produce epistemological uncertainty, as negation piles upon negation and the poet's meaning is increasingly obscured. Such an effect is not unique to litotes of course; excessive hyperbole can produce a similar effect, and "incomprehensibility" can threaten to become a poetic ideal, as if epistemological uncertainty were of a higher order than epistemological certainty. Hyperbole and litotes are conventionally categorized under irony, which names one's ability to say something other than what one means. With hyperbole one says a bit more and with litotes one says a bit less, but in both cases what one says is not exactly what one means.

As Christopher Johnson writes in *Hyperboles*:"With hyperbole the speaker . . . suggests that language is poorly suited to represent the *res*, but now he opts for too much, exaggerated, or conceptually audacious speech."[55] One might say something similar about litotes in Wordsworth. "Tintern Abbey" refuses straightforward description, as the poet turns to acts of linguistic negation to communicate language's seeming inadequacy fully to capture a referent. The question of language's adequacy or inadequacy is then transformed into the subject of the poet's meditation. In the poem's concluding lines the poet calls to his sister to bear witness to an experience the poet cannot accurately describe, or can only describe via double negation, and passes on nonetheless. Drawing out the idiom, the experience is passed on and, simultaneously, passed by. Perhaps, suggests Wordsworth's poem, one passes on what one misses, what one passes on.

Not Negative Enough?

In this chapter I have tracked a counterhistory to Baudelaire's argument that hyperbole is most necessary and most pleasing to lyric. Turning to a largely English literary tradition, I have sketched not a history of poetic uses of hyperbole but of understatement, specifically poetic uses of litotes. Many other poems might be included in this history.

One might think of the opening lines of Alfred Lord Tennyson's "Ulysses" ("It little profits that an idle king") or W. H. Auden's "Musée des Beaux Arts":"About suffering they were never wrong."[56] If one wanted one could imagine a taxonomy of poetry that aligned some poets with hyperbole and others with understatement, as we may conventionally align Walt Whitman with more and Emily Dickinson with less. Most poets wrestle with the messy middle, though, employing hyperbole and understatement at different times for different purposes. But interest in understatement shows off the ways poetic forms (like the sonnet or haiku) are unimaginable without various forms of restraint. Indeed, given the importance of form to poetry, one could argue that poetry is committed to the less imposed by formal constraints at least as much as it is committed to the more of imaginative play, as recent work in new formalism and historical poetics has shown.[57] But with Wordsworth we have arrived at a question of pressing importance to poetic language. Is less always more in disguise? Wordsworth, somewhat paradoxically, intensifies understatement through the repetition of figures of negation. Is litotes hyperbole by other means?

In *Labors of Imagination*, Jan Mieszkowski shows how for Immanuel Kant poetry is a discourse of understatement rather than overstatement, as the little the poet announces generates tremendous importance: "The poet," writes Kant in the *Critique of Judgment*, "promises little and announces a mere play with ideas; but he accomplishes something worthy of [being called] a task, for in playing he provides food for the understanding and gives life to its concepts by means of his imagination."[58] For Kant the little the poet promises always invites the plenty of interpretation, and in this way understatement gives way in turn to overstatement. When Friedrich Schlegel argues that Romantic poetry is always in a state of becoming [*ist noch im Werden*], he is responding in part to Kant's celebration of imagination. Romantic poetry is infinite, writes Schlegel, and "in a certain sense all poetry is or should be romantic."[59] One way poetry manifests its infinity is through continued extension as imaginative interpretation.[60] And one might then draw a line from Schlegel to Baudelaire and the more implied by hyperbole. Likewise, in *Theory of the Lyric,* Jonathan Culler suggests that hyperbole is necessary to lyric because lyric ("after" Baudelaire) stakes its significance on the poet's ability to discover tremendous importance in the seemingly inconsequential observation. Culler writes that a "presumption of significance is what permits one to speak, however counterintuitively, of the hyperbolic character of laconic poems," and he offers William Carlos Williams's "The Red Wheelbarrow" as example.[61] In this case, the briefness of "The Red Wheelbarrow" is transformed into the "so much" that depends on it. The inconsequential observation gives rise to a poem that in turn gives rise to extended interpretation. Paul de Man, in "The Rhetoric of Temporality," offers a different expression of the same difficulty when he writes of irony's destabilizing force: "Often starting as litotes or understatement, it contains within itself the power to become hyperbole."[62] De Man includes litotes only as a "starting" place, as if critical attention to litotes must give way to hyperbole. If litotes (less) is always hyperbole (more) in waiting, then Baudelaire's privileging of hyperbole can stand. Baudelaire helps us to see the various ways our conception of lyric (but not only lyric, also poetry, as lyric becomes synonymous with poetry, and even literature more generally) presumes the more of hyperbole.

But Wordsworth's conspicuous use of understatement in "Tintern Abbey" does not always convert double negation into exaggerated affirmation. Of the famous lines from "Tintern Abbey" in which Wordsworth asserts that the "beauteous forms" have not been "as is a landscape to a blind man's eye," Marjorie Levinson writes: "the simile protests too much, and its awkward and confusing litotes calls its claim into question."[63] Given the numerous examples of understatement in the poem, the figurative potential of litotes leads not to hyperbole but to another figure of understatement; frequently, one confusing litotes leads to another confusing litotes. In other words, the poem tests Kant's economics. On the one hand the poem is all about the possibility (the "vain belief") that something not large is not small either, as Wordsworth owes to the memory of "beauteous forms" (not nothing) the possibility of future restoration.[64] But on the other hand, the poem's preoccupation with negation leaves an after-image. At the poem's conclusion, Wordsworth's speaker turns to his sister as the future site of memory: "with what healing thoughts / Of tender joy wilt thou remember me, / And these my exhortations!"[65] But the poet's clear use of "remember" is soon replaced:

> Nor, perchance—
> If I should be where I no more can hear
> Thy voice, nor catch from thy wild eyes these gleams
> Of past existence—wilt thou then forget.[66]

"Remember" is quickly replaced by "Nor . . . wilt thou then forget," as the trope of litotes appears, even if in somewhat disguised form as the em dashes split "nor" from "forget." Perhaps on the off chance readers missed the trope, Wordsworth repeats the formulation in the closing lines:

> Nor wilt thou then forget,
> That after many wanderings, many years
> Of absence, these steep woods and lofty cliffs,
> And this green pastoral landscape, were to me
> More dear, both for themselves and for thy sake![67]

Wordsworth concludes "Tintern Abbey" by repeatedly foregrounding understatement and this late turn toward a female figure (the poet's sister) demonstrates keen awareness of the all-too-common association of women with modesty tropes. But why does the poet repeat himself?

Poets frequently employ litotes as an intensifier, as when the poet of *Beowulf* suggests that Cain "got no good" from killing Abel. What he got was very bad. When the speaker of Tennyson's "Ulysses" suggests that it "little profits" those whom he rules when he doles out unequal laws, what he means is real damage is being done. The poet of "Tintern Abbey" makes clear his awareness of such acts of rhetorical translation when, in closing, he offers his hope that absence (less) is more, "more dear." But the poem embraces a compulsion to repeat that does not lead simply, or completely, or entirely to intensified affirmation, as "remember" is dispersed into repetitions of negation. By repeating the formulation "nor forget," the poem shows how the negation of the negation leads but to another negation of negation, as if the epistemological questions the poem raises cannot be so easily controlled by a dialectical logic that transforms less into more. Does absence guarantee a return? At the same time that the poem asserts the "vain belief" that doubled negation is affirmation by other means, the poem also offers tautology. To not forget is to not forget. Offering direct criticism of Hegel's philosophy, but also, and not unseriously, offering a theory of understatement too, Theodor Adorno writes in *Negative Dialectics*: "To negate a negation does not bring about its reversal; it proves, rather, that the negation was not negative enough. . . . The thesis that the negation of a negation is something positive can only be upheld by one who presupposes positivity . . . from the beginning."[68]

In *Negative Dialectics* Adorno takes issue with Hegel's willingness to fetishize the positive-in-itself in order to develop and celebrate the power of his dialectic. Hegel famously defends tarrying with the negative, but if one's tarrying with the negative always results in movement toward the positive, then the negative is never quite truly negative, or not negative enough. And thus, one has tarried very little. Adorno takes seriously a negativity that cannot be so easily recuperated, one that risks throwing off the dialectic.[69] When Astrophil in Sonnet 63 of *Astrophil and Stella* "misreads" Stella's double protestation ("No, No") as invitation, because "Grammar sayes . . . / That in one speech two Negatives affirm," Sidney may use grammar to excuse harassment, or demonstrate the ways grammar can be used to harass; but he also anticipates Hegel (at least Adorno's version of Hegel).[70] I suggest only somewhat facetiously that Adorno is offering a theory of understatement too because litotes, as is by now familiar, frequently features a negation of a negation. I have asked whether the less of litotes is hyperbole by other means, and one can ask a different version of the question using Adorno's preferred vocabulary. Is litotes always committed to easy reversal? With relative ease readers can "do the math" and convert the double negative into a positive; but in so doing, readers impose grammatical logic on a stubborn rhetorical trope.

Wordsworth's almost incessant use of understatement, his repeated commitment to "nor forget" instead of remember in the closing lines of "Tintern Abbey," can help us to reread some of our earlier examples. In Milton's "Lycidas," for instance, the speaker's plea that Lycidas should not go unwept is not a plea for more intense weeping. "Lycidas" is often described as an elegy, but given the poet's final declaration that Lycidas is not dead, the poem is at most only minimally an elegy. Lycidas may not be alive but he is also not dead. The poem is not not an elegy and calls only for the smallest tear. Similarly, Phillis Wheatley's use of "not unregarding" in "A Farewell to America" to describe the ways the speaker looks upon another's grief does not intensify the feeling; instead, the use of the double negative showcases the possible flatness of the poet's response, thus frustrating the circuit of expected sentimentality. The speaker's feelings are minimal. When one translates less into more too quickly one can miss other effects understatement produces in poetry. I have turned to the poets for help exploring some of the ways poetry's commitment to litotes works to resist, through a minimal embrace, a reader's desire to translate less into more.

Baudelaire suggests that hyperbole is of structural significance to poetry, specifically lyric poetry. One can draw a line from Baudelaire's theory of the lyric to other modern theories of art. Oscar Wilde, for instance, writes: "art itself is really a form of exaggeration; and selection, which is the very spirit of art, is nothing more than an intensified mode of over-emphasis."[71] Many of our most powerful ideas not only about lyric, but also about literature in general, owe much to hyperbole. Poetry is poetry, for instance, because it means excessively, its linguistic structures are never exhausted. What looks small and insignificant in a poem is never just so; active struggle is always rewarded, for what is literary about literature is literature's capacity to signify in ever new and often surprising contexts. For this reason, as Jacques Derrida suggests in "Passions: 'An Oblique Offering,'" there may be "no democracy without literature."[72] There may be no democracy without institutions that encourage an excess of voices, perspectives, differences.

But when Baudelaire in "The Painter of Modern Life" attempts to describe an appropriate attitude toward the ephemeral givenness of the present moment, he too turns to litotes. Baudelaire makes fun of those painters who reject the present, deciding it to be ugly, and so paint contemporary subjects in costumes from the Middle Ages or the Renaissance. He argues that such an approach to one's subject is lazy; it is easier to decide in advance that everything is ugly than devote oneself to the slightly or minimally beautiful. "This transitory, fugitive element," writes Baudelaire, "you do not have the right to despise or dispense with it."[73] Baudelaire offers something like an understated maxim or a maxim of understatement. As Baudelaire shows, most have difficulty embracing these slight, minimal, fugitive elements. Building from Coleridge's fascination with various ephemera, which he termed "spectra," Rei Terada connects Coleridge to Adorno in *Looking Away* to explore what it might mean for perception not to compel endorsement or affirmative belief.[74] Instead of writing that one has the right to fancy the transitory, fugitive element, Baudelaire writes that one does not have the right to despise it, where "not despise" is not quite the same as "welcome." His conspicuous use of litotes—his negation of a negation—demonstrates his desire to hold back from calling directly for immediate acceptance, as if an encounter with the minimal can only be minimally claimed.

From Baudelaire to Wilde, poetry is associated with excess and read by the light of hyperbole. And this is, of course, not wrong, even if as a result one might sometimes miss the ways poetry struggles *for* less. Poetry, in other words, does not always follow Quintilian's offhand suggestion that it is better to go too far than not far enough. Poetry sometimes settles for less. But less is often difficult to accept, especially in a world that increasingly demands that one be always up and always on, a world increasingly committed to the more of surplus. To ignore modes of poetic thinking understatement makes possible, to see litotes as a failure of nerve, as archaic and unnecessary, perhaps even unpleasing, or to see it as hyperbole in waiting, is to miss the ways poets throw into sharp relief the ways more—under late capitalism, for instance—is more and more demanded. Poetry shows readers how remarkably difficult it is to accept what is given without investing in it or making more of it. To learn to read in an understated sort of way would be to learn how not to despise the little there is.

2. The Poetics of Downturns

Prepare for an unusual kind of downturn.

—*The Economist*

Taken together my first two chapters tweak Charles Baudelaire's understanding of the lyric, which he associates with hyperbole and apostrophe. In my first chapter, "Understating Poetry," I ask how our understanding not only of the lyric but also of poetry more generally might change when we foreground litotes (and other related tropes of understatement) in the history of poetry. If my first chapter substitutes understatement for Baudelaire's overstatement, this second chapter adopts a more speculative line of approach, one that owes much to the sounds of words and loose etymologies. The reverse of apostrophe would be something like description, suggests Jonathan Culler in *Theory of the Lyric*.[1] And though description has received recent attention, as critics question the importance of critique, "The Poetics of Downturns" substitutes *catastrophe* for apostrophe to reconsider lyric poetry. From the Greek *kata* ("down," but also "against" or "over") and *strephein* ("to turn"), *catastrophe* can translate literally as a "downturn." The word carries many of the same connotations as cataclysm, which similarly refers to a disastrous event, one marked by ruination, but unlike cataclysm, which refers to a downward flood, or the action of being washed down and away, catastrophe figures the act of "turning" and so is related, however tendentiously, to a rhetorical trope such as apostrophe (from *apo*, "away": to turn away). In this chapter I return to poems by Willian Wordsworth, this time paying particular attention to metaphors of "downturns" in Wordsworth's poetry, moments when heads are turned down toward the ground. Wordsworth is a poet of catastrophes and cataclysms; his poems chronicle the many disasters and calamities that befall the dispossessed. As in other chapters in this book that proceed by juxtaposing poetic tropes and contemporary discourse, here I focus attention on Wordsworth's "downturns" in order to discover in the rhetoric of poetry a chance to interrogate the rhetoric of contemporary capitalism and the effects of economic catastrophe.

Romantic poets make frequent use of the rhetorical trope of apostrophe, in which poet-speakers turn away from their present audience to address some absent or inanimate object. In *Theory of the Lyric*, Jonathan Culler cites numerous examples from canonical Romantic poems (like William Blake's "The Sick Rose," Percy Shelley's "Ode to the West Wind," and John Keats's "Ode to a Nightingale") and, following Baudelaire, argues for the importance of apostrophe to the idea of lyric in particular and to conceptualizations of poetry more generally. Culler takes seriously a poetic trope that readers sometimes avoid noticing. It can be a little embarrassing for readers, suggests Culler, when poets address absent, dead, or inanimate entities, but "apostrophe treats the subject's relation to the world as a specular relationship, a relation between subjects."[2] In other words, apostrophe has everything to do with poetic power, for through apostrophic address the poet claims the power to turn absent, dead, or inanimate entities into present, living, or animate interlocutors. As Barbara Johnson writes in *Persons and Things*, "apostrophe enables the poet to transform an 'I-it' relationship into an 'I-thou' relationship, thus making a relation between persons out of [what] was in fact a relation between a person and non-persons."[3] While the study of rhetorical tropes and figures may seem far removed from pressing issues of social life, apostrophe, like prosopopoeia (to be discussed in chapter 4), stages questions about the rhetoric of personhood. Literary scholars interested in apostrophe continue to raise compelling and important questions about figures that, as Johnson writes, refuse "to remain comfortably and conventionally figurative."[4] Virginia Jackson has recently returned to Johnson's "Apostrophe, Animation, Abortion" essay, from which the above quotation is drawn, to consider apostrophic address in the 1828 ode, "On Liberty and Slavery," by George Moses Horton, who was enslaved for sixty-eight years. Metaphors of confinement and slavery abound in white, Romantic writing, but, Jackson asks, "What happens when the fictional subject and the fictional object of a Romantic apostrophic ode are both constrained by the discourses of social death on which poetics (well, on which everything) has been built over the last two hundred years?"[5] In *The Calamity Form: On Poetry and Social Life*, specifically the final chapter "Apostrophe: Clouds," Anahid Nersessian similarly explores the ways apostrophe registers forms of precarity and dispossession that do not remain conventionally figurative.[6] Calamity form recalls, for Nersessian, Karl Marx's commodity form, and Wordsworth often uses "calamity" to refer to suffering, individual or national, caused when no provocation has been given.

But in this chapter, taking for granted the importance of lyric address to Romantic and post-Romantic poetry, I shift the focus from apostrophe to catastrophe, from turns away to turns down. Such downturns are not unrelated to tropes of falling, which have played a significant role in the critical discourse of romanticism, especially when romanticism is read with, against, and alongside the poetry of John Milton, but not only Milton. Amanda Jo Goldstein offers a powerful new understanding of romanticism's relationship to falling in *Sweet Science* by showing just how central Lucretius's mode of materialist, didactic poesis remained for Romantic writers.[7] But is it more than just the result of faux etymology work, and more than historical accident, that a certain preoccupation in Romantic poetry with the rhetorical trope of apostrophe should coincide with a certain fascination with catastrophes, with falling, with fallings from us, with vanishings, with decline? As Jonathan Sachs suggests in *The Poetics of Decline in British Romanticism*, "Anxieties about decline—national and imperial, economic and political, cultural and literary—are a pervasive feature of British public discourse in the later eighteenth and early nineteenth century."[8] What is the relationship between the animating power of turning away (apostrophe) and the potentially deanimating power of turning down (catastrophe)?

I ask these questions at a moment when catastrophe seems to have become all too common, and "common" in all the various senses of the word: shared, ordinary, ubiquitous, and so forth. Hannah Arendt identifies the origin of the modern world with the splitting of the atom in *The Human Condition*. The modern world begins, she argues, once a common catastrophe is imaginable, a catastrophe that happens to all life.[9] To be modern is to live in a world that can end, and since 1958, when Arendt published *The Human Condition*, the variety of ways the end of the world has been imagined has only increased, with images of environmental catastrophe added to images of nuclear catastrophe. But in *On Photography* Susan Sontag worries that as images of catastrophe become part of everyday experience in an age of mass communication, viewers become desensitized to extreme forms of violence, political oppression, and degradation, and these images lose any emotional or political effect.[10] Sontag identifies a risk present in the commonness of catastrophe: as catastrophe becomes common it can cease to appear fully catastrophic, or, to borrow from John Keats, one can feel the feel of not feeling it.[11] The more present something, the more difficult it can become to experience it. Though the devastating effects of climate catastrophe will not be evenly distributed, the commonness of catastrophe today, especially given the ways capitalism, as a world system, inspires and in turn benefits from natural and so-called manmade disaster, can make response difficult. How does one understand crisis in the midst of crisis, in the midst of so many crises? How does one think the ever present? In this chapter I ask how figures drawn from Romantic poetry might help us to think about the ubiquity of catastrophe differently.[12]

Apostrophes and catastrophes share a turn, the turn of figuration and figuration may be necessary for encountering that which has become ubiquitous. In "How Keats Falls," Jonathan Mulrooney reminds readers how difficult falling is to register, especially in a post-Newtonian world where the difference between "falling" and "standing still" remains stubbornly unavailable to sensation.[13] One stands still, in effect, only because one is already falling, even if one does not feel like one is falling. To *see* falling and to *know* falling may not be the same thing. Figure makes the difference. Catastrophe similarly demands the work of figuration, and importantly the word recalls a history of figure and figuration. Before meaning "a disaster," *catastrophe* in English referred to the change that produces the conclusion or final event of a play.[14] Wordsworth uses *catastrophe* this way in book 3 of *The Excursion*: "who should have grieved / At aught, however fair, that bore the mien / Of a conclusion, or catastrophe."[15] Put too simplistically, catastrophe named a figure before it named an event; only after several centuries of use in English does the aesthetic give way to the historical, as *catastrophe* comes to name a sudden disaster or calamity, an event of historical importance (not the end of a play but the end of the world).

I draw out this history of catastrophe to reopen and amplify catastrophe's figurative potential. In this chapter, and relying on the etymology of *catastrophe*, I take up figures in Wordsworth's poetry that are likewise down turned: human figures with heads turned down toward the ground, figures bent earthward, stooped, slumped, stumbling, falling, even hanging down. Wordsworth's figures can sometimes seem far removed from the real-world effects of catastrophe but his poetic—even philological—investigation of catastrophe through the downturn offers a chance for gentled engagement with the ongoing catastrophes of modern life that may otherwise, and more threateningly, overwhelm the mind. When Wordsworth in the advertisement to *Lyrical Ballads* anticipates that readers might look round for poetry, he also invites readers to discover poetry in that which does not "appear" as poetry. In moving from the rhetoric of economics to poetry and from poetry to the rhetoric of economics, my hope is that attention to the history of tropes and figures (however speculative) present in a word like *catastrophe* offers a chance to think the effects of world systems through the small, seemingly insignificant gesture: the downturned brow, the look down. Given the effects of downturns on the world economy, my interest is in the ways poets figure the downturn and in how, however anachronistically, poets might help us think the rhetoric and economics of downturns today.

Looking Up

Wordsworth's poetry is full of downturns. In "Lines Left Upon a Seat in a Yew-Tree" the poet-narrator remembers a youth nursed by science who first piled up stones near the yew-tree memorialized by the poem. The poet-narrator well remembers this "favored" being, now neglected, who turned himself from the world and sustained himself in solitude:

> Stranger! these gloomy boughs
> Had charms for him; and here he loved to sit,
> His only visitants a straggling sheep,
> The stone-chat, or the glancing sand-piper;
> And on these barren rocks, with juniper,
> And heath and thistle, thinly sprinkled o'er,
> Fixing his downward eye, he many an hour
> A morbid pleasure nourished, tracing here
> An emblem of his own unfruitful life.[16]

As Geoffrey Hartman notes, the inscription halts the traveler, the addressed "Stranger," in order to tell the story of this youth who fixed his downcast eyes for many an hour taking pleasure in his own morbid thoughts.[17] Here the downcast eye is a sign of the mind's potentially unfruitful introspection. But the youth soon looks up: "lifting up his head, he then would gaze / On the more distant scene" (ll. 30–31). In some important ways, "Lines" is a poem about the effects of looking up. The youth, as if trapped by his own morbid thoughts, thoughts that give him an unhealthily morbid pleasure, looks up to discover a distant lovely scene that disturbs him; the language used to describe the loveliness he sees is subtly violent, as his heart gives out: "his heart could not sustain / The beauty" (ll. 34–35). In "Lines," Wordsworth documents the potential cost of looking up for a youth unwilling to think of anything but himself, or unable to experience nature except as a reflection of his own consciousness. The youth's thoughts are ever on himself and this degree of self-consciousness occasions a potentially deadly experience of beauty.

The youth's looking up damages his heart. The beauty of the world is too much for him. Later lines of the poem warn readers that "The man, whose eye / Is ever on himself, doth look on one, / The least of Nature's works" (ll. 51–53). Wordsworth's poem offers a warning to all who might take too great an interest in themselves, for though one is a work of Nature one who looks "ever" on oneself mistakes the least for the greatest of Nature's works. The youth's eyes are fixed, meaning set firmly in position, but his fixed eyes signify a problem. By fixing his eyes he does not "fix" the problem of self-consciousness. His downcast eyes are otherwise fixed and as a result he precludes for himself an experience of Nature as something more than, or even simply something other than, an extension of himself. The youth casts his eyes down in order to fix his thoughts on himself and in the process the youth's eventual death is foretold. The youth's fixed eye cannot fix him. In this deep vale he dies. Here, the downward eye is a sign of intense self-interest, a self-interest that is always possibly debilitating.

Wordsworth revisits the figure of the downturn, or what I am referring to as the downturn, in two related and well-known poems: "A Night-Piece" and the Ascent of Mount Snowdon episode, with which *The Prelude* concludes. The passages are often productively paired. Lily Gurton-Wachter, for instance, takes them as epigraphs for the third chapter of *Watchwords: Romanticism and the Poetics of Attention*, "Bent Earthwards: Wordsworth's Poetics of the Interval," where she explores the potential risks of a too-fixed attention. She begins with Thomas De Quincey, who remembers Wordsworth applying his ear to the ground waiting for the mail carrier to arrive with news from the current war. When pressed by De Quincey Wordsworth explains that he focuses his attention so that he might relax it: "I have remarked, from my earliest days, that if, under any circumstances, the attention is energetically braced up to an act of steady observation, or of steady expectation, then, if this intense condition of vigilance should suddenly relax, at that moment, any beautiful, any impressive visual object, or collection of objects, falling upon the eye, is carried to the heart with a power not known under other circumstances."[18] Gurton-Wachter takes Wordsworth's experiment with his ear to the ground as a guiding figure, as she focuses on "the spontaneous and surprisingly productive moment of turning away—or *no longer*—paying attention," and discovers in Wordsworth's poetry a theory of perception that does not idealize hypervigilance but instead celebrates at least momentary distraction.[19] The relaxation of attention makes poetry possible and, suggests Gurton-Wachter, occasions alternative modes of observing history, especially in the context of ongoing and perpetual war.[20]

In both "A Night-Piece" and the Ascent of Mount Snowdon episode Wordsworth explores the possibility of looking up as a break from the potential trap of self-consciousness explored in "Lines." In "A Night-Piece" a traveler is startled by a pleasant instantaneous gleam on the ground. The poem describes a traveler moving though a landscape only barely lit by an obscured moon: "a pleasant instantaneous light / Startles the musing man whose eyes are bent / to Earth."[21] The traveler is bent earthward; he is turned down. Startled, he looks about. He looks around. In 1815 Wordsworth revises the lines, accentuating the preposition *up*: "At length a pleasant instantaneous gleam / Startles the pensive traveller as he treads / His lonesome path, with unobserving eye / Bent earthwards: he looks up—the clouds are split."[22] The traveler's "unobserving eye" makes possible the mind's delight, for like the youth in "Lines" the traveler looks up and views the clear moon and the glory of the heavens. Unlike the youth in "Lines," though, the traveler's look up occasions a poem. Whether the act of looking up causes the clouds to split asunder or whether the dash in 1815 simply records a chance coincidence: in either case the unobserving eye bent earthwards, bent toward the ground, conditions the possibility of a startle, a start. Looking down the pensive traveler is delighted, as the downturn conditions the possibility of poetic vision. He has vision; he has a vision. The clouds are split and glory revealed. Left to "muse upon the solemn scene," Wordsworth's traveler becomes a poet, one capable of musing.[23] "A Night-Piece" tells the story of a poet's beginning, as poetry begins with an eye bent earthwards followed by a look about, a look up that makes poetic musing possible. In marked contrast to the youth of "Lines Left Upon a Seat in a Yew-Tree," where looking up comes at a cost, as the youth's self-involvement leads to a dangerous heart condition, here the traveler's looking up in fact occasions the start of a poem, the traveler becomes a visionary as he is granted access to (a) vision. Significantly, the poem moves from an unobserving eye to a musing mind, from eye to mind. The sequence that begins with an eye bent earthward takes the place of a traditional Muse, the source of poetic inspiration, as muse is transformed into a verb.

Wordsworth reprises aspects of "A Night-Piece" in the Ascent of Mount Snowdon episode from *The Prelude*: "With forehead bent / Earthward, as if in opposition set / Against an enemy, I panted up / With eager pace."[24] As in "A Night-Piece," the poet walks with his head bowed, bent earthward, and likewise he looks up. Actually, in the 1805 *Prelude* the poet looks "about" and in 1850 the poet looks "up"—

> instantly a light upon the turf
> Fell like a flash. I looked about, and lo,
> The moon stood naked in the heavens at height
> Immense above my head[25]

> instantly a light upon the turf
> Fell like a flash, and lo! As I looked up,
> The Moon hung naked in a firmament
> Of azure without cloud[26]

—but in both versions, the poet's brow is no longer bent earthward. The poet discovers a scene worthy of poetic reflection by looking about, by looking up. As in "A Night-Piece" the traveler poet has been surprised and the poet turns the instant into an instance, an example. The downturned brow is no permanent state but sets the conditions for surprise; it sets the conditions for poetic creativity. The power of Wordsworth's poetry comes in part from moments like these, when the unremarkable event offers new poetic possibilities for noticing what one would otherwise have failed to notice. As one moves from "Lines" through "A Night-Piece" to *The Prelude*, one senses Wordsworth attempting to work out the sorts of looking up that enable poetic creativity. Much rests on the possibility of the bend; in opposition to the fixed eye, the bent brow introduces the possibility of future motion, motion necessary to poetic creativity and the creation of a musing mind. The fact that the youth in "Lines" dies suggests that much is risked by the look up. But "A Night-Piece" and *The Prelude* suggest what might also be gained when one's eyes are not fixed. In his reading of the scene from *The Prelude*, Geoffrey Hartman remarks that though Wordsworth "moves toward a self-recognition which will halt the traveler, erase the landscape, break the dream," though he moves toward "a fixed, abysmal, gloomy, breathing-place," "the fixating shock of self-consciousness is avoided."[27] One hears Hartman punning on the various meanings of fix, as if alluding to the youth's "fixed" downcast eyes in "Lines Left Upon a Seat in a Yew-Tree."

In his return to Geoffrey Hartman's reading, Joshua Wilner draws out the implicit contrast Hartman makes between the Ascent of Snowdon and the Apostrophe to the Imagination in book 6 of *The Prelude*, where Wordsworth's account of crossing the Alps is interrupted. In the Apostrophe to the Imagination "consciousness of self [is] raised to apocalyptic pitch," writes Hartman, but in the Ascent of Mount Snowdon "instead of apocalypse, there is only developing and self-displacing vision."[28] Wilner suspects that Hartman's reading of the Apostrophe to the Imagination has been more influential to readers, as imagination displaces literal description, than his reading of the Ascent of Snowdon. But as he shows, apostrophe and apocalypse are never far from one another in Wordsworth's poetry and in *Wordsworth's Poetry*.

But if there is no "apocalypse" in the Ascent of Mount Snowdon, there is at least one other catastrophe, one other downturn. In the 1805 version, while the poet looks about, the moon looks down: "Meanwhile, the moon looked down upon this shew."[29] Wordsworth places the subtly anthropomorphized moon in the position formerly occupied by the poet with brow bent earthward. The poet's brow cannot be lifted without leaving or noticing a remainder, someone or something still downturned. By virtue of the subtle anthropomorphism, the moon seems more idiomatically to look down on the show, as if the moon were not that impressed with all these upsides to downturns.

The moon's look down suggests that *The Prelude* resists any simple or final reversal. Similarly, up does not follow down, at least if one pays attention to the prepositions. In 1805 the poet looks *about* and the moon looks *down*. When Wordsworth revises the episode for the 1850 version of the poem, the poet looks *up* but the moon gazes *upon* the billowy ocean. I began thinking about Wordsworthian downturns in the wake of the Great Recession, which officially ended in the United States in 2009 and which, like many prior recessions, inspired new books for investors. As Geoff Colvin acknowledges in *The Upside of the Downturn*, downturns and even recessions—defined as two consecutive quarters of negative growth—are structural features of late, finance capitalism. For Colvin, the question is, how might one take best advantage of this structural feature:

> The terrible misery that people globally endured during the recession is tragic, and for many it isn't over. Economists say the US recession ended in 2009, but millions still can't find jobs, and pay isn't rising....The whole business world has turned upside down. The assumptions, strategies, practices, and basic truths that managers used to rely on don't seem to hold anymore....Yet I hope it's clear that for businesses and even for us individually, what many people regard as bad news ... can actually be good news. For this is that rare situation when we all face the greatest possible opportunity to make ourselves winners for a long time to come.[30]

Colvin's book is designed to help readers discover the economic upside to a downturn and reverse it. But Colvin's "we" in the quotation above does not include those for whom the downturn was more catastrophic. Colvin's imagined reader has not been overwhelmed by the crisis. Behind Colvin's book (and so many others like it) stands that common idiomatic expression: never let a good crisis go to waste. Wordsworth's poem is careful not to embrace this easy reversibility, as if *down* were just *up* in disguise. Colvin shows how this easy reversibility is supposed to work—for some.

Turned Down

Beyond those I have listed already, numerous examples of figures similarly described as bent or turned toward the earth can be found in Wordsworth's poetry, for instance when the poet-speaker of "The Discharged Soldier," later incorporated into *The Prelude*, turns and "through the trees look[s] down." Or when the pedlar, Armytage, in "The Ruined Cottage," which later became book 1 of *The Excursion*, describes Margaret: "evermore / Her eye-lids drooped, her eyes were downward cast."[31] Margaret's downward cast eyes contrast powerfully with both the poet-speaker and Armytage, both of whom are described elsewhere in the poem as "looking round," as capable of looking around.[32] In the second half of this chapter I linger over another of Wordsworth's downturned figures, the beggar from "The Old Cumberland Beggar," whose eyes, like Margaret's, are "evermore" on the ground. A figure for the downturn, his eyes are turned down. Emily Sun reminds readers in *Succeeding King Lear* that Wordsworth planned for "A Night-Piece," "The Discharged Soldier," "The Ruined Cottage," and "The Old Cumberland Beggar," to form one of the introductions to *The Recluse*, Wordsworth's unfinished encyclopedic poem.[33] And the poems, all written around the same time, share many thematic ties: including focused attention on the effects of war on the precarious poor.

The Old Cumberland Beggar does not look up. He does not look about. And he does not, recalling this book's title, look round. The poem "The Old Cumberland Beggar" investigates even as it challenges downturns as the conditioning possibility for future upturns. The old beggar

> travels on, a solitary Man,
> His age has no companion. On the ground
> His eyes are turned, and, as he moves along,
> *They* move along the ground; and evermore,
> Instead of common and habitual sight
> Of fields with rural works, of hill and dale,
> And the blue sky, one little span of earth
> Is all his prospect.[34]

"The Old Cumberland Beggar" was likely composed in 1798, sometime between "Lines" and "A Night-Piece," and published for the first time in the 1800 edition of *Lyrical Ballads*. Like many other poems in *Lyrical Ballads*, the poem tells the story of a dispossessed vagrant, an old beggar who moves through the village receiving "the dole of village dames" (l. 9). As Wordsworth explains in his note to Isabella Fenwick from 1843, the poem was written as "the political economists were . . . beginning their war upon mendicity in all its forms, and by implication, if not directly, on almsgiving also." "This heartless process," continues Wordsworth, "has been carried as far as it can go by the AMENDED poor-law bill."[35] By putting the poor to work, the amended poor law bill aimed to substitute paid labor for charity. Wordsworth's poem argues against houses of industry that would make the Old Cumberland Beggar "a captive" (l. 173). By confining him to the workplace, houses of industry also confine him to a limited, explicitly utilitarian purpose. As Philip Connell writes: the poem is "an implicit criticism of political economy as a legitimate approach to the problems of destitution and pauperism."[36] Wordsworth writes against houses of industry because they equate one's social value with one's industrial productivity, equate life with economic usefulness.

Unlike other moments in Wordsworth's poetry, where the downturn conditions the possibility for poetic vision, the Old Cumberland Beggar's vision, his prospects, are severely limited and the poem goes out of its way, with the use of the word "evermore," to suggest, however hyperbolically, that there will be no change. The lines of the poem that describe the beggar's downturned eyes also suggest forms of violence that do not remain comfortably figurative: "On the ground / His eyes are turned, and, as he moves along, / *They* move along the ground." Here "they" refers back to the beggar's eyes, but the line break separates the beggar from his eyes, as "he" and "they" are split, suggesting, for a moment, that he does not move along with his eyes. As he moves, they move as well, as if the beggar's eyes had fallen and now roll along the ground. This split is accentuated by Wordsworth's decision to italicize "they." The downturn has affected the beggar's vision and for a moment it can seem as if the beggar has lost his sight. In contrast to the youth nursed by science in "Lines," who gazes, and the traveler from "A Night-Piece," who looks, the beggar neither gazes nor looks. His eyes move along the ground but he does not "see" or "gaze" or "look." He is denied any "prospect," from the Latin *prospectus* ("distant view, look out; sight, faculty of sight"); in "The Old Cumberland Beggar" the chance to receive the poet's compensatory vision is buried deep in the noun form "prospect," and the action of the passage is similarly reduced to a static "is": "one little span of earth / Is all his prospect."[37]

The poem explores the effects on individuals of a political economy that centralizes wealth and expands economic inequality. In this way the poem is about downturns as they relate to prospects, the beggar's future prospects. Wordsworth contrasts the beggar's downturn with the "common" sight and thus positions "The Old Cumberland Beggar" in opposition to the tradition of the prospect or loco-descriptive poem (a tradition that, in turn, gives rise to what M. H. Abrams famously calls the Greater Romantic Lyric, discussed in chapter 1, poems in which a speaker describes a landscape and embellishes the description with reminiscence and meditation). As Joseph Addison writes in "Pleasures of Imagination," the man of polite imagination can experience "a secret Refreshment in a Description, and often feels a greater Satisfaction in the Prospect of Fields and Meadows, than another does in the Possession."[38] The loco-descriptive poem replaces the satisfaction of ownership with the satisfaction of description. The pleasure of describing a prospect is greater, Addison suggests, than actual, material prospects (transferred by possession). When the poet stands at the right spot, he has all he needs. Wordsworth engages this tradition throughout his poetry. In the Simplon Pass episode of *The Prelude*, for instance, Wordsworth takes as the poem's occasion the poet's failure to arrive at the appointed spot at the appointed time. Imagination rises up in the poet-narrator when he realizes that he has missed the chance to stand on the pass and describe what he sees. In "The Old Cumberland Beggar," Wordsworth plays the available pun. In contrast to the poet-figure who is offered a vision of the glory of the heavens upon looking up, the Old Cumberland Beggar will have for his prospect one little span of earth.[39] The beggar's future prospects are as dramatically limited as his view. And in this way Wordsworth shows the lie to the prospect poem. Addison's man of polite imagination can substitute the prospect of fields and meadows for the satisfaction of possession because he already possesses the basic material resources he needs.

I take Wordsworth's pun on prospects, as well as his pun on "common," as license for my own investigation into "downturns." John Barrell explores the relationship between the prospect poem, which celebrates the panoramic view of the gentleman, and the writing of eighteenth-century political economists like Adam Smith in *English Literature in History, 1730-80: An Equal, Wide Survey*.[40] To understand the workings of a modern political economy, to see the invisible hand at work, suggests Smith, one must view the whole as if from above. Wordsworth's poem suggests the opposite. The *Oxford English Dictionary* offers 1926 as the first instance of *downturn* as "a turning downward; a decline, esp. in economic or business activity." But Wordsworth, however anachronistically, however speculatively, unites prospects and downturns, and, to draw out this line of argument, unites downturns (turns down) with downturns (decline, even catastrophe), as a boom-and-bust political economy that increases precarity also produces a subject with eyes ever turned down. In "The Old Cumberland Beggar," Wordsworth reverses the title of Geoff Colvin's book, *The Upside of the Downturn*, and presents the downturns the upside requires. The beggar's prospects cannot easily be reversed. In a sense, Wordsworth's poem lingers with the first sentence from the quote above from *The Upside of the Downturn*: "The terrible misery that people globally endured during the recession is tragic, and for many it isn't over." Colvin's point, perhaps somewhat crassly put, is "don't be like them!"

But Wordsworth's poem does not oppose the general logic of Colvin's reversal in any simple way, for though the poem's language suggests that the beggar's prospects will not be reversed the poem nonetheless attempts a dramatic reversal of its own, strongly identifying an upside to the beggar's downturn. Critics frequently turn to "The Old Cumberland Beggar" to investigate Wordsworth's thinking about political economy and frequently note that Wordsworth's response to the problem of poverty is potentially shocking.[41] Wordsworth's poem defends the beggar's freedom by arguing that the beggar is not in fact useless to the village. Though there may be no upside for the beggar, there is an upside for the village: "While thus he creeps / From door to door, the Villagers in him / Behold a record which together binds / Past deeds and offices of charity / Else unremembered, and so keeps alive / The kindly mood in hearts which lapse of years ... Make slow to feel."[42] Arguing that the vagrant beggar has a social function, as the beggar binds together the village and so "keeps alive / the kindly mood" in others, Wordsworth suggests in closing that the beggar should be allowed to die: "As in the eye of Nature he has lived, / So in the eye of Nature let him die!" (ll. 188–89). The "uselessness" of the beggar is useful to the construction of the village community, as the villagers find themselves, like past deeds and offices of charity, bound together. A visible reminder of forgotten acts of charity, the beggar makes the village community a community, even as he remains excluded from that very same community. As readers have recognized, the poem strains to protect the possible upside that accompanies the beggar's downturned gaze, the catastrophe, that keeps alive kindly moods. If the beggar is made a captive in a "House, misnamed of industry" (l. 172), then not only will the beggar's freedom be curtailed (as he is subjected to demands of usefulness and put to work) but the village will also potentially lose the "bind" that makes kindly moods live between villagers. Both the beggar and the villager, the poem suggests, will be adversely affected. But the solution the poem offers is potentially shocking: "let him die!" So that kindly moods might live, the beggar must (be let to) die. David Simpson damningly characterizes this moment: "We must all have wondered, in reading and teaching 'The Old Cumberland Beggar,' for example, whether Wordsworth might have been devoid of certain basic human sympathies for the intrinsic well-being of aging vagrants."[43] Lamenting that Wordsworth does not express enough dissatisfaction with a political economy that produces poverty, Gary Harrison quotes an early reader of Wordsworth's, Orestes Brownson, who writes in the *Boston Quarterly Review* in 1839 that "Wordsworth sings beggars, we admit, and shows very clearly that a man who begs is not to be despised; but does he ever fire our souls with a desire to perfect our social system, that beggary shall not be one of its fruits?"[44] Eric Lindstrom qualifies such readings by focusing on Wordsworth's use of the fiat, where the weakened "let" formulation repeats in the closing lines: "let the light," "let him ... sit down," "let him die!" "Wordsworth's fiat," suggests Lindstrom, "knowingly falls short of efficient instrumentality. It is deliberately ineffectual."[45] Though

Wordsworth's identification of an upside to the beggar's downturn remains potentially shocking, Lindstrom lingers over those aspects of the poem's language that may challenge this easy reversal.

The Downturn's Downside

I have placed "The Old Cumberland Beggar" in relationship to several other Wordsworth poems in which figures are downturned, with brows bent toward the earth. Wordsworth's preoccupation with such downturns becomes more unavoidable the more frequently such turned figures appear. But before concluding this chapter, I want to place Wordsworth's downturned old beggar among a wider tradition of similarly downturned figures, a tradition that includes texts by Wordsworth's frequent interlocutors: Plato, Dante, and Milton. Figures that look down or bend to the earth are used for many purposes: to signify concentration, as a response to defeat, devotion, or hard labor, etc. Plato, for instance, repeats the story of Thales of Miletus, the pre-Socratic philosopher so focused on looking up that he repeatedly falls down into a well, in *Theaetetus*, and the story of Thales is frequently used to satirize the philosopher-academic-dreamer so preoccupied with "higher" order thinking that he forgets to attend to more mundane matters. Looking up too often or for too long can come at a potential cost. But significantly for "The Old Cumberland Beggar," given the poem's focus on precarious economic conditions, texts from Plato, Dante, and Milton also frequently associate the downturned figure with greed. In a poem about the effects of economic policy on the poor, Wordsworth takes up this tradition but makes of the downturn a sign of want.

In *The Republic*, Plato several times refers to figures with downturned heads, and in *The Republic* these examples are almost always negative. In book 8, for instance, Plato describes the money lenders who, instead of looking up to see the numerous inhabitants of the city now burdened with debt and disenfranchised, keep their heads down. Here keeping one's head down is a sign that one refuses to bear witness to the effects of one's economic decisions. Keeping their eyes down on their ledgers, the money lenders pretend not to see the suffering they cause: "money-makers with down-bent heads [*hoi de dē khrēmatistai egkupsantes*], pretending not to see them [those burdened with debt], but inserting the sting of their money into the remainder who do not resist."[46] Keeping their heads down allows the money lenders to continue their potentially abusive lending practices. The head bent earthward is willed, a conscious decision to forge ahead with lending practices that are known to cause pain and suffering. Looking down offers the money lenders a way to defend themselves from full recognition of the negative effects they are having on the Republic. A similar image recurs in book 9 of *The Republic*, where those uninterested in wisdom sway and roam without direction: "They have never . . . turned their eyes to the true upper region . . . nor ever been really filled with real things, . . . but with eyes ever bent upon the earth and heads bowed down over their tables they feast like cattle."[47] With eyes looking ever down [*katō*] they bend [*kekuphotes*] toward the earth. For Plato those who look always at the ground refuse the truth of wisdom; they do not look up and away from the earth. If Thales never looks down until it is too late, those who feast over their tables like cattle similarly do not look up until it is too late. Plato's condemnation of those unwilling to look up appears throughout his writing; from the *Symposium* to *Cratylus* looking down for too long is a sign of one's willingness to sacrifice eternal truth for momentary pleasure. Dante and Milton pick up the trope, and Wordsworth turns it dramatically around in "The Old Cumberland Beggar."

Canto XIX of Dante's *Purgatorio* offers a short treatise on downturns, one Wordsworth may have had in mind while crafting "The Old Cumberland Beggar." Dante's speaker is pulled along by Virgil: "I followed him, bearing my brow like one / whose thoughts have weighed him down, who bends as if / he were the semiarch that forms a bridge." Like Wordsworth's traveler in "A Night-Piece" and the poet of *The Prelude*, Dante's speaker travels with his head down until Virgil interrupts his thoughts. As they begin to climb, Virgil asks: "What makes you keep your eyes upon the ground [*Che hai che pur inver' la terra guati*]?" Virgil tells Dante to look up, and, as if this advice anticipated the next encounter, Virgil and Dante enter the fifth level of Purgatory and see stretched prone upon the ground, all weeping, a people turned down: "my eyes discovered people there who wept, / lying upon the ground, all turned face down [*a terra tutta volta in guiso*]." Dante discovers the avaricious and one of them, still turned down, explains: "Just as we did not lift our eyes on high / but set our sight on earthly things instead, / so justice here impels our eyes toward earth."[48]

One last link in this loosely associated chain of figures, from Milton's *Comus*. As Comus attempts to convince the Lady to partake of his feast, Comus offers a familiar argument: the Lady should partake of the feast because what is Nature for if not providing in abundance. "Beauty is Nature's coin," asserts Comus, and must not be "hoarded."[49] If one does not partake of Nature's goodness and beauty, the all-giver "would be unthanked, would be unpraised."[50] In response the Lady offers an argument about inequality:

> If every just man that now pines with want
> Had but a moderate and beseeming share
> Of that which lewdly-pampered luxury

Now heaps upon some few with vast excess,
Nature's full blessings would be well-dispensed
In unsuperfluous even proportion,
And she no whit encumber with her store,
And then the giver would be better thanked,
His praise due paid, for swinish gluttony
Ne'er looks to heaven amidst his gorgeous feast,
But with besotted base ingratitude
Crams, and blasphemes his feeder. Shall I go on?[51]

This passage is particularly interesting for a number of reasons. First, the Lady offers a response to Comus that embraces the redistribution of wealth, thus drawing a line between Plato, Milton, and Wordsworth, as "The Old Cumberland Beggar" defends acts of charity as one privileged response to economic inequality. Here in *Comus*, though, while the Lady defends charity she does not limit her response *to* charity. Instead, she comes across as a bit more radical. Luxury heaps upon some few a vast excess. And in this way the Lady is responding to fortune, recognizing that chance has distributed wealth unevenly. An argument in favor of charity often assumes that those with more should distribute some of what they have to those who have less; but rarely does charity result in "unsuperfluous even proportion." While charity is a good, the Lady suggests that it only goes so far in redressing the problem of inequality as it keeps in place an economic system that disadvantages some (or many). Charity does not disturb the status quo. By contrast, it keeps the status quo in place by making some dependent on others, on their charity. The Lady argues that those who do not dispense in "even proportion" Nature's blessings are not unlike those who, with besotted gluttony, cram themselves full, never looking to heaven, and so blaspheme their feeder, God. In *Comus*, Milton draws on the image from Plato's *Republic* and Dante's *Purgatorio*, as those who stuff themselves like cattle, those preoccupied with worldly gain, the avaricious, look only on the ground (and never up to Heaven) and offers his own criticism of charity.[52]

I began this chapter with Wordsworth's experiments with downturns, and to a point the downturned Old Cumberland Beggar resembles other figures in Wordsworth's poetry. But when the beggar is placed in the context of similarly downturned figures from literary history, like some of those found in Plato, Dante, and Milton, Wordsworth's downturned beggar begins to resonate differently, for in "The Old Cumberland Beggar" Wordsworth places a figure of want in the position frequently held by figures of excess. He describes the beggar's downturned eyes using much the same language Plato,

Dante, and Milton use to describe the avaricious, those who keep their heads down in order not to see the ways particular economic practices damage the lives of others. And in this context, Wordsworth's poem confronts the cost of downturns for an economic system that increases inequality and promotes individual self-interest, an economic system that has taught those with material resources to expect (and so profit from) downturns, even economic crises and catastrophes. Substituting the harmed for the harmer, the poem associates the figure of the downturned brow with the harmed and makes legible the human cost of increasingly common economic practices.

In taking on houses of industry, Wordsworth takes on economic policies that imagine the poor more fully integrated into a capitalist world system. In drawing a figurative link between downturns and poverty, downturns and downturns, as one discovers in the downturned eyes of the beggar an echo of money-lending practices that helped produce the very poverty the poem describes, "The Old Cumberland Beggar" invites its own sort of speculation. Economists have explained that under capitalism one downturn leads inexorably to another, turns up alternating with turns down, so that at least for those with ready-at-hand capital a downturn is hardly ever a downturn, a crisis hardly a crisis: such volatility offers chances for profit. The tropology of Wordsworth's poem draws together downturns and downturns, and thus the poem shows up the ways downturns (the downturns of money lenders, for instance) produce and expand poverty. The poem smuggles in its sharpest criticisms of a political economy still very much our own under the guise of a half-forgotten literary history.

This weave of textual figures may extend beyond Wordsworth's intentions, but the poem repeatedly draws attention to the workings of figure. If the poem tests a version of economic thinking that prioritizes the upsides of downturns, transforms catastrophes into opportunities, the poem also associates this transformation with the trope with which we began, apostrophe. The poem argues against utilitarian versions of political economy, where the answer to rampant poverty is useful employment in houses of industry, and in favor of uselessness, the Beggar's uselessness and even the poem's own. But the poem's antiutilitarian defense of uselessness requires explaining the "usefulness" of the Old Cumberland Beggar through a quite dramatic use of apostrophe: "deem not this man useless—Statesmen! ye / Who are so restless in your wisdom, ye / Who have a broom still ready in your hands / To rid the world of nuisances."[53] The poem calls on the power of apostrophe to make the absent present, as the absent Statesmen become the poet's present interlocutors. Rhetorically, the apostrophe demonstrates, or works to demonstrate, the power of the poet to drag before him even the rich and powerful to make his case. But in this way, the poem associates apostrophe with attempts to secure an upside for the downturn. Unlike the beggar's eyes, which are evermore turned on the ground, apostrophe—the poet's turn away—transforms possible powerlessness into power. Here, Wordsworth's turn risks instrumentalizing something of the look away that Rei Terada describes, as she charts a course between the coerced acceptance of the given and a modernist aesthetics of negation.[54] Wordsworth's poem makes legible the tension between the poet's turn away and the beggar's turn down, a tension between apostrophe and catastrophe. The beggar's catastrophe conditions the possibility of the poet's apostrophe. As if a good materialist, Wordsworth shows how the poet's turn away depends on the beggar's downturn. Forest Pyle takes the title of his introduction in *Art's Undoing,* "From Which One Turns Away," from a review of Théodore Géricault's painting *The Raft of the Medusa* (1819). As the author of the review describes it: "The picture is a heap of corpses from which one turns away."[55] Wordsworth's apostrophe acknowledges what Pyle calls a poem's radical dimension, a radical aestheticism, as Wordsworth's poem recasts the turn away, apostrophe, as a turn away from catastrophe's literalization. Wordsworth's turn away (the apostrophe) turns away from a figure that cannot not look down.

Thinking Words Poetically

Wordsworth is a poet of apostrophes. And in recent decades, readers have learned to be less embarrassed by his turns away from his audience to address some absent or inanimate entity. But he is also a poet of catastrophes (turns not only away but also down). As Kevis Goodman writes of Wordsworth in *Pathologies of Motion,* "Few if any writers have been more attuned to the effects of historical dislocation and economic change."[56] *Downturn,* when used to refer to a decline in economic or business activity, to a fall in rate or value, appears in English only in the mid-nineteenth century, according to the *Oxford English Dictionary.* Though Wordsworth's downturns predate the emergence of *downturn* as an economic metaphor, poets have long associated downturned eyes and brows with avarice and greed, as one turns one's eyes away from others to one's own material benefit. As a euphemism, *downturn,* when used to refer to economic or business activity, extends this poetic trope, as *downturn* focuses collective attention on the curve of a line and away from lived economic realities.

Wordsworth's interest in downturned eyes and brows comes after such downturns became a common poetic trope for narrow economic self-interest but before *downturn* became a common metaphor for economic decline. Moving into the twentieth century, the metaphor of downturns joins related metaphors. John Maynard Keynes writes repeatedly of "slumps," for instance in "The Great Slump of 1930" and "How to Avoid a Slump" (from 1939). In "The Old Cumberland Beggar" and elsewhere, Wordsworth explores the commonness of catastrophe, as he associates a downturned brow with economic reality and the lived slump. Keynes similarly recognizes and reconfigures the etymology of catastrophe, drawing attention to the ways slumps are always potentially catastrophic (for some, if not for all). "The Great Slump of 1930" begins: "The world has been slow to realize that we are living this year in the shadow of one of the greatest economic catastrophes of modern history." And a bit later, "the extreme violence of the slump is to be noticed. . . . Hence the magnitude of the catastrophe."[57] Keynes's slumps have increasingly become a feature of commodity capitalism, a system that rewards those with the resources to benefit from such slumps. Wordsworth's poems offer readers a chance to interrogate an economic metaphor that has become common in contemporary discourse, for as Anna Kornbluh suggests in *Realizing Capital*, "poetry is the medium of financial life."[58]

In this way, Wordsworth's use of downturned figures makes legible his commitment to old forms of philological thinking that draw on the history of words and enable attention to poetic forms of thought. Responding to a world in which catastrophes have become the norm, a world in which no crisis should ever go to waste, Wordsworth turns not to the word *catastrophe*, which he uses relatively rarely, but to a figurative potential present in the word itself. Wordsworth unfolds his translation across numerous poems, developing through poetry a vocabulary to describe a predicament that has become so present as to become otherwise unknowable or indescribable. To borrow language from Anahid Nersessian, Wordsworth's interrogation of the figure makes partially legible, even sensuous, the "manifestation of bounded but evanescent experiences of historical change."[59] The poetic figure of the downturn emerges as if from within its history (a history, going back to Plato, that associates downturned brows with the refusal to acknowledge the potentially devastating effects of economic systems). As Wordsworth's poetic exploration of catastrophe foregrounds the logic of downturns so integral to capitalism, he also anticipates passages like this one from an issue of *The Economist* published after the Great Recession of 2008 and 2009:

> Some argue that recessions speed up the process of productive economic churn—what Joseph Schumpeter called "creative destruction." The destruction

part is easy to see: downturns kill businesses, leaving boarded-up windows on the high street as their gravestones. But recessions may also spur the creation of new businesses.[60]

In an attempt to discuss the effects of downturns on businesses, writers for *The Economist* produce a world in which businesses live and die. Businesses are killed by creative destruction and, extending the metaphor nicely, *The Economist*'s writers reimagine windows as gravestones. But the effects of downturns on actual people have been removed from view. In this version of a familiar story, downturns kill businesses (not people). Wordsworth's poetic investigations anticipate the violence of this catastrophe: a world of downturns in which businesses, not to mention "kindly moods," live and die—a world in which people register only by hardly registering.

3. I Wandered Lonely as an iCloud

I think that I cannot preserve my health and spirits unless I
spend four hours a day at least—and it is commonly more than
that—sauntering through the woods and over the hills and fields
absolutely free from all worldly engagements.
—Henry David Thoreau, *Walden*

What purchase might there be for loosening the grip of
capitalism as an oppressive instance? . . . One critical orientation,
which is seemingly paradoxical given that mobility and
liberation have hitherto been closely associated, is to be sought
in challenging mobility as a prerequisite and incontestable value.
Is the project of liberation still compatible with an unlimited
extension of the exigency of mobility, contact and connection
which . . . can be a source of new forms of exploitation and new
existential tensions?
—Luc Boltanski and Eve Chiapello, *The New Spirit of Capitalism*

We always read in the present, in the present moment, but of course we never
do. The present always remains at least a little absent, out of touch, ghostly,
out of time. Dissatisfied with older historicist methods that strove to place
a literary text back in its proper context (though no historicist method was
ever quite so naïve), readers of literary texts today have embraced forms of
strategic presentism, anachronism, and unhistoricism. Perhaps because texts
from every historical period can rightly seem to anticipate contemporary
concerns readers of literary texts have worked to discover the present "in" the
past and the past "in" the present, accentuating not the differences between
literary periods that generate historical narrative but a sameness across periods that in effect challenges historical narratives. In "Queering History," and
in opposition to versions of history based on (hetero) difference, Jonathan
Goldberg and Madhavi Menon propose unhistoricism, a "homohistory" that
expands the possibilities of the nonhetero by thinking history through "connotations of sameness, similarity, proximity, and anachronism."[1] The project of
unhistoricism would, they continue, take seriously the idea of the *idem*, Latin
for "same," in contrast to versions of historicism that prioritize alterity and

insist on identifiable chronological disjunction. Critical methods in literary study that similarly foreground resonances across periods and flashes of surprising conjunction have proliferated in recent years.[2]

Romanticism plays a particularly complicated role in this unfolding critical story. In *Why Literary Periods Mattered*, Ted Underwood explores how the promise of literature's power to cultivate readers still "depends on vividly particularizing and differentiating vanished eras, contrasting them implicitly against the present as well as against each other."[3] As Underwood explains, this organizing principle emerges in the early nineteenth century, with romanticism and with new versions of historicism that separated different ages by profoundly different modes of life and thought, the so-called "Spirit of the Age." Quoting a letter from Blackwood's *Edinburgh Magazine*, James Chandler notes that by 1830 the Spirit of the Age had absorbed the attention of the world. Romantic historicism emerges as the study of "comparative contemporaneities."[4] The version of historicism against which much critical energy has been marshalled in recent years, by Goldberg and Menon for instance, is in many ways a Romantic invention.

But if romanticism is the age of the Spirit of the Age, then Romantic texts afford unique opportunities to interrogate this and related concepts, like epoch and period, even "contemporaniety," all concepts that continue to shape historicist discourse and historical methods. In other words, if Romantic texts are in some way responsible for what Goldberg and Menon refer to as "conservative" historicisms that prioritize difference, they also allegorize the efforts to secure (and know) such differences. For this reason, as Cynthia Chase suggests, romanticism "resists being defined as a period."[5] Though Romantic texts are responsible for generating powerful historicisms, they also relentlessly question the ability of any text to "know" its own moment, which may be why so many figures in Romantic poems wonder who they are and how they fit in.[6] By anticipating and allegorizing the very questions asked of them, Romantic texts question the fit between poem and period, spirit and age, in advance of any critical reading. "Was it for this?" Wordsworth's poet-narrator asks famously in *The Prelude*; "And what is this?" asks Shelley's poet-narrator in *The Triumph of Life*.[7] As efforts to narrate possible fits and possibilities for fit between text and context, Romantic poems allegorize the work of periodization. Romanticism, in other words, names not a period but the work of periodization, and more often than not these allegories demonstrate the ways fit can resist fitting in the end. One distinguishing feature of "Romantic" poems may be their tendency toward unromanticism, a fit that still throws something of a fit, which is lost when romanticism is collapsed into a long century, either "The Long Eighteenth" or "The Long Nineteenth," period designations that remove from romanticism this questioning, allegorizing potential and fit romanticism within a familiar chronological narrative.[8]

In Romantic studies, the recent embrace of critical anachronism, strategic presentism, and unhistoricism raises particular challenges in part because concerns over Romantic Ideology still powerfully resonate across the field. In "Against Presentism," Lynn Hunt worries that presentism "encourages a kind of moral complacency and self-congratulation." To interpret the past through the present "usually leads us to find ourselves morally superior."[9] History no longer offers a chance for critical reflection but only for un-critical admiration, implies Hunt. And Hunt's presentist historian can seem like a familiar Romantic character, self-involved but hardly self-aware. But just as no literary historian was ever so naïve to believe that a text could be returned unproblematically to its original context, so no reader committed to critical anachronism, strategic presentism, or unhistoricism aims (I hazard) to make of the past nothing other than an admiring reflection. For readers of Romantic texts, though, any celebration of romanticism's presentist power may risk seeming another sign of Romantic Ideology, where the desire to detach from context disguises a desire to detach from historical, political, and social reality. One might wonder, in other words, whether the desire to make romanticism present today continues what Jerome McGann powerfully describes in *Romantic Ideology* as "uncritical absorption in Romanticism's own self-presentation."[10] If romanticism is in some way responsible for the rise of historicism, romanticism also offers readers strategies for resisting it, but then resisting history can seem a fully "Romantic" project too.

Building on the previous chapter, "The Poetics of Downturns," in which I juxtapose Wordsworth's many downturned figures with the rhetoric of the economic downturn, in this chapter I similarly try the fit between poetry and history, paying particular attention to the ways a canonical Romantic poem, perhaps the most canonical (and most lampooned) Romantic poem, fits the contemporary rhetoric of technology. I begin with an observation: that Wordsworth's "I wandered lonely as a cloud" anticipates (with the first and last words of the poem's first line) Apple's iCloud, which I take as repre-sentative of cloud computing more generally and a figure for technological innovation that has profoundly reshaped the knowledge economy. As the poem wanders free of the "Romantic Period" it anticipates twenty-first-century discourse about technology, and to the extent to which it has only become more difficult, if not impossible, today to disentangle technology from capitalism, the accidental conjunction between a "past" poem and a "present" rhetorical discourse raises complicated questions about mobility under capitalism. So, this chapter is hopelessly unhistoricist, fully committed to an opening anachronism, as it embraces the play of reference, the play of an aberrant referentiality. In her introduction to *Utopia, Limited: Romanticism and Adjustment,* Anahid Nersessian abbreviates romanticism to "Rcsm" as a way to mark the minimal in the context of capitalist expansion, though "Rcsm" might suggest to readers "racism" as well as romanticism.[11] Abbreviating "I wandered lonely as a cloud" to "i . . . Cloud," I take the accidental conjunction as an occasion to think not only about the ways poems wander free from specific contexts but also the ways they become entangled in new ones, keeping in mind all the while, however impossible it may be to do so, that if Romantic poems encourage such conjunctive efforts they also throw them into question.

"I Wandered Lonely as an iCloud" attempts to look round for poetry and, in the process, discover something of the untimeliness of Romantic poems. In "Anachronistic Reading," J. Hillis Miller writes that "a poem encrypts, though not predictably, the effects it may have when at some future moment, in another context, it happens to be read and inscribed in a new situation." "Another way to put this," continues Miller, "is to say that the poem, though not the poet, foretells, foreshadows, foresees, prefigures, or even brings about performatively the meaning and force it comes to have."[12] Careful to distinguish the poet from the poem, Miller, quoting Jacques Derrida's *Specters of Marx,* explores how interpretation transforms the thing interpreted. As a way to keep in mind a poem's potential, this challenge that encourages and simultaneously throws into question the force of a conjunctive flash, I prefer the term untimeliness, and draw from a critical inheritance that includes Friedrich Nietzsche's *Untimely Meditations,* Derrida's *Specters of Marx,* Giorgio Agamben's "What is the Contemporary?" and more. A poem's untimeliness makes possible conjunctive flashes of aberrant referentiality. As Natalie Melas suggests, "untimeliness usefully complicates an unexamined historicism that presumes an exact coincidence between a poem, a poet, or an event and a punctual moment in time."[13] To read a poem as untimely is to attend to the ways the poem exceeds its moment and conditions the possibility of a future reading. But one significant risk that possibly accompanies an untimely reading (and so as well an anachronistic, strategically presentist, or unhistoricist reading): the untimely can come to seem too timely, nothing but timely, as one puts one's reading to work to grasp the immediacy of the present moment. The greater the sense of present emergency, the greater the pull to turn the text one reads into all-too-knowing a prophet. As a term, untimeliness serves to remind readers that when the untimely becomes too timely, it ceases to be untimely. For the untimely to be worthy the name, for an untimely reading to be truly untimely, it always must remain, somehow, still untimely and so a little useless, irreverent, irrelevant.

In teasing out the untimely, accidental conjunction of Wordsworth's cloud and the rhetoric of cloud computing, I am most interested in how this metaphor that runs throughout Wordsworth's poetry can occasion forms of materialist critique. The test is whether a poem so often taken to exemplify an idealist fantasy, as the speaker transcends his material condition on the couch to dance with the daffodils, can also function otherwise. In other words, I am interested in how we might discover in Wordsworth's poem resources for thinking a contemporary predicament that is not unromantic, as cloud computing advances a knowledge economy predicated on ever-increasing mobility and flexibility.

Dancing the Cloud

As one of the most canonical of Romantic poems, "I wandered lonely as a cloud" has inspired a broad range of critical responses. In *Thinking Through Poetry*, Marjorie Levinson describes it as "an old warhorse" of a poem "that has done duty for several varieties of Romanticism."[14] Levinson situates her reading in the context of postclassical life and physical sciences, where nature, following Spinoza, is a self-organizing network of interactive agencies. She puts pressure on the lonely cloud simile, situating the poem in the context of Luke Howard's popular treatise *On the Modification of Clouds* from 1803, as she observes that "a cloud (or poet) is lonely only if its natural condition of being is plural, composite, or collective."[15] Like Levinson I am interested in Wordsworth's simile, as I follow the poem toward the material and informational interconnectedness of our own day. My own reading will hardly get off the first line, in much the same way the speaker, by the end of the poem, seems hardly to get off the couch, but I quote the full poem here as it was published in 1807:

> I wandered lonely as a Cloud
> That floats on high o'er Vales and Hills,
> When all at once I saw a crowd
> A host of dancing Daffodils;
> Along the Lake, beneath the trees,
> Ten thousand dancing in the breeze.
>
> The waves beside them danced, but they
> Outdid the sparkling waves in glee:—
> A Poet could not but be gay

> In such a laughing company:
> I gazed—and gazed—but little thought
> What wealth the shew to me had brought:
>
> For oft when on my couch I lie
> In vacant or in pensive mood,
> They flash upon that inward eye
> Which is the bliss of solitude,
> And then my heart with pleasure fills,
> And dances with the Daffodils.[16]

Anticipating some uses of cloud metaphors today, the poem moves from a wandering detachment to an organized freedom (one predicated on movement-as-form or form-as-movement). As the poem opens, the poet-speaker reports wandering lonely as a cloud. He encounters "all at once" the host of daffodils. Often, when he is on his couch, the daffodils flash upon his inward eye and his heart dances with them. The poem celebrates forms of connection that memory and imagination (and, so, poetry as well) make possible and offers a story of development, as the detached speaker discovers new forms of attachment. Though the poem begins with a detached speaker the poem does not celebrate detachment. The speaker moves from wandering lonely as a cloud to dancing with the daffodils, from wandering to dancing, as if the poem were about the power of form, about the ways the natural world, and, more importantly, memories of the natural world, shape experience and make a life burdened by modernity more livable. The poem is about the power of form to make attachment possible in a world that threatens to make attachment difficult, if not impossible.

This chapter owes much to scholars working on cloud metaphors in Romantic writing, including Mary Jacobus, Marjorie Levinson, and Ana-hid Nersessian.[17] It also owes much to scholars working at the intersection of romanticism and media studies.[18] Celeste Langan and Maureen McLane begin their foundational essay "The Medium of Romantic Poetry" with an epigraph from Niklas Luhmann, "The recognition that every form is a form-in-a-medium dates back to romanticism."[19] Langan and McLane go on not only to explore how media studies approaches can inform Romantic writing but also how Romantic writing anticipates contemporary media theory. Despite the desire for an unmediated condition explored by Romantic writers, despite the drive to achieve the impression of immediacy, Romantic writers "frequently call attention to the book, the page, the line, the drop of ink," and so even before the term media comes into wide use Romantic writers allegorized something like a technological unconscious.[20]

If Romantic poetry anticipates contemporary media theory, contemporary media often extends Romantic theory into the future. Romantic idealism has often been understood as a celebration of imagination over the materiality of lived reality. Cloud computing makes a hauntingly similar promise: companies and individuals can rise above the brute materiality of hardware and labor costs. Float free in the cloud. One can access one's files from anywhere, just as Wordsworth's poet-speaker imagines he might access his memory of daffodils from anywhere, or at least from the couch. If Wordsworth's poem discovers itself differently legible as it anticipates its own abbreviation, then the poem also offers a chance to think with and through an idea of the cloud it could not (and yet seems always already to) have anticipated. In other words, the poem's materialist critique of cloud computing emerges only as a result of this chance to wander, as one metaphor (lonely as a cloud) shifts into another (cloud computing).

Like Wordsworth's poet-speaker, designers of various cloud computing technologies celebrate the ways the cloud connects users and increases freedom, where organized connection does not come at the expense of freedom but conditions its possibility. The simile that Wordsworth associates with detachment has become the metaphor technology companies associate with attachment and new forms of connectivity. Cloud computing came to prominence in the early 2000s, as technology companies reduced dependence on local hard drives. In 2006, Eric Schmidt, Google's then CEO, described the emerging technology, in which data services and architecture are stored on servers: "We call it cloud computing—they [data services and architecture] should be in a 'cloud somewhere.'"[21] Schmidt and Jonathan Rosenberg explain the metaphor's origin in *How Google Works*: "It's called 'cloud computing' because the old programs to draw network schematics surrounded the icons for servers with a circle. A cluster of servers in a network program had several overlapping circles, which resembled a cloud."[22] Cofounder of Cloud Camp, a course for programmers, Reuven Cohen explains that the cloud is "a rebranding of the Internet."[23] As metaphor, the cloud replaces the earlier metaphor of the net. Cloud computing products make it possible to access various files from anywhere instead of having files only accessible from a particular machine, because the files are not stored on the machine itself, on the hard drive, but on servers that are located elsewhere, that are located "somewhere." Precisely because the files are "somewhere," they are, in theory, accessible from "anywhere."

In this opening frame, my point is rather simple. "I wandered lonely as a cloud" raises questions about the possibility for connection when one lies at some distance from one's jocund company, as one lies on a couch alone in vacant or pensive mood, but not lonely. As if borrowing Wordsworth's initial metaphor (though, admittedly, one rarely discovers a "lonely" cloud in the Lake District), cloud computing attempts to realize Wordsworth's dream. As John Durham Peters writes in *The Marvelous Clouds*, the single, lonely cloud has become the symbol of cloud computing: "The cloud metaphor has been a smashing success for the information technology business, and fluffy, benign cumulus clouds are now the standard iconography of online storage."[24] Scholars are increasingly aware of the material costs of cloud computing, which is expanding quickly and requiring greater and greater amounts of energy. The cloud may neither be fluffy nor fully benign. But to hear the echo of iCloud in "I wandered lonely as a cloud" I want to play up the ways the poem explores the working of figure and metaphor. For while the single cloud on one's desktop recalls Wordsworth's simile, the poem moves from metaphor to metaphor, from wandering as a cloud to dancing as a daffodil. What does Wordsworth's poem tell us about not only the metaphor of the cloud today but also the workings of metaphor in the discourse of technology?

Romanticism and Materialism

To think about romanticism, and in particular Romantic poetry, and materialism today may still strike some as quite odd. Are not poets the least materialist of writers and Romantic poets the least materialist of the poets? This at least is how Jerome McGann characterized Romantic poetry so powerfully in *Romantic Ideology*, where he argues that Romantic poetry "is everywhere marked by extreme forms of displacement and poetic conceptualization whereby the actual human issues with which the poetry is concerned are resituated in a variety of idealized localities."[25] What distinguishes Romantic poetry is the recurring displacement of material life.

McGann's new historicism still presents a compelling challenge, but writers from before and after the publication of *Romantic Ideology* have struggled with the many ways Romantic texts neither fully displace nor embrace "actual human issues." In his preface to *Black Jacobins*, first published in 1938, C. L. R. James associates Wordsworthian tranquility with political conservatism and resistance to revolutionary struggle. But even as James turns away from Wordsworthian tranquility, he embraces what he calls the fever and fret, borrowing from Keats's "Ode to a Nightingale." In his preface and as he begins his history of the Haitian Revolution, James does not so much turn away from romanticism but turn from one version of romanticism to another. Romanticism proves a particularly complicated object of study.[26] Scholars of romanticism have found numerous ways to discover in Romantic writing this tangled and knotty dynamic, especially scholars interested in questions of imperialism and empire. Is Romantic writing complicit in an imperialist, even white nationalist, project? The answer, following various lines of inquiry by scholars, is both yes and no. Does Romantic writing offer resources for criticizing the workings of empire? Again, the answer is both yes and no.[27]

But to judge from recent publications by specialists in contemporary poetry and poetics, the answers to such questions have rather more straight-forward answers. Romanticism is idealism, nothing but idealism. And con-temporary poetry, unlike Romantic writing, demonstrates its repeated com-mitment to materiality. Marjorie Perloff's *Uncreative Genius: Poetry by Other Means in the New Century*, Kenneth Goldsmith's *Uncreative Writing: Managing Language in the Digital Age*, and Craig Dworkin and Kenneth Goldsmith's *Against Expression: An Anthology of Conceptual Writing* show how contempo-rary writing has distanced itself from the tropes that preoccupied—or at least have been understood to preoccupy—Romantic poets: genius, imagination, individuality, creativity, emotion, and so on. Dreams of originality strongly associated with Romantic discourse have themselves been transformed by technologies that enable new writing practices. As Goldsmith writes: "writ-ers are exploring ways of writing that have been thought, traditionally, to be outside the scope of literary practice: word programming, databasing, recycling, appropriation, intentional plagiarism, identity ciphering, and in-tensive programming, to name but a few."[28] Summarizing Perloff, and almost alluding to Wordsworth's "I wandered lonely as a cloud," Goldsmith explains: "because of changes brought on by technology and the Internet, our notion of genius—a romantic isolated figure—is outdated."[29]

Technological change in recent years is largely responsible for an increase in nonexpressive, conceptual, and material poetics, a poetry, following Charles Olson, that aims to get "rid of [the] lyrical interference of the individual as ego" so strongly associated with romanticism and embrace self-consciously "unoriginal" practices common in the digital age.[30] In the introduction to *Against Expression*, called "The Fate of Echo," Dworkin describes the original online collection from which *Against Expression* emerged and which "hap-pened to gather a particular kind of writing to make a secondary argu-ment: some of the presumed hallmarks of poetry—the use of metaphor and imagery, a soigné edited craft, the sincere emotional expression of especially sensitive individuals—might be radically reconsidered, and poetry might be reclaimed as a venue for intellect rather than sentiment."[31] In the original foreword published online at UbuWeb, Dworkin contrasts recent develop-ments in contemporary poetry and poetics with romanticism and Wordsworth in particular. He writes: "what would a non-expressive poetry look like? A poetry of intellect rather than emotion? One in which the substitution at the heart of metaphor and image were replaced by the direct presentation of language itself, with 'spontaneous overflow' supplanted by meticulous procedure and exhaustively logical process?"[32] A metonym for romanticism more generally, "spontaneous overflow" stands for an expressive poetry that foregrounds the "heart" of the poet over direct presentation of language. Unlike an expressive poetry that foregrounds the lyric ego and aims to transmit or communicate some expressive content, nonexpressive poetry renders words opaque and material thus making possible forms of "social, economic, and political critique," as Goldsmith writes in *Uncreative Writing*.[33] Dan Graham's "Schema" is one of Dworkin's examples of nonexpressive poetry, "where the self-regard of narcissistic confession [is] rejected in favor of laying bare the potential for linguistic self-reflexiveness."[34] Graham's poem consists of publishing information about the appearance of the page upon which the poem is printed. As Dworkin explains:

> Graham submits a template—not unlike the portion of XML source used to order and display the information pulled from various databases—which the editor of the magazine was to calculate and complete, providing information about the physical characteristics of the publication. Rigorously and recursively self-referential, the completed piece parses itself, collapsing form and content. The result focuses attention onto the most minute particulars of the physical aspects of print.[35]

The scheme, and so the text of the poem, includes the weight of the paper sheet, the type of paper stock, the name of the typeface, and so forth; and of the pages selected, the number of words, the number of adjectives, the percentage of area occupied by type. The poem attempts to turn attention to the materiality of the printed object. It has no "content" but its material context. Dworkin continues: "The radical implications of Graham's work follow from that combination of an insistence on the cultural materiality of language and a rejection of the romantic author as a unified locus of interior authority."[36] In this way, the poem forces readers to attend to a material context that more often is ignored by a tradition of Romantic poetry, to return to McGann, that privileges an ideal or idealized content over historical and material context.

From James to Dworkin, Wordsworth stands for a romanticism, or at least a version of romanticism, that must be resisted if one is to gain access to materiality and lived reality. But it can sometimes seem like readers reject Wordsworth's writing in order to simplify the question. Few readers would confuse Wordsworth's "I wandered lonely as a cloud" with Graham's "Schema," but just how easy is it to access materiality? Unlike an expressive poetry structured by figure (and the various forms of substitution figurative language foregrounds in a poem like "I wandered lonely as a cloud"), a nonexpressive poetry would "replace" metaphor with what Dworkin describes as the "direct presentation of language itself." The readily apparent difficulty of such a presentation arises from the fact that the effort to replace "the substitution at the heart of metaphor" already depends on the logic of substitution—or replacement—that defines metaphor, as one replaces a substitution. To supplant "spontaneous overflow" with the direct presentation of language itself is already to participate in the logic of substitution that defines figurative or expressive poetry.[37] The poet's effort to substitute for metaphor the direct presentation of language depends upon, well, metaphor.

In this way, critical arguments that assert romanticism's outdatedness reproduce certain "Romantic" structures and preoccupations. Goldsmith, for example, begins *Uncreative Writing* with something of a Wordsworthian problem: "faced with an unprecedented amount of available text, the problem is not needing to write more of it; instead, we must learn to negotiate the vast quantity that exists."[38] Goldsmith develops "uncreative" writing practices to manage, parse, and organize "this thicket of information," just as Wordsworth offers *Lyrical Ballads* to "manage" the rapid communication of intelligence.[39] Famously, Wordsworth laments the craving for extraordinary incidents produced in the minds of readers by the proliferation of information (newspapers for instance) and argues for poetry to play a role in offsetting the blunting of the mind that results from this craving. Goldsmith and Wordsworth respond to the same problem. Similarly, Dworkin characterizes the shift from expressive to nonexpressive poetry and poetics using familiar Romantic tropes: contemporary nonexpressive poets choose Echo over romanticism's (perhaps specifically Wordsworth's) Narcissus, language over ego, materialism over idealism. Such an opposition is complicated, though, by the very poetry under discussion. The opposition Dworkin sets up between Echo and Narcissus maps easily onto the opposition Keats, for instance, sets up between Shakespeare and Milton. Shakespeare was already something of a remixer and a model of sorts for Keats, for romanticism too. Like the poets Dworkin celebrates, Keats distinguishes the poetical character from Wordsworth's "egotistical sublime." "A poet," writes Keats famously in a letter to Richard Woodhouse from October of 1818, "is the most unpoetical of anything in existence, because he has no Identity."[40] Dan Graham's "Schema," like Keats's poet, is similarly empty of content of its own. Sometimes the difference between a Romantic and a contemporary poetics is difficult to define. And one might say that, from the start, what distinguishes a Romantic poem as

"Romantic" are all its various attempts to move away from romanticism, if by romanticism one names any untroubled belief in the correspondence between meaning and the conditions of meaning.

I started this section by suggesting that poets are the least material of writers and Romantic poets the least material of poets. This suggestion is true of course only if one defines romanticism in the terms employed by those who collapse romanticism and idealism, a drifting into mind of language merely as a vehicle to explore the self. But what if the Romantic poet's turn inward is not a turn away from materiality but a turn toward the question: where is the material? The rejection of romanticism common in contemporary poetics—a rejection that aligns romanticism with idealism and contemporary poetry with materialism—always risks transforming materialism into an ideal idealism, as the auto-referentiality of text becomes indistinguishable from Wordsworth's ego-ideal.[41] When one thinks one has at last the material referent, one discovers it instead dispersed, a cloud; when one thinks one has finally rid oneself of the material referent, one discovers it instead a stone.

New Materialisms

Recent advances in technology are helping us not only develop new writing practices but also rethink what we mean by matter, material, materiality, and so call for what Diane Coole and Samantha Frost term "new materialisms." The more we come to understand about atoms—but also genes, networks, and so forth—the less comfortably solid material becomes, for, as Coole and Frost write, "The microscopic atom consists of a positively charged nucleus surrounded by a cloudlike, three-dimensional wave of spinning electrons." They continue: "Even when vast numbers of atoms are assembled in the kind of macrostructures we experience in the 'condensed matter' of the perceptible world, their subatomic behavior consists in the constant emergence, attraction, repulsion, fluctuation, and shifting of nodes of charge: which is to say that they demonstrate none of the comforting stability or solidity we take for granted."[42] What formerly we thought "material" is now, we discover, more dispersed, more cloudlike than we might prefer. To be a good materialist today one cannot simply kick a stone and feel good about having returned oneself to the hard stuff that matters most. We cannot, as Wordsworth famously did when confronted by the immateriality of self and world, simply reach for some tree, branch or wall—as he explains in his discussion of "Ode: Intimations of Immortality" with Isabella Fenwick: "I was often unable to think of external things as having external existence, and I communed with all that I saw as something not apart from, but inherent in, my own immaterial nature. Many times while going to school have I grasped at a wall or tree to recall myself from this abyss of idealism to the reality."[43] Wordsworth's fear when a boy was that he would fall into an abyss of idealism and so he grasped for some wall or tree in an effort to encounter a world that threatened to disappear—as the world became merely an extension of his own immaterial self. The threat, Wordsworth realizes, is himself, his own self. In later years, of course, Wordsworth's fear is the reverse: that the world is too much with us, a large stone on a small chest. We read too quickly when we imagine Romantic texts as referring unproblematically to some external reality; but similarly, we read too quickly when we imagine Romantic texts as fully self-referential.

How does one get to what matters? Bruno Latour begins *Pandora's Hope* with a question from a colleague that takes him by surprise, as Latour positions his essays on the reality of science studies against a philosophical line that follows Kant through romanticism to deconstruction. The question results, Latour implies, from social, cultural, and scientific discussions common in the twentieth century: "'I have a question for you,' [Latour's colleague] said, taking out of his pocket a crumpled piece of paper on which he had scribbled a few key words. He took a breath: 'Do you believe in reality?'"[44] In other words, the question from Latour's colleague is, given the various concerns over reality as socially constructed, as virtual: is it still possible to "believe" in reality? Latour's answer is "But of course!" The colleague is here the young Wordsworth and Latour simply the closest wall or tree. One does not ask if another believes in reality unless one already worries that something has happened to it, and so, like a young Wordsworth, the colleague reaches out.

Latour's is no naïve materialism and his writing has been widely influential, but he is compelled to begin the book with this story so as to foreground some of the ways critique has run out of steam, as he imagines those who celebrate the loss of the world planning a sad celebration: "they will 'deconstruct,' as they say—which means destroy in slow motion—anyone who reminds them that there was a time when they were free and when their language bore a connection with the world."[45] Polemically, Latour caricatures "deconstruction" as an attempt to slowly destroy any reminder of language's referential function, as if questioning language's referential function were the same as denying it. The fact that the so-called linguistic turn has made it possible to ask such a question— "Do you [still?] believe in reality" (uttered with a shaking voice)—is precisely why Coole and Frost assert the necessity of new materialisms: "Textual approaches associated with the so-called cultural turn are increasingly being deemed inadequate for understanding contemporary society, particularly in light of some of its most urgent challenges regarding environmental, demographic, geopolitical, and economic change."[46] Textual approaches have left us all a nervous colleague clutching a crumpled piece of paper.

Like a young Wordsworth we reach for something else, something more, something more material—or at least one sometimes feels one should be reaching out in this way, reaching for books like *Pandora's Hope* and *New Materialisms*. But if reaching for this crumpled piece of paper repeats Wordsworth's questioning search, then these various linguistic and material turns are perhaps not so easy to date and differentiate. We risk repeating a familiar story over and over again. I suggested earlier and only half-facetiously that perhaps what makes Romantic texts Romantic is their resistance to romanticism, as if romanticism were nothing other than a resistance to romanticism, understood as the naïve belief that one can know for sure that language is free from reference, as if the mind could know with certainty the "connection" between language and world. Is idealism similarly the resistance to idealism, materialism the resistance to materialism?

Latour foregrounds a form of material textuality in his opening anecdote as his colleague takes from his pocket a scrap of paper upon which he has written a few key words. He holds a material text. In recent years, scholars have worked to complicate the opposition of romanticism and materialism. In *Sweet Science: Romantic Materialism and the New Logics of Life*, Amanda Jo Goldstein teases out the importance of Lucretius to romanticism and so discovers in romanticism a Lucretian materialism, which is a materialism not divorced from questions of figure, and so not divorced from questions of textuality. While Goldstein is frustrated with any rigid sense of "materialism" invoked in Marxist ideology critique and deconstruction, she does not proceed "as though their tasks were finished."[47] Instead she attends to the sometimes surprising work of figure, a material semiosis that accentuates the commonality between sign and referent. Likewise, in Latour's opening scene, the colleague's question appears possible only because he has written, and so Latour's opening story foregrounds technologies of inscription even as the colleague's question seems to lament a linguistic turn that embraces theories of textuality that are perceived to threaten reality. With the introduction of a linguistic vocabulary, "writing" itself becomes complicated. And writing, understood as a system of marks that simultaneously obscures and conveys meaning, is the cause of the colleague's question; but it also conditions its possibility, for there would be no chance for reassurance without the scrap of writing, without the very system that produces the need for reassurance in the first place. We don't always know what it is we hold.

But what if one imagines Latour's colleague holding a copy of "I wandered lonely as a cloud"? When Latour suggests that a textual approach like deconstruction, which emerged with and after the linguistic turn, celebrates the destruction of reference, he simplifies not only deconstruction but also the linguistic turn. The question may not be whether or not language has a referential function but whether one can ever guarantee that reference hits the mark (or whether a mark ever hits its referent). To read Wordsworth's "I wandered lonely as a cloud" as commentary on cloud computing is to discover in the poem an accident of reference and to try and take seriously for a moment the effects of such an accident, an accidental conjunction, not only for the poem but also for the rhetoric of cloud computing. Given his caricature, Latour implies that textual approaches like deconstruction resulted in a purely formal linguistic model in which reference (and the chance of reference) is forestalled from the start. But this is the model that Paul de Man, by contrast, associates with aesthetic ideology, which de Man's rhetorical, deconstructive reading means to complicate (if not oppose).[48] As has so often been the case in the past, and perhaps will be the case again, the turns of criticism (from a linguistic to a material one) are predicated on a reading that is also a misreading (where the difference between reading and misreading may not be so easy to know or secure). In his posthumously published book, *Aesthetic Ideology*, de Man argues that the encounter with something one might call matter or materiality occurs not when textual approaches are eschewed but only "by way of an epistemological critique of tropes."[49] To oppose textuality and materiality is to fall into aesthetic ideology, suggests de Man. Textual approaches make encounters with materiality possible, for de Man, even as matter turns out to be something other than what we thought. Literary attention to signs, words, tropes, and figures, does not result in a rejection of materiality; it offers an attempt to encounter it, in whatever minimal way possible. Materiality is not opposed to writing even if it is "opposed to some extent to the notion of cognition," opposed, that is, to our ability to know for sure what it is that is opposite.[50] Latour's caricature of "deconstruction" risks reducing his own position to caricature, as if, for Latour, all we really need do is look out the window. Latour's position is more complicated than this caricature, but his rejection of textual approaches is shared by Coole and Frost, who similarly deem textual approaches inadequate in *New Materialisms*, as if the choice were simple, as if the difference between materiality and textuality could be known ahead of time.

The dream that we can somehow frame language, cordon it off, and so free the stuff that matters most from linguistic interference, is a longstanding one. For Wordsworth and for those interested in poetry, for those committed to the work of poetry and to forms of thought poetry makes possible, the question is not how to cordon off linguistic interference. Instead, one might ask, following Geoffrey Hartman's take on formalism, how does poetry lead one, for lack of a better word, beyond poetry?[51] The question is not how cordon off linguistic interference but how acknowledge linguistic reference, however aberrant, however anachronistic, however untimely. The metaphors of Romantic poetry recur today in displaced form. Critique may be running out of steam, as Latour suggests, but more and more clouds are forming. "I wandered lonely as a cloud" turns out to be a poem about materiality but maybe only accidentally, not the materiality of stones to be kicked but the materiality of figure, as Wordsworth's poem discovers itself within new figurative networks.

Steam, Clouds, Scattered Materialisms

When Coole and Frost write that "the microscopic atom consists of a positively charged nucleus surrounded by a cloudlike, three-dimensional wave of spinning electrons," they mean, of course, that to be a good materialist today one need take an interest in clouds.[52] If so, then there may be no more materialist a poet than Wordsworth, famous for beginning both of his long epic poems with clouds and subjecting himself to ridicule for "I wandered lonely as a cloud." Because the present always possibly allows the past to signify differently, Romantic conventions that may have felt outworn in the twentieth century have inspired new vocabularies for critical intervention in the twenty-first. In recent years scholars have returned to cloud metaphors in Romantic poetry and discovered in these familiar conventions something other than idealism. In *Romantic Things*, Mary Jacobus moves from common Romantic tropes (trees and rocks and clouds) to thinking about versions of materiality. As Jacobus writes, clouds "constitute one of the most elusive 'materials' of Romantic lyric," and Jacobus, in her first chapter on clouds, takes the "invention" of clouds in the early nineteenth century, when Luke Howard produced his classification of clouds as part of the embryonic science of meteorology, as point of departure.[53] Jacobus focuses on the cloud, both in art and poetry, in order to think about form and vacancy, mobility and change, and, perhaps most importantly for her, mood. In *The Calamity Form*, Anahid Nersessian takes the cloud as an occasion to think romanticism's relationship to capitalism, a way to think the disappearance of nature on the edge of capitalism's triumph.[54] As Marjorie Levinson argues: "Our totaled-out and thoroughly post-organic and commodified present—the ozone layer above, wall-to-wall mall below, and the Web in between—gives us a fresh perspective on Romantic naturalism, organicism, pathetic fallacy, personification, and other central conventions of the period."[55] In this concluding section, I return to the accidental conjunction of various "clouds" (as Wordsworth's metaphor reappears in the rhetoric of cloud computing) in an effort to draw out Wordsworth's materialism, or the materialism of "I wandered lonely as a cloud." I am interested in what sorts of materialist approaches to poetry result from attention to language's aberrantly referential effects.

Wordsworth builds the poem around a powerful substitution, as wandering gives way to dancing. The poem moves from one form of movement to another.[56] With reference to Friedrich Schiller's *Letters on Aesthetic Education*, David Simpson notes in *Wordsworth, Commodification and Social Concern* that dance is a common figure within aesthetic ideology for a social and political model in which all works in harmony. When one prioritizes the poem's move from wandering to dancing, one reads the poem as embracing formalized movement. But the harmony of the dance can also conceal the violence that makes it possible. For this reason, and though Wordsworth's poem is often read "as a standard expression of Romantic pantheism," Simpson situates Wordsworth's dancing daffodils in the context of Karl Marx's dancing table, Marx's figure for the commodity in *Capital*.[57] The poem offers a record of the poet-speaker's move toward commodity form as it stages the becoming-commodity of ghostly things like poets and poems. If the dancing heart is not read through Schiller, where formal movement is a sign of harmony, but through Marx, where the dancing heart, like the dancing table, is already a commodity, then the poem is a record of the poet-speaker's resistance to and simultaneous drift into commodification. As Simpson suggests, the poet-speaker discovers an economy "where a high rate of interest is assured [as the poet generates tremendous interest through his memory of the initial encounter] and no one else can drive down prices because they cannot get into the market."[58]

In my opening epigraph from Thoreau's *Walden* mobility offers respite from a capitalist economy that exploits workers, but mobility may no longer offer respite. Thoreau celebrates his ability to move through the world unencumbered by worldly engagements and contrasts his mental and physical health, preserved and strengthened by his freedom to saunter, with that of mechanics and shopkeepers. He continues: "When sometimes I am reminded that the mechanics and shop-keepers stay in their shops not only all the forenoon, but all the afternoon too, sitting with crossed legs, so many of them—as if the legs were made to sit upon, and not to stand or walk upon—I think that they deserve some credit for not having all committed suicide long ago."[59] Thoreau ramps up his rhetoric quite quickly and associates mobility with resistance, resistance to new and emerging forms of labor. I draw my second epigraph from a more recent text that likewise takes seriously the relationship between mobility and capitalism. But if for Thoreau mobility makes resistance possible, for Boltanski and Chiapello it represents capitalism's latest and most advanced form of oppression. In the new spirit of capitalism, mobility is key to a knowledge economy that idealizes workers who are flexible, creative, and reprogrammable. The new spirit of capitalism demands that workers learn a particular dance. As Boltanski and Chiapello explore, mobility and flexibility today are sources for new social anxieties and forms of exploitation.[60] What once offered respite from capitalism for Thoreau is now a source of anxiety for workers under capitalism, as workers anticipate a near future when they may no longer be mobile or flexible enough to secure adequate material resources.

In an economy that values mobility and flexibility, one is expendable when others are more mobile and flexible. Mobility and flexibility can often seem like code in the new knowledge economy for a purely formal process of substitution or interchangeability. In *The Laws of Cool: Knowledge Work and the Culture of Information,* Alan Liu explores the subtly destructive effects of a late capitalism that privileges a worker's ability to wander with the help of a cloud that promotes new forms of creative knowledge work. Mobility and flexibility are now a source, suggests Liu, for new anxieties as "global competition legitimates restructuring, downsizing, outsourcing, and the replacement of career workers with permatemps—the social law of a new nomadism."[61] In a postindustrial sociality, "'lifelong learning' demands perpetual reeducation at 'Internet speed,' but bodily, family, community, ethnic, gender, and other duties of everyday life pose an incalculably great counter-demand that makes it almost impossible, for instance, to study at night."[62] On the level of the individual, one must remain always mobile, flexible, and connected else one discover oneself replaced, exchanged, obsolete. Paradoxically, absolute mobility increases insecurity.

In the cloud, processes of near-immediate substitution make new forms of mobility possible. As a technology, cloud computing is designed to function seamlessly, masking the various processes of substitution that make the technology work. The work of substitution (even the substitution of one worker for another) becomes almost illegible, a nonevent. Only the figure of the cloud is visible. The cloud as figure unites mobility and processes of substitution. In *A Prehistory of the Cloud,* Tung-Hui Hu explores the reliability and ubiquity of the cloud. The cloud makes it possible to imagine an interconnected world, a fully integrated system. Hu subjects computing infrastructure to history and makes legible the work of this now seemingly ubiquitous metaphor. He writes: "As a piece of information flows through the cloud . . .

it is designed to get to its destination with 'five-nines' reliability, so that if one hard drive or piece of wire fails en route, another one takes its place, 99.999 percent of the time. Because of its reliability and ubiquity, the cloud is a particularly mute piece of infrastructure."[63] The cloud is mute because it only "speaks" when the system fails. When something goes wrong, one recognizes a principle of articulation at work. Here I draw on both senses of the term *articulation*. When the cloud fails it articulates (speaks) its failure to articulate (connect). When Hu describes the cloud as mute, one might not only recognize the cloud as a Romantic metaphor but also the ways tropes that animate speech advance an idea of lyric poetry. The goal for Hu's materialist critique of computing infrastructure is to make infrastructure less mute, to give infrastructure, the cloud, a chance to speak. Infrastructure remains mute as long as hard drives and pieces of wire are replaceable with "five-nines" reliability, so that muteness is predicated on systems of substitution that occur immediately, or almost immediately. If Hu aims to give the cloud a voice, he repeats Percy Shelley's poem "The Cloud," where Shelley animates the cloud, throws his voice to the cloud through the use of a particular trope, prosopopoeia, and gives the cloud a chance to speak directly to readers.

Marketing and advertising campaigns for cloud computing rely on the power of substitution. In the language of Apple's original advertising campaign, the cloud is ideal not only because it will make one's life easier but also because it might replace one, where substitution is not a threat but a sales pitch: "iCloud is so much more than a hard drive in the sky. It makes it quick and effortless to access just about everything on the devices you use every day. . . . No syncing required. No management required. In fact, no anything required. iCloud does it all for you."[64] Apple is relying on a consumer's lack of interest in managing various files. To discover one's files already managed relieves one of some contemporary headaches. Cloud computing participates in a broader fantasy, that technology will reduce the need for work.[65] But what exactly does the "it" of "iCloud does it all for you" refer to? If iCloud does it *all* for you, does iCloud risk replacing you? These questions resonate more powerfully when Apple's advertising campaign is read in the context of *The New Spirit of Capitalism*, where the threat of substitution looms large. Anxiety about cloud-enabled Artificial Intelligence, for instance, has only increased in recent years, as new technologies threaten to make various sorts of work (and so various workers) "obsolete." My point is that cloud computing is built on systems of substitution that go unrecognized and this structure, increasingly, mirrors contemporary working conditions. Cloud computing has become itself a figure for processes of substitution designed to go unnoticed with "five-nines" reliability. The cloud "speaks" when the sixth nine sticks.

Against some of the versions of materialism I lingered over in earlier sections of the chapter, versions of materialism that associate Romantic metaphor with idealism or deem textual approaches inadequate, I argue in closing that a poem like "I wandered lonely as a cloud" gets sticky precisely because it foregrounds the work of metaphor so explicitly. Theories of metaphor often begin by foregrounding the importance of movement. Metaphor carries a word from its normal use to a new one; it transfers a word from one place to another. A vehicle is involved. In *Metaphor*, Denis Donoghue develops this line of thought and like Thoreau in a way associates metaphorical substitution—the movement of metaphor—with freedom.[66] But in the context of cloud computing, an infrastructure that disguises processes of substitution through the imposition of a powerful figure, the lonely cloud, a poem like "I wandered lonely as a cloud" may signify differently. If cloud computing is built around processes of substitution that are designed to make substitution invisible, nonphenomenal, what make of poetic metaphor's sometimes sticky substitutions? Put differently, if Romantic poetry foregrounds the work of substitution, can we discover in Romantic poetry a material residue? Wordsworth's poem embraces figurative potential as the poem is built around the power of substitution, as it moves from one form of movement to another, from one figure (the cloud) to another (the daffodil). But far from disguising this power of substitution, the poem foregrounds it and, precisely because it foregrounds it so powerfully, the poem has invited caricature.

"I wandered lonely as a cloud" has often been read as a poem about removing oneself from the discomfort of the material world through the power of imagination: "For oft, when on my couch I lie / In vacant or in pensive mood, / They [the daffodils] flash upon that inward eye." The couch is now a powerful figure for emotional disquiet on the one hand and general apathy on the other. Instead of getting off the couch, one might argue, Wordsworth finds a way to live there happily. If so, then Wordsworth's poem and the idealist position it advances can easily be read as contributing to a work ethic that cloud computing fully realizes. One no longer needs to leave the couch to work all of the time. And for this reason a nonexpressive poetry that distrusts the lyric ego and metaphor more generally, a poetry committed to the materiality of the letter offers some resistance to an aesthetic ideology that displaces material life, embracing the fantasy of transcendence for the stuff that matters most.

But what Wordsworth's presumed idealism—his collapsing of subject and object—cannot have controlled is itself newly legible with the insistent presence of "as," the conspicuous use of figure now removed from Apple's rewriting of the poem's first lines: "iCloud / That floats on high o'er hills and vales." With "iCloud" the process of articulation conveyed by simile has become the absence of articulation as Wordsworth's conspicuous use of figure disappears. With five-nines reliability, the processes of substitution that make cloud technology possible go unnoticed. In this way late capitalism sells us back Wordsworth's dream as the imagined disarticulation of Wordsworth's dream. In other words, if figure makes transcendence possible then Wordsworth's figures make this dream of transcendence too legible. Cloud computing, in the shape of iCloud, similarly advances a dream transcendence and does so by abbreviating the work of figure, by making processes of substitution less visible in order to advance a knowledge economy predicated on the interchangeability of workers. The apparent absence of figurative language (iCloud as compared to "as a cloud") becomes ideal as the rhetorical structures that document and make visible various resistances to dissolution in effect disappear from view. If the aesthetics of late capitalism now includes the elimination of figure, an elimination of figure because there is nothing but figure—all parts are interchangeable—then paradoxically it is now Wordsworth's simile that stubbornly remains immobile. Perhaps there's a chance for materialism even if it is indistinguishable from idealism. Wordsworth of course never leaves the couch—at least not within the world the lyric imagines—but what the insistence of "as" makes legible is, and this might be the simplest if also the most puerile way to put it: Wordsworth is unwilling to work his "as" off. What we have not yet come to terms with are the ways that the absolutely formal system of late capitalism—one that advances mobility and interchangeability—needs, somewhat paradoxically, to eliminate the very figurative potential of language that seems to give it its form.

4. On the Poetry of Posthumous Election

Old Exit 9 Ran for sheriff against a dead man
& lost.

—Kevin Young, "Old Exit 9"

Discovering the tropes and figures that give poems shape in sometimes new and surprising contexts, *Look Round for Poetry* foregrounds the untimeliness of poetry, its sometimes aberrantly referential force, as lines of thought flash into constellation. In the previous chapter, "I Wandered Lonely as an iCloud," I read the metaphor of the cloud in Wordsworth's famous poem alongside the rhetoric of cloud computing to show how the poem anticipates and prefigures contemporary anxieties under capitalism. Spurred by Wordsworth's simile, readers might see cloud technology's fuzzy cloud icon as a not entirely un-Romantic metaphor. Continuing to foreground the untimely power of figurative language, in this chapter I focus particular attention on figures of address, among them prosopopoeia, a trope common to lyric poetry in which the absent, dead, or inanimate entity is granted a face and a voice to address a living reader. I read these figures of address in lyric poetry alongside a still sometimes surprising (if not uncommon) event in electoral politics, the election of the dead to public office. Voters today who throw their voice (and vote) to the dead lay claim (knowingly or not) to a power that poets have long professed.

Often the best way to win an election is to die during the campaign. Numerous examples of posthumous election exist and almost every election cycle in recent years has included at least one instance. To list a few examples: in October of 1962, US Representative Clement Miller of California died in a plane crash but was reelected in the November election that year. In October of 1972, US Representatives Hale Boggs of Louisiana and Nick Begich of Alaska disappeared in the Alaskan wilderness. Rescue parties never found their plane and both men were declared presumptively dead. Both won reelection. More recently, in April 2010, Carl Robin Geary died several weeks before the election but defeated Barbara Brock for mayor of Tracy City, Tennessee; in 2012, Janice Canham won posthumous election to mayor in Jackson's Gap, Alabama; in 2016, Dennis Hof won posthumous election to the Nevada State Assembly. The dead won in 2020 too. In October, David Andahl died of COVID-19 but his name stayed on the ballot in North Dakota, and in November he won election to the state House of Representatives. But perhaps the most famous example in the United States is Mel Carnahan, who won posthumous election to the US Senate in November of 2000.[1] Like Miller, Boggs, and Begich, Carnahan died tragically in a plane crash just weeks before the election, but by Missouri State Law his name could not be removed from the ballot. The recently deceased Carnahan defeated incumbent and former Missouri Governor, John Ashcroft. As a result of Carnahan's posthumous victory, his widow, Jean, was appointed to the Senate in his stead.[2] Missouri Republicans briefly considered challenging Mel Carnahan's victory and Jean Carnahan's appointment on the grounds that to win one must reside in the state one has been elected to represent.[3] As Pat Robertson argued in *The Washington Times*, "A dead man is not a resident of [a] state. There is no way a dead man can be elected—it doesn't compute."[4] Ashcroft, however, refused to challenge the election result in court. He would have risked losing twice to the same dead man. *The Toronto Star* somewhat glibly described the election in a headline, "Ashcroft is Pro-Life, but Voters were Pro-Dead," contrasting Ashcroft's position on abortion with Missouri voters' support for a dead politician. The article continues: "Ashcroft is coming under fire for various reasons—his opinions on abortion and dancing (he's against both), among others—but his inability to defeat a deceased Democrat seems to be the biggest albatross around his neck." By alluding to Samuel Taylor Coleridge's famous poem, "The Rime of the Ancient Mariner," *The Toronto Star* brings together Romantic poetry and posthumous election, turning to Romantic poetry for help with this still surprising event: voters giving the dead a chance to represent and so "speak" for them.

Given the etymological ties between *vote* and *voice*, when constituents cast a vote for a dead candidate they give the nonliving the chance to speak (again) and speak for them as their representative. Constituents perform a rhetorical act familiar to readers of Romantic and post-Romantic poems. Wordsworth describes why he hopes to limit the presence of personification in his poetry in his preface to *Lyrical Ballads*, but Romantic poetry features numerous animating tropes (apostrophe and prosopopoeia among them) that throw into question the difference between the living and the dead, the animate and the inanimate. When Percy Shelley calls upon the West Wind to animate him in "Ode to the West Wind," he calls on the wind to do what he, the poet-speaker, has already in a sense done, as the poem's opening apostrophe imagines the wind a living interlocutor: "O wild West Wind, thou breath of Autumn's being /. . . Make me thy lyre."[5] Though the speaker of Shelley's poem worries that he has lost his creative power, become almost inanimate himself, he begins the poem with an animating trope, an apostrophe that humanizes the wind through the power of lyric address. In early chapters of this book I investigate the importance of apostrophe to various conceptions of the lyric that emerge from critical encounters with Romantic poems. In this chapter I shift attention from apostrophe to prosopopoeia, a trope that also appears at key moments in Romantic and post-Romantic poetry. Shelley experiments with prosopopoeia in his poem "The Cloud," as he grants a cloud the ability to address readers directly: "I bring fresh showers for the thirsting flowers."[6] In giving a cloud the power to speak, Shelley transforms a mute, inanimate entity into an almost human one and in the process confuses the difference between the animate and inanimate, the living and the dead, persons and nonpersons. John Clare likewise employs the trope to powerful effect in "The Lament of Swordy Well," where he grants the land itself the power to voice the devastating effects of human greed on the environment. Clare embraces prosopopoeia to lodge a political critique. Poets repeatedly invoke the trope. In *Dying Modern*, Diana Fuss explores the curious paradox she calls the "corpse poem," a modern elegy that similarly features prosopopoeia, as poets produce first-person poetic utterances spoken in the voice of the deceased. Fuss foregrounds the ways prosopopoeia enables new forms of elegy and explains that though poets deployed the form in the nineteenth century "as a vehicle of comedy or theology, the corpse poem evolved in the twentieth century into a critique of politics, history, or even literature itself."[7] From Clare to twentieth-century poets Fuss discusses, like Richard Wright and Randall Jarrell, throwing one's voice to the dead, giving the inanimate a chance to speak, makes legible ongoing forms of dehumanization, depersonalization, and objectification.

Who or what counts as living, as having a voice, as having a say is a question Romantic and post-Romantic poets ask with some increasing frequency, and voters, like poets, raise the question whenever a deceased candidate is granted the power to speak in their stead. When a candidate dies and voters cast their vote for them, voters borrow power from the poets and throw their voices to the dead to make them live (rhetorically if not biologically). A vote for the dead throws into question who or what counts as living.

For several decades literary criticism has attempted to demonstrate that poetry is intimately involved in political discourse. Revising the "Romantic" understanding of poetry as divorced from history and politics, an understanding of poetry that emerges from various conceptualizations of the aesthetic after Immanuel Kant, contemporary literary criticism has worked to show that poetry is deeply embedded within historical and political discourse and responds sometimes implicitly, sometimes explicitly to historical and political conditions. In *John Keats and the Culture of Dissent*, for instance, Nicholas Roe reads the Tory campaign to suppress John Keats's poetry in journals of the day as a sign that Keats's poetry is potentially more dangerous, more political than has generally been acknowledged.[8] In *Brown Romantics*, Manu Samriti Chander acknowledges the many ways white English Romantic poets were complicit with the project of imperialism, but turns to representative figures he calls "Brown Romantics" who "struggled to challenge the dominance of English poets, mobilizing Romanticism against Romanticism."[9] Chander turns in conclusion to the poetry of John Keats and discovers in canonical romanticism strategies for resisting imperialism and white supremacy. We will explore some of the implications of these readings of Keats in chapter 5, "Keats for Beginners." My interest in this chapter, though, is not limited to the various ways a poem engages the politics of its own historical moment. Instead, I begin with some of the surprising ways political discourse relies on poetic tropes, specifically tropes of address, tropes scholars associate with the emergence of the Romantic lyric. The election of the dead to public office makes newly legible the poetic tropes, like prosopopoeia, that condition representative government, as one's vote (one's voice) is lent to another, even a deceased other. In this way, the election of the dead offers readers a chance to think differently the relationship between poetry and politics. Just as poetry is political, so too is politics poetical (and, by extension, not a little Romantic too). In the second half of this chapter I turn to a late twentieth-century poem by Lucille Clifton, "jasper texas 1998," a poem readers might not think of immediately in the context of Romantic poetry but a poem that extends questions about poetry and politics to issues of racialized violence, to questions of voice and muteness, life and death. Composed in response to the brutal, racially motivated murder of James Byrd Jr. in the United States in 1998, the poem grants Byrd posthumous life, giving him a chance to speak from beyond the grave and bear witness to his own death. Clifton animates Byrd's dismembered head, whose voice, he explains in the opening lines, results from his having been chosen to speak by the other members of his body. Clifton places Byrd's first-person poetic utterance in the context of an election. Through a double act of figuration, prosopopoeia and posthumous election, the poem raises complicated questions about how life is determined and whose lives count.

Death in Politics

Many reasons exist for why any particular deceased candidate might receive enough votes posthumously to win an election: voters might wish to register their deep admiration for the candidate; they might feel great sympathy for family members of the deceased; they might wish to express their extreme animosity toward the deceased's opponent. But in attempting to understand the frequency of posthumous election, the author of the *Toronto Star* article concludes with a more general pronouncement: "The truth is, beating a dead man in an election is a difficult task. We love dead people, and that's understandable because they no longer talk."[10] The *Toronto Star*'s witticism plays on our love of peace and quiet. Politics is noisy business, the author implies, and electing the dead to "speak" quiets the political arena. If the *Toronto Star* directly alludes to Coleridge's "Rime of the Ancient Mariner," it might also remind some readers of Kant's essay "Perpetual Peace," which opens with a pun on politics and the death-drive. Kant remembers "Perpetual Peace" inscribed on a Dutch innkeeper's sign above the picture of a church cemetery.[11] A desire for perpetual peace, so the innkeeper's sign puns, is a desire one can satisfy not in life but only in death. Kant in "Perpetual Peace" and the author of the *Toronto Star* article, "Voters were Pro-Dead," draw our attention to the same questions: is the surety and stability of death the dream and desire of political life? Is the model state a cemetery?

Sigmund Freud suggests an answer when in *Beyond the Pleasure Principle* he offers a fable of life's origin. Life itself comes as a shock to the previously inanimate entity. The tension of life is too great, and the first drive of life, writes Freud, is to reduce life's tension. Counterintuitively, Freud suggests that animate life endeavors to cancel itself out: "In this way the first drive came into being: the drive to return to the inanimate state."[12] Similarly, from Kant to the *Toronto Star*, the first drive of politics is toward the end of politics. An ideal politics is the absence of politics. In this case, the election of the dead is no random event; instead, voting for the dead expresses a political desire innate to politics, one that structures political life, as if the goal of politics were perpetual peace, as if the most perfect parliament were a parliament of the dead.[13] One of the ironies of contemporary democratic elections especially in the United States is that politicians often campaign to put an end to political strife and rise above partisan bickering. The desire for politics without politics is always also an attempt to put the struggles of politics, the strife and debate, the possible anger and disagreement, to an end.[14]

From this point of view, an ideal citizenry is an inanimate citizenry. In

Necro Citizenship, Russ Castronovo further explores the relationship between politics and death. He argues that "the U.S. democratic state loves its citizens as passive subjects, unresponsive to political issues, unmoved by social stimuli, and unaroused by enduring injustices."[15] The democratic state aims to eliminate through pacification the very subjects it purports to represent. This investment by the state in passive subjects amounts, writes Castronovo, "to a sort of political necrophilia that fuels fascination with a citizenry immune to public commotion and insensible to contestatory energy."[16] The "or" that divides liberty from death in Patrick Henry's famous phrase, "Give me Liberty, or Give me Death," may no longer hold, as the democratic state pursues liberty so that citizen-subjects will become politically apathetic, insensible, even inanimate. In the light of Castronovo's description of political necrophilia, the election of the dead to public office can seem a sign of the state's success in producing an inanimate citizenry, a citizenry that has come so to embrace its own inanimacy that a corpse seems the best possible representative. What happens when a candidate is posthumously elected varies from state to state. In the United States, the governor often appoints a temporary successor. In casting a vote one always throws one's voice, offers one's voice to another; when one throws one's voice to the dead, one risks muteness. One participates only enough in the process to put an end to one's participation.

Following this line of thinking, a vote for the dead is a sign of one's acquiescence to the status quo (one's acquiescence to a version of politics that has perhaps always been the dream of politics, a politics without dissension). But when voters embrace a dead politician they may also wish to register a protest against versions of politics that seem similarly "dead" or deadened. Jacques Rancière suggests in *Disagreement* that the rise of extremism and fundamentalism in the twentieth and twenty-first centuries should be viewed not as exceptions to but consequences of consensus—a means to preserve politics from a growing conformity that threatens to do away with politics and the possibility (even necessity) of disagreement.[17] When voters dissatisfied with both major parties in the United States argue that there is no difference between them, they argue that Republicans and Democrats conform more than they differ. Rancière's suggestion helps explain why some voters choose not to vote or choose to vote for third-party candidates that may have no hope of winning. Does the election of the dead express growing dissatisfaction not only with modern representative democracy but also with the available models of political and social critique? Can we think of a vote for the dead, in other words, as a form of minimal protest, a form of what Anne-Lise François in *Open Secrets* calls "recessive action"?[18]

Poets, Talking, Politics

We love dead people, reports the *Toronto Star*. The defense of politics from talk, from too much talking, from too many voices, is long-standing and predates the modern state. Who has the right to be heard is one of the first political questions. Who is of the *polis* (a citizen) and who of the *demos* (the people)? Not all who have a voice have the right to be heard, argues Aristotle, in *Politics*, referring specifically to enslaved persons. As Aristotle explains, political power is consolidated when some limit the rights of others to speak *and* be heard, which is why democracy is always, in a sense, against democracy, a democracy worthy the name. All so-called democracies today limit the power of some to speak and be heard.[19]

Because political power is consolidated by determining who has the right to speak, whether through legislation, police brutality, or corporate mechanisms that disincentivize political involvement, it may be no surprise that the poets, accused of excessive talking, are exiled from Plato's Republic. The security of the Republic depends upon the control and even elimination of speech, but the ability of the Republic to control speech is threatened by poets, who, even if they do not seem to know what they are talking about, talk and talk.[20] Through various animating tropes, personification and anthropomorphism, apostrophe and prosopopoeia, poets have long muddled the difference between who (or what) has the ability to speak. As literary scholars have shown in recent years, poets across the eighteenth century increasingly turn to figurative language to explore the differences between persons and nonpersons, between persons and things, showcasing the ways "persons" and "things" are, themselves, rhetorical figures. From so-called it-narratives in which a material object tells its own tale, as Jonathan Lamb discusses in *The Things Things Say*, to various creaturely poems that feature talking animals, as Tobias Menely and Heather Keenleyside discuss, poets not only talk too much but also make it possible for some "things" to act as "persons" too.[21] And as Monique Allewaert and Angela Naimou show—with attention to the dehumanizing processes of colonial expansion and the slave trade—writers take up the power of such animating tropes at a moment when who has the right to claim legal personhood is a question asked with increasing urgency.[22]

Poets investigate the many animating tropes that challenge the difference between persons and nonpersons at a key moment in the history of political power. In his final lecture, "*Society Must Be Defended*," Michel Foucault suggests that new versions of biopolitical sovereignty emerge in the nineteenth century around the same time poets throw into question the knowable differences between persons and things, the voiced and unvoiced. With the early nineteenth century, the power of the sovereign to kill is replaced by the power of the sovereign to make live (and let die).[23] Who counts, who counts as alive, and who has the power to determine who counts and who counts as alive: these are biopolitical questions, explains Foucault. In "The Romantic Rhetoric of Life," Alastair Hunt and Matthias Rudolf extend Foucault's thinking to explore the importance of romanticism, and the common preoccupation of Romantic writers with the concept of "life," to the emergence of biopolitics and new versions of sovereignty.[24] The rhetoric of "life" in Romantic poetry raises questions about sovereignty. As Sara Guyer suggests in *Reading with John Clare*, Romantic poets lay frequent claim to the power to make live, showing the ways "life" cannot be thought apart from rhetoric. For this reason, Guyer argues that biopolitics may always already be biopoetical. The power to make live depends on various animating rhetorical tropes familiar to Romantic poets: "questions of sovereignty and representation are simultaneously but impossibly poetic *and* political."[25] Romantic poets preoccupied by animating tropes trope the power of a biopolitical sovereign.

If the election of the dead seems very far from poetry, prosopopoeia is not. Discussions of lyric poetry often invoke the poet's "voice"—as if the poem itself were audible. In reading a poem as a lyric one grants the mute text a voice that can be heard. For this reason, prosopopoeia, argues Paul de Man, is the master trope of poetic discourse: "The principle of intelligibility, in lyric poetry, depends on the phenomenalization of the poetic voice. Our claim to understand a lyric text coincides with the actualization of a speaking voice."[26] One grants the mute text a voice, the dead new life. But what is true of lyric, of lyric poetry, of poetry may be true more generally of reading. Dismissing writing, Plato suggests that writing does not know to whom it should speak and so "speaks" to any and all. As a result, argues Barbara Johnson, prosopopoeia is not only the master trope of poetic discourse but also "*the* figure for reading."[27] In summarizing a text one often tries to explain what someone "said." The meaning of a text is supposed to conform to structures of speech. In reading one grants the dead writer the power to speak from the grave. Like posthumous election, reading is all about throwing voices.

But poets also explore the potential complications that accompany prosopopoeia and these potential complications are likewise introduced with the election of the dead to office, for the principle of intelligibility, in representative government, depends on the phenomenalization of the public's collective voice. John Milton's poem to William Shakespeare explores the potential risks that accompany powerful animating tropes. As Milton writes to Shakespeare:

> Thou in our wonder and astonishment
> Hast built thyself a live-long Monument.
> For whilst to th' shame of slow-endeavouring art,
> Thy easy numbers flow, and that each heart
> Hath from the leaves of thy unvalued book,
> Those Delphic lines with deep impression took,
> Then thou our fancy of itself bereaving,
> Dost make us Marble with too much conceiving.[28]

Confronted by Shakespeare's "live-long Monument," the folio of his plays, Milton discovers himself reduced to marble. The living Milton is struck dumb with too much conceiving and transformed into an inanimate object before Shakespeare's "living" book. As de Man writes in "Autobiography as De-Facement," "'Doth make us Marble' . . . cannot fail to evoke the latent threat that inhabits prosopopoeia, namely that by making the death speak, the symmetrical structure of the trope implies, by the same token, that the living are struck dumb, frozen in their own death."[29] In response to a very difficult text, readers might want to know what the author meant to say. At moments like this one, the author's voice can be invoked to silence discussion. Reading no longer names a struggle with what is written but a process whereby what the author meant to "say" is newly heard. Once what the author said has been determined, then reading is quickly—and all too quietly—transformed into nothing other than the reception of information. In granting life to the formerly mute text (as the text is transformed into the author's speech) the living reader risks becoming passively mute just as Milton is reduced to marble.

Granting life to the inanimate always risks stripping life from the living. This is what Pat Robertson, in his response to Mel Carnahan's victory, seems to have known without knowing it when he suggested that the election of the dead did not "compute." In granting life to Carnahan, voters simultaneously transformed Robertson into an inhuman "computer." Or more to the point, in granting a deceased Carnahan the right to speak in their stead, Carnahan's constituents risked their collective political voice. Constituents had no say over who would be appointed in Carnahan's place. But the threat of political muteness is not introduced with posthumous election. As Castronovo's own rhetoric shows, the control of speech (achieved through pacification of the citizenry) grants life to the state: "The U.S. democratic state loves its citizens as passive subjects," he writes, thus transferring life (in particular the ability to love) from the citizen to the state. Death to the citizen is life, through personification, to the state. And the reverse may be equally true, as Milton explores in his poem to Shakespeare. Granting life to the state may always risk turning voters into passive subjects.

Giving Voice to the Dead

Poets have not always been as preoccupied by prosopopoeia as they may be today, but the use of prosopopoeia, as Diana Fuss argues in *Dying Modern*, has increased in recent centuries along with expanded democracy and representative government. For Fuss the prevalence of corpse poems after romanticism is evidence for a growing dissatisfaction with elegy, in which the dead are often addressed through apostrophe. Recent years, however, show an increase in the number of poems in which the dead are not addressed but speak directly to the living. As a poem of mourning, an elegy offers consolation for loss. And in offering consolation, such poems also work to compensate for and overcome that loss. Fuss argues that in offering compensation for loss the elegy creates distance from the lost love object. The modern corpse poem counters mourning with melancholia, as the dead speakers of corpse poems remain present to the living and so refuse the distance that successful mourning demands. Mourning, unlike melancholia, enables one to move on but in moving on one also moves away from the love object. Melancholia marks instead a refusal to move away from the lost love object. Following Freud's understanding of mourning and melancholia, R. Clifton Spargo argues that melancholia refuses compensation. Maintaining contact with the love object, the melancholiac remains committed to loss.[30] And this commitment to loss describes an ethical relation to the love object, to the other. The other cannot, will not be forgotten. The one suffering from melancholia rejects that which might allow one to move on (and forget the pain of loss).

The corpse poem, with its dominant rhetorical figure, prosopopoeia, refuses the distance from loss that the elegy offers. The dead remain intimately present. They do not recede into the past. They continue to speak. These are poems not of mourning but of melancholia. As Fuss writes, "The corpse poem is not a substitute for loss but a vehicle for it, not a restitution for loss but a means to achieve it."[31] The corpse poem does not allow for the comfort of moving on because the dead, in speaking, have refused to become silent and mute. If the consolation the elegy offers is also a denial of loss, then the corpse poem remains committed to loss. The loss itself is never overcome but repeated with each iteration of the poem, with each renewed call of the dead to the living. Fuss suggests that the corpse poem has another purpose: to give death back to the living in a modern age that works to deny the possibility of loss, for instance through technological innovation and commodity capitalism. Nothing is lost for long. Everything is always available (and so replaceable in a moment). The corpse poem stands as a reminder of loss, a reminder of the impossibility of ridding the world of loss even as it calls attention to the fact that modern society works not only to overcome the possibility of loss but also the necessity of death. Fuss, for instance, discusses Randall Jarrell's World War II poem, "Losses":

> It was not dying: everybody died.
> It was not dying: we had died before
> In the routine crashes—and our fields
> Called up the papers, wrote home to our folks,
> And the rates rose all because of us.[32]

In an age in which casualties of war approach unimaginable numbers, Jarrell's poem attempts to secure for the individual a death that is not reducible to the abstraction of number. As Fuss writes, "The soldiers of World War II are not individuals who have died but mere numbers on an ever-rising mortality index. Sucked out of bombers or scattered on mountains, these soldiers' violent deaths are barely recognized as such."[33] By reducing death to a number, one limits the emotional force of loss: individuals do not die, numbers just go up. Death is not dying anymore. Prosopopoeia makes death present again and again by refusing the modern refusal of death.

The trope stages a tension between acknowledging and refusing loss, especially the loss of death (death as loss and death as lost). On the one hand, prosopopoeia acknowledges death and prevents the reader from moving away from the dead. The dead (as dead) call again and again. But poetic uses of prosopopoeia also refuse to allow the dead to fall silent (and die). In speaking as the dead, the poet also gives life to the dead; but in giving life back to the dead the poem repeats the very thing it works against. Death (and so loss as well) is overcome. The dead are no longer simply dead. I have spent this much time on prosopopoeia because poets, as Fuss argues, are increasingly preoccupied with poetic tropes that give life to the dead. From apostrophe, which transforms the absent, dead, or inanimate into a present, living interlocutor, to prosopopoeia, which grants the dead or inanimate a chance to speak, turning "things" into "persons," poets challenge the knowable difference between the living and the dead. Voters similarly challenge the knowability of this difference by electing the dead to represent (speak for) them. In giving their voice(s) to the dead, the electorate, like the poet, animates the dead, gives life to the dead. It is not clear, however, whether the dead are given new life in order to silence the living or if the dead are given new life in order to demonstrate to the living a truth about death that the living deny in our democratic age.

"Who Is the Human in This Place"

Most of the chapters of this book draw examples from nineteenth-century poems conventionally categorized as Romantic. The first three chapters turn on poems by William Wordsworth. The last two chapters will focus on poems by Keats and Percy Shelley. But here, just past the midpoint, I turn to a poem, "jasper texas 1998," by a twentieth-century poet, Lucille Clifton. I decided against a chronological arrangement for the chapters of *Look Round for Poetry* because my method in this chapter shares much with my method in preceding chapters like "The Poetics of Downturns" and "I Wandered Lonely as an iCloud." When one looks round for poetry, one discovers surprising constellations, as Wordsworth's preoccupation with cloud metaphors makes newly legible the metaphors of information infrastructure. Tropes are untimely. Their untimeliness makes it possible to read differently the structures that surround us. This chapter began with the unlikely event of posthumous election; as voters throw their voices to the dead, animating them, they recall not only the power of poetry but also the importance of poetry to politics. And we have explored how representative democracy itself relies on similar poetic tropes that throw into question the knowable difference between the voiced and the voiceless, the living and the dead, the human and the nonhuman. Posthumous election makes the poetics of politics newly legible. Clifton's poem extends into the twentieth century some of the rhetorical investigations pursued by more conventionally Romantic poems and shows how poets continue to challenge violence that does not remain comfortably figurative. Clifton addresses literal violence through a poem that amplifies its own figurative potential and she does so by staging a posthumous election.

"jasper texas 1998" responds to an historical event of racialized violence and does so with attention to the power of figure. But the literal event is difficult to narrate from the safe distance of scholarship. On July 7, 1998, James Byrd Jr., a Black man, was murdered by three white men: Shawn Allen Berry, Lawrence Russell Brewer, and John William King. They wrapped a heavy chain around Byrd's ankles, hooked the chain to a pickup truck, and then dragged Byrd for several miles until his body struck a culvert, severing his head and arm. Berry, Brewer, and King left Byrd's torso in front of the town's Black cemetery and then went to a barbeque. In court they testified that Byrd's throat had been slashed prior to his being dragged but the autopsy revealed that Byrd had been alive for several miles until being beheaded. The violence of the historical event may demand a literal language, a language that can refer directly and unsparingly to the horror of the event, of the violence, of the hatred. But Clifton writes the poem in the voice of the dead, which does not minimize the horror of the violence but does foreground the importance of rhetorical fiction:

> i am a man's head hunched in the road.
> i was chosen to speak by the members
> of my body.   the arm as it pulled away
> pointed toward me, the hand opened once
> and was gone.
>
> why and why and why
> should i call a white man brother?
> who is the human in this place,
> the thing that is dragged or the dragger?
> what does my daughter say?
>
> the sun is a blister overhead.
> if i were alive i could not bear it.
> the townsfolk sing we shall overcome
> while hope bleeds slowly from my mouth
> into the dirt that covers us all.
> i am done with this dust.   i am done.[34]

Who is human ("the thing that is dragged or the dragger")? Who counts as alive? In granting the head the ability to speak, Clifton produces a powerful protest poem.[35] Byrd returns from the grave to question humanity. To ask, why? To ask, what must be done? Because injustice continues, Byrd returns from the grave to address the living and testify to the crime committed against him. As Brian Norman has written about the prevalence of dead women talking in American literature, from Edgar Allan Poe's "The Fall of the House of Usher" to Toni Morrison's *Beloved* to Suzan-Lori Parks's *Getting Mother's Body*, "the dead talk more often than we might expect."[36] The dead return to protest justice's failure and to make a claim on the attention of the living. Clifton's poem shows how troublingly easy it was for Berry, Brewer, and King to deny Byrd his humanity, to make a human a thing. But in granting Byrd the ability to speak, through the power of figure, Clifton returns Byrd to the living to claim the right to further recognition.

In Clifton's poem, the figure that is Byrd seems more exhausted than angry as he reverses the difference between living and dead. The human is aligned with the "thing" that is dragged, as the head is given the ability to speak. And the draggers are imagined as things. They are less than human. In this way the poem may remind readers of Richard Wright's "Between the World and Me," a poem Fuss discusses and that opens: "And one morning while in the woods

I stumbled / suddenly upon the thing," the site of a lynching, a pile of dry bones and a stony skull.[37] At first it is unclear what the "thing" is upon which the speaker of the poem has stumbled, for the poem's second stanza consists of a list: white bones, a charred stump, a vacant shoe, butt-ends of cigars and cigarettes, a drained gin-flask, lipstick. The poem does not describe the event of a lynching from the start; readers, instead, encounter a list of things and imagine a scene of violence. The poem's second half consists of the speaker's imagining himself murdered as he relives the event. Clifton's poem does not afford such an imaginative act of identification. Instead the poem dramatizes the difference between the speaking dead (Byrd) and the living reader. Byrd is done. But what of the reader? What of the poet, Clifton? The final line of the poem in its very denial of life calls for something to be done but it does so through repetition. The head hunched in the road, granted second life through Clifton's employment of the figure of prosopopoeia, falls silent.

Clifton grants the severed head a voice, but in closing the poem focuses on the "dirt that covers us all," implying that "we"—the us of the poem—have all been buried. And metaphorically, the poem imagines readers, the towns-folk, as if in a grave and so gives expression to despondency, hopelessness, and the fear that racism and racialized violence cannot be defeated. This closing reversal returns readers to the risk that accompanies prosopopoeia; giving life to the dead always risks robbing the living of theirs. Here, the dirt that covers "all" already carries with it a vague threat: that the living have been buried too. The townspeople sing but the hope that bleeds from Byrd's mouth seeps into the dirt that covers all, that covers "us" all. If the dirt covers all, how do the townspeople sing? Clifton grants the dead a voice but the poem closes by suggesting, however subtly, that the living, like the dead, are buried beneath dirt, beneath racism and violence. The dead Byrd is done with this dust. He is free from it. But the living are now the ones buried.

On the one hand, prosopopoeia offers Clifton a chance to overcome the violence perpetrated against Byrd. Berry, Brewer, and King silenced Byrd by murdering him. Byrd returns from the grave to confront readers with the help of Clifton's poem; he refuses to remain mute. In speaking for Byrd, on the other hand, Clifton risks silencing him. Byrd does not speak for himself. Clifton speaks for him. In this way prosopopoeia raises a number of ethical questions. The elegy, unlike the "corpse poem," is a poem of mourning and as such it aims to bring about some form of healing. But in offering healing it also looks to generate distance from the loss mourned. In order to heal, the pain of loss must in some minimal way be forgotten, the importance of the lost object diminished. Prosopopoeia offers Clifton a chance to refuse this forgetting. Byrd has not receded into the past. He is present in his own voice. And yet of course, this is not Byrd's poem; this is not Byrd's voice. Clifton speaks on his behalf. The rhetorical trope of prosopopoeia presents both poet and reader with a problem. To refuse to allow the dead to be forgotten the poet speaks as and for the dead; however, in speaking as and for the dead the poet also effectively silences him. The dead do not "speak." The poet writes and so substitutes her voice for Byrd's. This dilemma is in part why prosopopoeia always threatens to silence, to freeze, the living reader. How does one respond? To "hear" Byrd is to accept Clifton's voice in his stead. Not to "hear" Byrd is to allow the perpetrators of the murder to succeed in silencing him. The townsfolk sing "we shall overcome," but the poem allows readers neither to celebrate nor lament the singing. A powerful call for justice, the poem also shows how difficult it can sometimes be to tell the difference between making live and letting die.

"I Was Chosen to Speak"

If Clifton's choice to employ prosopopoeia in the poem raises complicated questions about voice and representation, she further complicates these questions by making Byrd's voice dependent on an election. Clifton recasts her poetic decision as an electoral one. What politics follows from speaking for and as another? How does the poet's use of prosopopoeia reflect on a posthumous election in which the dead are given (back) a voice? Why does the poem associate posthumous election and racialized violence? Clifton's poem grants Byrd the chance to bear witness to his own murder. The reader encounters first-person testimony. But Clifton reflects on the animating power of tropes by situating Byrd's speech in the context of a posthumous election. The second line of the poem ("i was chosen to speak by the members / of my body") reminds readers that prosopopoeia (*the* trope of poetic discourse, *the* figure for reading) also structures representative democracy. Just as Clifton speaks for Byrd in giving him a voice from beyond the grave, so too does the elected official speak on behalf of constituents. The elected official is the "face" of the people, the phenomenalization of their "voice." The trope that conditions poetic discourse is also the trope that conditions representative democracy, and the election of the dead calls attention to the poetics of such a political system.

The poem unites questions about race and violence in the United States with questions about representation (in poetry and in politics). The voice of the poem is not that of Byrd himself, at least not simply or unproblematically.

More precisely, the "I" of the poem is that of "a man's head," where the genitive noun (*man's*) modifies the predicate noun. The head functions as Byrd's representative (and more terrifyingly, as a synecdoche). And the poem develops this complicated representational logic over the course of its opening lines. The head claims the right to speak by virtue of a choice, as described in the second line, and though "choice" suggests intent (as if the head had been nominated, chosen, and elected by its constituents), the poem plays on the rhetoric of election as the metaphor of "choice" substitutes for the more literal mechanics of bodies in motion. With "members of my body," the poem situates itself in the context of existing metaphors about politics and bodies, and the body politic. At least since Hobbes the state has dreamed of itself as a healthy body, one at peace with itself and not torn asunder by division and conflict. One goal of politics is the production of a unified populace, as disagreement (politics) substitutes for physical violence (war), but elections frequently disclose the numerous ways in which the body politic is torn asunder by conflict. In the poem, the violence done to a Black body is not dissociated from the mechanics of political representation. The head in the poem is elected to speak by virtue of a literal dismemberment. The arm as it pulls away (as it was pulled away) points toward the head, and the head takes this indexical mark as a sign and begins to speak. Violence is transformed into an election. And while Byrd finds a voice, the poem, by staging an election in the context of violence, also comments on the literal and metaphorical violence that politics inspires and conceals.

If elections substitute politics for war, Clifton's poem foregrounds the violence that makes elections possible; the violence of substitution, even the seemingly innocuous substitution of one voice for another, is never far from actual violence. In speaking for one's constituents, a representative always risks silencing them. To speak as a representative requires substituting one's speech for the speech of one's constituents. And while speaking for another may always risk silencing them, for a representative not to speak for one's constituents would likewise risk silencing them. One's voice is silenced, in a sense, when one's representative chooses not to speak or is prevented from speaking. "jasper texas 1998" is a poem about racial violence that also interrogates the conditions of possibility of representative government with its opening lines and use of a rhetorical trope, prosopopoeia. A "post-Romantic" poem, "jasper texas 1998" extends Romantic explorations of animating tropes into the twentieth century, as it showcases some of the ways representative democracy depends on the animating tropes that political theory may often assume only pertain to poetics.

Something Awry in the Social

If prosopopoeia is the trope of reading, it is also the trope of representative democracy. There is no representative democracy without the power to throw one's voice; there is no representative democracy without the power to throw one's voice even to the dead. Posthumous election, in other words, discloses a truth about the rhetorical structures that determine representative democracy. It may be that without the possibility of posthumous election there would be no chance for democracy. For a free election to be truly a free election, one must not know in advance the outcome. There must be a chance for surprise. And posthumous election is one form such surprise might take. If the result of a free and democratic election is absolutely "computable," then the election is neither free nor democratic. No democracy worthy the name exists without the possibility that an election, to return to Pat Robertson's phrase, not compute. But in Clifton's poem, posthumous election follows from, responds to, and resists depersonification. Posthumous election in Clifton's poem is a sign that something is awry in the social.

Questions about voice are intimately related to questions about personhood. In sometimes surprising ways, tropes determine social and political structures, the social and political structures that make personhood thinkable in the first place. To explore these structures fully requires poetic training, as Barbara Johnson suggests in *Persons and Things*, when she argues that a rise in the use of prosopopoeia discloses a truth about capitalism.[38] Persons get in the way of capitalism, which is why capitalism promotes the commoditization of persons (the transformation, for instance, of persons into billboards). With attention to various forms of violence that reduce persons to things, Achille Mbembe offers necropolitics in response to Foucault's biopolitics, where necropolitics describes the many ways contemporary social and political structures subject life to the power of death, with war the end and necessity of democracy, politics, and culture; and he explores how the subjection of life to the power of death affects relations among resistance, sacrifice, and terror. In *Necropolitics*, Mbembe identifies the "new and unique forms of social existence in which vast populations are subjected to conditions of life conferring upon them the status of *living dead*," a figure that may remind readers of Coleridge's "Night-mare LIFE-IN-DEATH," from "The Rime of the Ancient Mariner."[39] Mbembe demonstrates how necropower blurs "the lines between resistance and suicide," voice and its negation.[40]

A vote for a deceased politician can always be understood in broadly psychological terms, as an expression of distaste for the deceased's opponent or sympathy for the families of the dead. And the reasons will vary for why any one specific candidate was elected posthumously. But in closing, and with the help of a poet like Clifton and a poem like "jasper texas 1998," a poem that takes up and extends some familiar Romantic lyric preoccupations, I focus on the ways posthumous election shows an electorate struggling with the figures and tropes that determine representative democracy. In contrast to various examples of active protest, where protesters celebrate people's willingness to put themselves in danger in the service of political action, the self-muting that results when one elects the dead to speak for one can seem a retreat from political action. But if election of the dead also calls attention to the tropes that structure representative democracy, if the election of the dead raises questions about contemporary necropolitical regimes, then a vote for the dead shows up the ways the living are given a voice in politics only to the extent to which that voice is also negated. There may be no representative democracy without this double bind, one the poets know well and explore with rigor and focused attention. In throwing one's voice one always risks throwing one's voice away. In the case of posthumous election, then, when one throws one's voice—one's vote—to a dead politician, one literalizes the risk that structures representative democracy: in throwing one's voice to the dead, one makes explicit the structures of negation that make one's participation legible in the first place. Active participation in representative democracy—as one throws one's voice to another—may always risk the very voice one throws.

Following the poets, the election of the dead can seem a response to a version of politics and a conception of the state that already risks (even desires) a muted citizenry. "We love dead people, and that's understandable because they no longer talk," quips the *Toronto Star*.[41] If the state suffers from political necrophilia, as Castronovo argues, then one electoral response is to give the state exactly what it seems to want: a silent state, a state of silence. One sends the dead to Washington. But as Lauren Berlant writes in the final chapter to *Cruel Optimism*, "All politically performative acts of vocal negation are pedagogical, singular moments inflated to embody something generally awry in the social."[42] As neither an embrace nor a rejection of representative government, a vote for a corpse publicly performs an act of vocal negation. One says "something is awry" by negating one's vocal performance, calling attention to what Mbembe describes as a death world.[43] Clifton's poem suggests that necropolitics may be winning this contest over democracy, as those who murdered Byrd may be understood to function as agents of the State. But Clifton's poem also suggests that posthumous election makes new acts of voicing possible. That the dead so often win election may, in other words, be a small sign that the many, the people, the demos, are not yet ready to give up their voice(s)—however timidly this "not yet ready to give up" is expressed, however difficult it may be to hear what it is that is expressed. Unfortunately, it may not be possible to tell in advance the difference between performative acts of vocal negation and exaggerated cynicism, even in the wake of ongoing racialized violence. But by continuing to trope the voice and its possible negation, life and death, Romantic and post-Romantic poetry offers readers a chance to describe the difference it might still make to try and describe this difference.

5. Keats for Beginners

I would like to begin before beginning.
—Jacques Derrida, *The Death Penalty*, volume 1

The previous chapter, "On the Poetry of Posthumous Election," turned specific attention toward a twentieth-century poem by Lucille Clifton. I risk a potentially jarring return to nineteenth-century poems with my final two chapters, this one which takes poems by John Keats as points of departure and the next which does the same with poems by Percy Bysshe Shelley. But if the opening chapters of *Look Round for Poetry* explore the untimeliness of poetic tropes and figures through various possible conjunctions—as tropes of lyric address, for instance, mingle with representative democracy—then with these last chapters I return to Romantic poems and let political questions come to the fore, as poems by Keats and Shelley theorize what it might mean to live amidst the possibility of conjunction, juxtaposition, or constellation, what it might mean, in other words, to live among others. In *Necropolitics*, Achille Mbembe identifies the contemporary social, economic, and political pressures that "engulf us in the hallucinatory dream of a 'community without strangers,'" a world of people who "aspire only to take their leave of others."[1] A community without strangers is one that precludes from the start the possibility of surprise. As I show in this chapter, Keats's poems address this hallucinatory dream through the trope of beginning. Like poems, and the grammatical and rhetorical structures that shape them, beginnings are always possibly a little untimely. They can surprise. And the surprise of beginning is possible only because one lives among others, Keats's poems suggest. In my final chapter I extend this insight by focusing on the force of prepositions, specifically the force of the preposition "among," in several of Shelley's most famous poems.

In a letter to Coventry Patmore, Gerard Manley Hopkins describes John

Keats as "one of the beginners of the Romantic movement," by which he means one of the poets who helped start the movement away from neoclassical poetry and poetics.[2] Given that Keats published his first book of poems in 1817 when Wordsworth was in his mid 40s, calling Keats "one of the beginners" seems almost anachronistic. But Hopkins's letter evokes another sense of "beginner," one that I turn round in this chapter. An awareness of Keats as a beginner—one invested in the principle of beginning—lurks within Hopkins's letter. Of the poets one might associate with the Romantic movement—Charlotte Smith, Wordsworth, Samuel Taylor Coleridge—Keats is "one of the beginners," as if only some Romantic poets ought to be considered "beginners," as if only some poets are interested in the question of beginning. Following Hopkins, or, at least, following this hint in Hopkins's letter, I want to ask: what does it mean to call Keats a beginner? Who or what is a beginner?

Such questions can seem far from the discourse of politics but in *The Human Condition* Hannah Arendt suggests that beginning "may be the central category of political, as distinguished from metaphysical, thought."[3] For Arendt, politics exists only because sometimes something unanticipated occurs. And one name for this chance is "beginning." There is politics only because there are beginnings. Keats has often been read as either too political or not political enough. Given Hopkins's decision to call Keats one of the beginners and Arendt's suggestion that beginning is the central category of political thought, how might thinking of Keats and beginning offer a chance to rethink Keats's relationship to politics? The event of beginning, I show with specific reference to the closing lines of "Sleep and Poetry" and the opening lines of *Endymion*, raises questions about the possible relationship between perception and cognition, understanding and experience—and so the relationship between commitment and action.

In recent years, the question of beginning has taken on added importance in the context of contemporary political life. Calls to "Make America Great Again" play on a version of romanticism likewise committed to the past, as Romantic writers returned, for instance, to medieval tropes to keep a threatening modernity at bay. Romantic celebrations of childhood can be read similarly as calls for a return to a lost moment of wholeness and self-satisfaction. More often than not, Romantic texts challenge such calls and show them to have been fantasy as if from the start. Far from celebrating the play present, for instance, in "now and again," which I discuss in the introduction, the *again* in "Make America Great Again" aims to secure the future for the present and make of the future nothing other than a repetition of the past, a past perceived as simultaneously lost and better—better for some, for those who "matter" most. If a *beginning* is another name for that which was unanticipated, if it exposes one to the possible surprise of otherness, then those who regularly employ a slogan like "Make America Great Again" position themselves self-consciously against the unanticipated. For instance, in *Great Again: How to Fix Our Crippled America*, Donald Trump, a former president of the United States, offers his own take on beginnings and for Trump, at least, there is never any surprise at the beginning of any project: "At the beginning of any kind of project I know what I need to know," he writes.[4] If the dangerous effects of such hyperbolic self-confidence were not so well known, a sentence like this one might lead simply to caricature, but what the sentence conveys is an absolute denial of beginning, if by beginning one means exposure to possible surprise, exposure to what cannot have been fully anticipated. Trump knows what he needs to know, and he knows it all from the beginning. The sentiment (and the sentence) fulfills the promise of repetition present in the "again" of the book's title. Everything that happens happens only ever as an "again," one known from the start. The threat of iterability present in the writing of Jacques Derrida, for instance, has been transformed into all-knowing self-confidence. If from the beginning, one knows what one needs to know, and if one knows that one knows (or feels that one knows) what one needs to know, then a beginning is, in essence, always and only a repetition; and any event just a gradual unfolding of what one already knew beforehand. This quote from *Great Again* captures a political mentality prominent today, one that assumes from the start that one already knows what one needs to know; a mentality that assumes that at the beginning—and from the beginning—one needs to know nothing other than what one already knows. Such self-confidence situates itself in opposition to the surprise of beginning. And if we take Keats (and Arendt) seriously, then this self-satisfaction also opposes politics itself. It offers a strategy for putting politics (and the surprise of politics) to an end. To read Keats as a beginner, to read Keats for beginners, is to discover in Romantic writing not only the threat of beginning, as beginning challenges confident self-understanding, but also its astounding potential, for there is no principle of beginning without a principle of freedom.

"One of the Beginners"

Almost from the start, Romantic poets have been accused of turning away from active involvement in politics, understood as instrumental action or intervention in the world of human affairs. The defining turn of the poet inward to explore his own thoughts and feelings, it has been argued, constitutes simultaneously a turn away from the poet's own historical moment. Turning inward, the poet turns away from others. Keats for instance is most famous for addressing not his fellow man but a nightingale and an urn. Indeed, of the Romantic poets accused of turning away from history and politics, Keats is often a prime example. As Stopford A. Brooke writes in 1907: "[Keats] has . . . no vital interest in the present, none in man as a whole, none in the political movement of human thought, none in the future of mankind, none in liberty, equality and fraternity."[5] Brooke offers a particularly damning picture of Keats, and one still prominent: the dreamer-poet far removed from (and even uninterested in) the world of human affairs.

More damning than Brooke's argument that Keats has no interest in "the political movement of human thought" is Jerome McGann's later suggestion that Romantic poets use art as a means to escape the world. It is one thing to take no interest in politics; it is quite another actively to flee all things political. In response to a world turned topsy-turvy—with the French Revolution's dramatic failure, marked by the violence of the Terror and the rise of Napoleon as dictator—the Romantic poet, argues McGann, sticks his head in the sand (or, perhaps more precisely, sticks his head in the idealized work of art). Romantic poetry, writes McGann, "is everywhere marked by extreme forms of displacement and poetic conceptualization whereby the actual human issues with which the poetry is concerned are resituated in a variety of idealized localities."[6] The poet uses poetry to transport himself into an idealized world and so away from actual human issues, and once again Keats is a prime example.[7] In more recent years we have begun to think again (and differently) about Keats and politics.[8]

We have not tended to think about Keats and beginnings, even though he is, to quote Hopkins again, "one of the beginners," in part because we have tended to focus on Keats's intense preoccupation with endings, on what Keats himself in a letter to Charles Brown calls his "posthumous existence," an existence that carries on as if after the end.[9] Even before Keats knew he was going to die of tuberculosis, he was preoccupied by mortality and tended to think together mortality and poetic production: as Moneta explains in *The Fall of Hyperion*, to feel "What 'tis to die and live again before / Thy fated hour" is, at least in part, what makes one a poet.[10] The poet is haunted by a future death that, in some sense, has already occurred. It has been "felt." "Crucial to the figuration of Keats as Poet," explains Andrew Bennett, "is an early death which is presciently inscribed within the poet's life and work—an early death which he knows about."[11] Keats enters history a poet whose life had already ended.[12]

In *Lives of the Dead Poets*, Karen Swann writes powerfully about the ways her chosen poets, Keats, Shelley, and Coleridge, resist the forms of life expected of them, which, she argues, also "suggests that they bear a critique of the culture that would enlist art and artists into its designs."[13] With respect to Keats, Swann shows how Keats's "posthumous life" refuses "narratives of progress or even of working through" and, instead, "convey[s] a sense of a world suspended and withdrawn."[14] Keats's care for evacuated poetic conventions thus speaks to what Swann describes as, following Baudelaire and others, experience under modern commodity capitalism, where life becomes abstracted and phantasmagorical. Keats's exploration of a vanished life bears within itself a critique of the modes of life available to him.

To think about Keats and beginnings (and beginnings and politics) is to depart slightly from two dominant threads of Keats criticism—the apolitical poet, and the poet preoccupied by his own end—and take seriously a Keats who writes for beginners and of beginnings, a poet who attempts through beginning (as concept and act) a rethinking of poetry under modern commodity capitalism. What sorts of beginnings might be possible? What does beginning tell us about experience now, and now and again? From within the question of beginning Keats bears witness to a politics conceived around what we do not yet know about the world, about ourselves, and about our being in the world with others without foundation or guarantee.[15] One might always commit oneself to politics conceived around returns, knowing returns, in an attempt to secure for some a foundation or guarantee.[16] Keats's poetry offers readers a chance to think the revolutionary character of beginnings.

Keats's Beginnings

Discussions of Keats's beginnings often themselves begin with "On First Looking into Chapman's Homer," as both Lawrence Lipking and Helen Vendler do in their attempts to identify the moment a young, fledgling poet became the mature poet now anthologized. How did Keats become Keats? This question is of great importance, at least for Lipking, because "Keats seems to hold the key to everything we would like to know about how one becomes a poet."[17] Just as Keats looks into Chapman's Homer so too do readers of the poem look into Keats. One sees here Keats's beginning, as if a beginning were something one could see. To know something about Keats and beginning is to know something about poetry and beginning.

But the decision of Lipking and Vendler (and others) to focus on this poem from 1816 confirms much of what one knows about beginnings, those startling and unexpected events that take one most by surprise and that change things moving forward. If readers discover "Keats" in "On First Looking into Chapman's Homer," then this discovery is not in any simple way true for Keats himself, who is plagued by doubts about his own poetic powers. Unsurprisingly, numerous examples of such self-doubt are found in his letters even after "On First Looking in Chapman's Homer," the poem that marks Keats's emergence, his beginning, as "Keats."[18] As he writes to B. R. Haydon in May of 1817 about the first lines of *Endymion* (begun toward the end of April), "Truth is I have been in such a state of Mind as to read over my Lines and hate them."[19] What Keats bears witness to in beginning, from within beginning itself, may be distinguished from what others discover there. Lipking and Vendler see a beginning. Keats sees only more of the same, confirming one of Sigmund Freud's most basic insights. Challenging any idea of history as a series of known events, and challenging the idea that history is most historical when known, Freud argues that the individual subject often testifies unknowingly, unconsciously, to precisely those historical occurrences that have most shaped her. The most forceful events may even be those we do not know, did not experience, those events that failed to enter consciousness and are legible now only in their recurrence.

In an influential essay, Vendler attempts to locate what she calls the experiential beginnings of Keats's odes.[20] With reference to "To Autumn" and following a letter from Keats to J. H. Reynolds from September of 1819, Vendler argues that the experiential beginning of the poem is found twenty-six lines in, with the stubble-plains. As Keats writes in the letter to Reynolds: "How beautiful the season is now—How fine the air. A temperate sharpness about it. Really, without joking, chaste weather—Dian skies—I never liked stubble-fields so much as now—Aye better than the chilly green of the spring. Somehow a stubble-plain looks warm—in the same way that some pictures look warm—This struck me so much in my Sunday's walk that I composed upon it."[21] "To Autumn" becomes a different poem, argues Vendler, when one understands it to emanate from the stubble-plains instead of working leisurely toward them. She acknowledges that her reconstruction of the experiential beginnings of Keats's odes may be conjecture, but revealing the hidden beginnings "can help define the shape and course of each ode as it completes itself to wholeness."[22] A sense of the whole poem is possible, argues Vendler, only if one identifies its origin, only if one, in other words, distinguishes the poem's literal from its experiential beginning.

What one learns from attending to Keats's "hidden beginnings," following Vendler's argument, is that Keats is unlikely to begin a poem with the experience that occasioned it. For Vendler, these experiential beginnings are hidden but may be revealed through critical intervention. As a result another question is raised: why should the experiential beginnings of the poems time and again be moved to the middle or end of the poems? Why should Keats postpone the poem's beginning? In identifying a split between a poem's literal and experiential beginning, Vendler highlights the ways Keats's poems allegorize the difficulty of knowing a beginning. As a result of moving the "beginning" to the middle or end of the poem, "a beginning," for Keats, is no longer purely phenomenal.

And indeed, Keats, in the same letter to Haydon quoted above, troubles the very idea that a beginning is an event available to consciousness and understanding. "I read and write about eight hours a day," writes Keats about his preparation for writing *Endymion*. He continues: "There is an old saying well begun is half done—'tis a bad one. I would use instead—Not begun at all 'till half done so according to that I have not begun my Poem and conse-quently (a priori) can say nothing about it."[23] But how does one know when one is half done if one has not yet begun? For Keats, it seems, a beginning does not happen at the beginning (or first) but only after the poem is well underway; a poem begins only after reaching its midpoint, as if one all of a sudden discovered that one had begun a poem only at the point at which one also discovered that one was half done with it. "Oh, I didn't even know I'd begun!" One can "say something about" a beginning only later and in this way one is always attempting to catch up to a beginning that has escaped one—one's attention, one's understanding.[24]

Beginnings are not simply "hidden" but often missed, and as a result, it seems, readers repeat the difficulty of beginning. When is a beginning? How does one know one has begun? My thinking about missed events—and my thinking about beginnings as missed events—has been shaped heavily by Cathy Caruth's reading of Sigmund Freud's *Beyond the Pleasure Principle*, where the traumatic event fails at first to enter consciousness and so happens for the "first" time only in its recurrence as a flashback.[25] Emily Rohrbach and William H. Galperin have recently focused attention on the importance of similarly missed events to the makeup of the everyday. In *Modernity's Mist*, Rohrbach foregrounds the verbal play of "mist" and "missed," where the mist that offers resistance and makes thought possible is always possibly missed, not encountered or only encountered in its absence; and for Galperin in *The History of Missed Opportunities*, the everyday begins with romanticism but be-gins only as a result of its having been missed.[26] Readers of Keats register the force of this temporality in sometimes surprising ways. Vendler's own essay, for instance, announces its own beginning more than once. "Let me begin with the one factual instance," writes Vendler after an introductory paragraph. Straining against some invisible force that labors to prevent a beginning ("let me begin"), even after the essay has already, in another sense, begun, the next paragraph announces a second (or third) beginning, "I will begin with the other ode."[27] Even as Vendler attempts to locate the experiential beginnings of Keats's poems, her own writing registers the impact of beginning—or not. The beginning of her own essay, in other words, is, like Keats's odes, divided, dispersed, and deferred. Vendler's essay reproduces Keats's difficulty locating beginnings and so bears witness to the surprise of beginning.

The character of surprise is inherent in all beginning. To the extent to which they happen, beginnings, like traumatic events, happen belatedly (for us, to us). That is, precisely because a beginning takes one by surprise it is not an event for which one is prepared. A beginning happens too soon (before one is prepared for it) and as a result it happens also too late (it is missed, understood only after the fact). One only has a chance to understand the event later. And for this reason, one does not know a beginning as a beginning as it happens. Such is the awkward temporality that beginnings mark and that Keats explores. The awkward temporality of beginning is not unlike the awkward temporality produced by a phrase I discussed in my introduction: "every now and again." To suggest that romanticism is every now and again suggests simultaneously that romanticism, like beginning, is ever-present *and* only ever intermittent.

A Resolution to Begin

If not all then most poets struggle with beginning in that more common sense: how to begin to write a poem? But not all poets thematize beginning itself in quite so enigmatic a way as Keats. Keats's thematization of beginning, though, may be, to return to Hopkins, what helps make him "one of the beginners" of the Romantic Movement. I would like to turn now to a specific passage from one of Keats's early poems, "Sleep and Poetry." Here, as in the letter to Haydon, Keats struggles with and so explores the enigmatic temporality of beginning.

In "Sleep and Poetry," the final poem from his first book, Keats attempts to work through various anxieties about his future as a poet. The poem stands, in other words, as the summation of his previous attempts at making a beginning. He bounces between multiple and sometimes conflicting fears: what if I do not have enough time before I die to write the best I have to write; what if some "say that I presumptuously / Have spoken"; what if the reception of my poems is negative and hastens my disgrace?[28] After asking for "ten years, that [he] may overwhelm / [Him]self in poetry," Keats resolves in conclusion to make a beginning, and in part "Sleep and Poetry," like *Endymion*, lays out the necessary conditions for his future career as he resolves to begin even though he does not yet feel confident enough to begin.[29] He finds relief from the questions listed above in the thought of the poet's house, where cold and sacred busts smile. Posterity will disclose all. There is no need to worry now: "happy he who trusts / To clear futurity his darling fame."[30] Keats convinces himself and in a sense this is the aim of the poem, to convince himself that worrying about whether or not he is prepared to write the poems he longs to write, poems that will have the desired effect on his reading audience and so guarantee his place in the poet's house, will only prevent him from beginning.

But in concluding the poem, Keats tells a strange story *of* the poem's beginning. At the end of the poem, Keats resolves to begin the poem that announces his beginnings as a poet. The final lines of the poem read:

> There came
> Thought after thought to nourish up the flame
> Within my breast; so that the morning light
> Surprised me even from a sleepless night;
> And up I rose refresh'd, and glad, and gay,
> Resolving to begin that very day
> These lines; and howsoever they be done,
> I leave them as a father does his son.[31]

The poem's final lines introduce a number of textual complexities. The poet awakens from a sleepless night but feels refreshed nonetheless. And he resolves that very day to begin "these lines," "Sleep and Poetry." With the semicolon in the next to last line, though, there is a jump from the description of the past when the poet rose refreshed and resolved to begin and the present moment in which he reflects on the poem he has, quite suddenly, concluded. Now reflecting on what he has written, the poet is unsure how well these lines have been composed; he wonders whether they successfully constitute a poem. But howsoever they be done, he must leave them to their future audience. The final determination on the quality of the poem is not for Keats to decide. Only posterity will tell whether or not he has a place among the poets in the poet's house. To worry too much about how well the poem will do would prevent the poet from leaving the poem to others, to a future he cannot know. Following poetic convention, the poet must leave the lines as parents must always possibly leave a child—to a future beyond their control. This reading of the final lines follows from the anxieties expressed earlier in the poem.

And yet the lines might be read differently, as indicating the poet's ignorance of how the lines came to be "done" (in other words, how they came to be begun in the first place). The poem moves very quickly, almost immediately, from the poet's resolution to begin writing to the very writing of the lines having been concluded. The lines, in other words, might be taken as a sign of the poet's lack of confidence ("I do not know how good a poem this is"); but they also suggest that the poet does not know how the lines came to be composed: "howsoever these lines came into existence, howsoever they be done, I leave them now." The line acknowledges—in however subtle a way—the absence of the poet during the actual composition of the poem. The line does not just communicate the poet's worry that the poem is unworthy of publication, and he is not simply worried that the poem will be deemed unsuccessful. The final lines also disclose the poet's absence during the composition of the very lines that were begun and now stand concluded, ready to be left to others. The poet resolved to begin but the lines following the semicolon suggest that the poet may have been absent to what in fact was begun. He encounters them now "done," howsoever they came to be done.

Faced with this strange unawareness of the poem's beginning, the poet claims the lines he finds before him as his own. Howsoever these lines came to be present on the page, the poet leaves them as a father does a son. Here, the paternal/filial kinship between the poet and his lines results from the positing power of language. Paternity, for instance, is never determined empirically with absolute surety (at least not without the aid of technology). It is performed and enacted in the absence of any guarantee of biological relationship. A father, like the poet, must posit the existence of a relationship that is not simply or entirely natural because it is also linguistic.[32] Howsoever these lines came to be, the poet claims them as his son and leaves them as a father. On the one hand, the poet resolves to begin and concludes the poem with the same anxiety expressed earlier: what if these lines are not great poetry? I must now leave them. The conclusion to the poem attempts to secure the poet from this worry that the lines are unworthy of publication. On the other hand, the lines might be read, as I have been suggesting, as disclosing a strange unawareness on the part of the poet as to how exactly the lines came to be written, foregrounding once again and with some intensity the ways in which one may always be ignorant of what, of all that, is begun. Keats takes up this difference again and again in attempting to begin and in reflecting on beginnings. Given-to-be-read, a beginning cannot posit what it means.[33] And so, a beginning is also always a call to another to witness what may not have been experienced directly.

Politics and Beginning

Hannah Arendt begins *On Revolution* with the French Revolution. Her thinking begins, in other words, with the same event to which Keats and other Romantic poets found themselves returning. "Revolutions," she writes, "are the only political events which confront us directly and inevitably with the problem of beginning."[34] And she begins with a literary reading of the word *revolution*. She focuses on the fact that *revolution*, from the Latin *revolvere*, to roll back, refers both to a circular course or orbit and a dramatic change. *Revolution* can signify repetition (more of the same, as a chalk mark on one's tire revolves and so returns always to the same spot) or its opposite, a new beginning, a departure from all that has come before. In *On Revolution*, Arendt argues that actors in the French Revolution did not mean to begin something new but "pleaded in all sincerity that they wanted to revolve back to old times when things had been as they ought to be."[35] For Arendt, the revolution, the force of the revolution as the beginning of something new, occurred unwittingly, as if by accident, without conscious intention. Later revolutionary actors, following the events of the French Revolution and hoping to bring about dramatic change, failed, suggests Arendt, precisely because they consciously intended to bring about a revolution, something new.

A beginning is a beginning, Arendt posits, only to the extent to which it cannot have been expected. It interrupts what one may have been led to expect, or even what one intended, given all that has come before.[36] As Arendt writes in *The Human Condition*, "It is in the nature of beginning that something new is started which cannot be expected from whatever may have happened."[37] To actively seek to make a beginning one must expect what one will begin. As a result, one may simply bring about more of the same.[38]

In *The Human Condition*, Arendt aligns the principle of beginning with the conditions of possibility of politics. Drawing from Augustine's political philosophy, she writes: "With the creation of man, the principle of beginning came into the world."[39] Before the human, there were no beginnings because there existed no possibility for surprise. With humanity, following Augustine's reasoning, surprise is possible. Man, the human, is a beginner, one capable of action, of calling into being that which did not exist before. Before the human, there were no beginnings and without beginnings, without the surprise of beginning, no freedom: "With the creation of man, the principle of beginning came into the world itself, which, of course, is only another way of saying that the principle of freedom was created when man was created but not before."[40] Arendt argues that without the chance of something unexpected happening, there is no freedom and without freedom no politics.[41]

Arendt's larger argument in *The Human Condition* is that humanity seeks actively to resist this condition. Humanity, in other words, seeks actively to avoid beginning, preferring what is known and expected to what startles unexpectedly. This resistance to beginning is due in part to the fact that a beginning is also always a sign of one's ignorance. A beginning, writes Arendt, "must necessarily be hidden from the actor himself, at least as long as he is in the act or caught in its consequences."[42] The French Revolution constituted a beginning, but what "happened" is not what the actors wanted, expected, or intended to have happen. A beginning, as Keats's resolution discloses in "Sleep and Poetry," happens all too often beyond one's awareness, which means that it cannot have been expected even by the one who acts—like those who, during the French Revolution, wanted a revolution but not a *revolution*. One who begins is always dumb to the fullness of what has been begun. Howsoever it be done, a beginning is not an object of cognition. It, instead, marks a gap between what is known or understood and what is enacted or done. Keats's poetics (even as he focuses on figures of passivity: sleep, dreaming, indolence) and Arendt's politics (with her strong calls for action) share a commitment to the potential power of beginning, a disruptive power that is also full of hope. Twenty-first-century democratic political discourse is, in some ways, a record of attempts to erase the revolutionary character of revolutions, where the ungraspable difference between a revolution and a *revolution* makes beginnings possible even as it inspires increasingly violent attempts to grasp that which relentlessly eludes one's grasp.

Writing Politics

The final lines of "Sleep and Poetry" are complicated by the poet's claim that he leaves the lines as a father does a son, which, while a poetic convention, also foregrounds the fact that this paternal claim results from language's ability to posit a natural or biological relationship in the absence of the guarantee that one exists. The resolution to begin is followed almost immediately by the poet's admission that what was begun (what was written and so stands now "done") was missed—and so the poet must claim some relationship to his own writing after the fact. The claim of kinship cannot help but raise the relationship between poet and poem as a question. If one could take for granted some kinship with what one begins, then it would not be necessary to claim this kinship. Keats's resolution to begin turns on the chance that what is written, these lines, are not entirely his; he finds them awaiting him. Keats, with his resolution to begin, discovers the need to claim some relationship to writing (whatever it might be said to mean, whatever actions it may go on to perform). As Jacques Rancière suggests in *The Politics of Aesthetics*, "By stealing away to wander aimlessly without knowing who to speak to or who not to speak to, writing destroys every legitimate foundation for the circulation of words."[43] Following Arendt, beginnings pose a similar problem and she links them to freedom and the possibility of politics. One misses one's own beginnings—howsoever they be done. Keats's poems draw together "beginning" (as event and structure) and writing. One cannot fully know the significance of what one has written or what it will be possible to find there.

After "Sleep and Poetry," Keats returns to his preoccupation with beginnings in the preface to *Endymion*, where he struggles with his regret for making *Endymion* public. He attempts to ward off (though in attempting to ward off also, of course, invites) the negative reception the poem will receive from reviewers. His disavowal of the published poem also implies that he has not yet finished "beginning" the poem. Or, the proper beginning of the poem remains, in a sense, just out of reach and not yet known. Keats leaves off the 1817 volume with "Sleep and Poetry," resolving to begin "these lines," but the resolution to begin is quickly followed by lines that introduce the necessary, or at least possible, absence of the poet to the very beginning the poem marks. The existence of the lines comes as a surprise. Keats returns to the question of beginning in the opening lines of *Endymion*, thus demonstrating not simply a desire to begin, a desire both to announce and to know a beginning, but also an awareness of the ways beginnings bar full understanding. When Keats attempts to mark or describe—whenever he attempts to make—a beginning, the language of the poem discloses something more than can easily be accounted for; the language of the poem seems to open itself to ambiguity and undecidability.

Keats has been haunted, he writes in the opening lines of *Endymion*, by the story of Endymion and because the tale, like "an endless fountain of immortal drink," pours into him, he will trace the story:

> Therefore, 'tis with full happiness that I
> Will trace the story of Endymion,
> The very music of the name has gone
> Into my being, and each pleasant scene
> Is growing fresh before me as the green
> Of our own vallies: so I will begin . . .[44]

In contrast to "Sleep and Poetry," in which Keats resolves to begin, here he announces his beginning with "so," "so I will begin." "So" either marks a decision ("and now" or "as a result") or offers itself as a simile. Just as the "name has gone into my being," so Keats will begin. Or, just as the pleasant scene turns green as the valleys, so Keats will begin. On the one hand the colon marks a break; it interrupts the syntax previously established. And with the break, the poet declares his desire to begin: "So I will begin / Now."[45] "Now" is withheld for a moment as the syntax carries over to the next line. The story of Endymion has stayed with the poet and gone into his very being, but to begin requires an act of will. The effort to begin requires a break and a declaration: "I will now begin." Yet on the other hand, "so" establishes continuity with what precedes the colon. Each pleasant scene of *Endymion* grows before the poet as the valleys turn green. Just as the pleasant scenes have grown green, that is organically, so too will the poem begin without break or interruption, emerging organically from the very music of the name and like the green of the valleys. The opening of *Endymion* stages two competing senses of beginning: through trope (metaphor, like the valleys) or performance (the speech act, "I will"). Unclear however is whether the opening of *Endymion* attempts to merge trope and performance and so overcome the potential instability of the closing lines of "Sleep and Poetry" or if the opening of *Endymion* merely repeats and extends the unreadability that the previous poem discovers with its own attempt to begin.[46]

The above quoted lines tell the story of a beginning that the reviews of *Endymion* came to acknowledge even as they labored to contain a poet who seemed to them highly political. Reviewers of *Endymion* objected to Keats's style and aligned Keats's style with Leigh Hunt's and so with Hunt's politics.[47] John Gibson Lockhart writes of *Endymion* in *Blackwood's*: "This romance is meant to be written in English heroic rhyme. To those who have read any of Hunt's poems, this hint might indeed be needless. Mr. Keats has adopted the loose, nerveless versification, and Cockney rhymes of the poet of Rimini."[48] And John Wilson Croker writes in the *Quarterly Review*:

> At first it appears to us, that Mr. Keats had been amusing himself and wearying his readers with an immeasurable game at *bouts-rimés*. . . . He seems to us to write a line at random, and then he follows not the thought excited by this line, but that suggested by the rhyme with which it concludes. There is hardly a complete couplet inclosing a complete idea in the whole book.[49]

The early reviewers of Keats's volumes responded to what they considered Keats's "loose rhymes"—his departure from a more conservative poetic style. Keats's couplets do not always come to a close and instead the ideas exceed the form meant to hold them. As a result, he draws attention to the ways in which form polices content.[50]

Lockhart quotes extensively from the opening of *Endymion* and is critical of the reasons that induced Keats to compose it, though he does not elaborate much on his criticisms. "The poem sets out the following exposition of the reasons which induced Mr. Keats to compose it," writes Lockhart, who then quotes the first thirty-three lines of the poem, breaking off the quotation just prior to the lines quoted above. He italicizes "therefore" and includes three exclamation points: "*Therefore* 'tis with full happiness that I / Will trace the story of Endymion!!!"[51] Dissatisfied with the reasons Keats offers in the opening lines for choosing Endymion, Lockhart is confused (or at least pretends confusion). "Therefore" is offered by way of explanation but at least for Lockhart this "therefore" does not suffice. Lockhart wants Keats to know what he has begun and why, but this would seem to be the thing that Keats does not know and in this way *Endymion* returns readers to the resolution to begin that concludes "Sleep and Poetry," a resolution made possible by a difference between what words mean and the actions they might perform.

Keats's interest in beginnings and his attention to the ways in which what words do may be distinct from what they mean, a difference that makes possible beginning even as it undoes what one knows about beginning(s), has consequences for his reviewers, just as Vendler's attempt to locate Keats's "hidden beginnings" results in her own stuttering beginning. Keats focuses on the "music of the name" and extends his interest in form to the signifier "Endymion." From "Endymion," from the music of the name, Keats announces he will begin and move on. Because the music of the name has entered his being, Keats is inspired to trace the story. In both instances, the poet is figured as passive. The music does not inspire him to imagine something new, but merely to "trace"—as an almost mechanical or mindless activity—the story.[52] As Croker complains, too often Keats seems more interested in the sounds of words than their semantic content. Instead of moving from idea to idea, Keats moves from sound to sound, allowing the rhyme sounds to determine the poem's content; this may always have been, it may continue to be, the purview of poets and one way of distinguishing poetry from prose, but Croker and Lockhart align an interest in the sound and shape of the signifier with a repugnant, even dangerous, politics. Lockhart breaks off his extended quotation just prior to Keats's announcement of his intention to follow the music of the name. Keats becomes fixated on Endymion, he suggests, because of the sound of the name ("The very music of the name has gone / Into my being"). In translating sound into semantic content, Keats finds in the "end" of Endymion the chance to begin the poem that will make him one of the poets. The music in the name that has gone into his being offers Keats a chance to begin—and it may be impossible to know for certain whether "being" refers to something prior to language or to the word itself (as an anagram for "begin") and to the authority to begin that is hidden in the word.

These reviews are critical of Keats's interest in words as words. Words make possible a beginning even in the absence of cognition and this beginning is something the reviewers align with a potentially disruptive politics. Of further interest, though, may be the ways in which Keats's attention to the "music of the name" (his interest in the ways rhyme precedes thought) is contagious and infects the language of those writing about Keats. Lockhart himself seems to allow the "music" of the word to propel his writing forward. An example may suffice. Lockhart writes, "To those who have read any of Hunt's poems, this hint might indeed be needless." This sentence is constructed around a loose pun, as the subject, "this hint," is sonically determined by the prepositional phrase; and the loose pun occasioned by the sound of Hunt's name carries the sentence forward as "indeed" becomes "needless."[53] Keats's investment in the material signifier gives rise to a mode of writing— an attention to writing—that is carried not only across Keats's own lines but also into the writing of others. Keats's conservative reviewers repeat the event even in the attempt to put an end to the practice of writing that gives Keats his beginning. Just as Keats traces the story, so too do Keats's reviewers trace Keats. In this way, Keats's focus on words makes something happen in the writing of those attempting to respond to and curtail the forms of attention Keats's writing makes possible. Keats's readers bear witness to his beginnings.

For Beginners

I have borrowed the title for this chapter from the well-known series that introduces readers to particularly difficult philosophers through cartoons and word balloons, the *For Beginners* series (*Marx for Beginners*, *Heidegger for Beginners*, *Derrida for Beginners*, etc.). A number of similar series have emerged on the market in response to the difficulty of literary theory; the list includes, among others, Oxford's "Very Short Introductions" and Norton's "How to Read X" series. Literary theory may not in fact be dead, as has often been suggested, but word balloons may be required to make it "live." To reconcile the force of beginning that emerges in Keats and Arendt with the notion of beginning at play in the *For Beginners* series, or for that matter the notion of beginning at work in any "beginner's guide," may be quite difficult, since a beginning, following Keats and Arendt, cannot have a guide, one who knows how to arrive at the unexpected. The very idea of a guide counters the possibility for surprise that constitutes a beginning. A guide who is a guide should not be surprised. And a "beginner's guide" is meant to prevent the occurrence of the unexpected.

But what is at stake for beginning in Keats is not simply learning to choose the unexpected over the expected, as if the unexpected were inherently more valuable. Precisely because beginnings question one's ability to know them as beginnings (in advance or even as they happen), a beginning is not an event one welcomes or rejects. With the human, suggests Arendt in *The Human Condition*, the principle of beginning came into the world. And she outlines the ways human society protects itself from the possible disruptions beginnings initiate even though humanity cannot be rid of beginnings without ridding the world of humanity itself. One is (a) beginning. Both Keats and Arendt offer a chance to think beginning as event (and not as being). For Arendt the fact that the human is a beginner results in a call to action. For Keats, though, it results in a defense of passivity.

A poem like "Ode on Indolence" may help Keats's "beginnings" to emerge.[54] If beginnings are possible only because there is a difference—one that cannot easily be overcome—between knowledge and action, between what is understood and what is done, then what appears as indolence may constitute a beginning as well. One cannot know in advance: "How is it, shadows, that I knew ye not? / How came ye muffled in so hush a masque," writes Keats in "Ode on Indolence."[55] One who begins might just look like one sitting idly by. Keats's passivity, his sometimes hard-fought indolence, is not simply activity in disguise; but it can stand as a reminder of the ways beginnings are not available to phenomenological models of perception. A beginning? Where? "I knew ye not."

This account of beginning, discovered in Keats, and in particular, as I have discussed, in the closing lines of "Sleep and Poetry" as well as the opening lines of *Endymion*, may be particularly difficult for readers of Keats to acknowledge, precisely because calls to action are not easily avoided. One feels today a steadily increasing demand always to be doing something, to be always "up" and "on," ready to take on what comes next—ready to begin (hence the near ubiquitous presence of "energy drinks," part of late capitalism's attempt to bolster consumption by selling the energy that makes consumption possible). One must finish what one is doing—be done with it—so that one can begin something new. But this perceived need to begin in all-too-knowing a fashion is at odds with, it labors to overcome, the discontinuity of perception and cognition that makes possible a beginning for Keats. Precisely because Keats misses his beginnings, beginning is not something Keats chooses (just as readers of Keats find themselves repeating Keats without choosing to).

Keats's investment in beginnings does not offer readers any concrete recommendations for political action, precisely because action is too often conceived around what gets done. Instead, he aims to preserve the chance that beginnings are always elsewhere, known after the fact and only via marks and traces (as Keats mindlessly "traces" the story of Endymion). And though the work of preservation keeps Keats from offering a program of action, the preservation of beginning (the awkward resolution to begin something one has already missed—howsoever it be done) keeps politics—and the chance for politics—from coming to an end, as ideology, as what Arendt calls totalitarianism. In the close of "Sleep and Poetry" Keats must leave his lines as a father does his son only because it is not clear "howsoever they be done," only because, that is, he is unsure how they came to be composed and so unsure of all that they will do. The poem-as-written and so the poem as given-to-be-read discloses this difference, a difference that makes possible another beginning precisely because it happens unawares, and is recognized only belatedly in the attempt to begin *Endymion* a few months later.

Keats's preoccupation with beginning, one to which he returns throughout his short career, offers a chance to rethink poetry as a mode of political thought, as a way of giving-to-be-read contradictions that one might more often look to overcome in the effort to intervene in the struggles of one's day. In a later letter to Coventry Patmore, Gerard Manley Hopkins returns to his focus on Keats and beginnings. In response to the view of Keats as a dreamer, a poet only ever partly of this world, a poet laboring to escape politics and history—the view of Keats that remains more or less intact today after almost two hundred years—Hopkins writes: "[Keats] lived in mythology and fairyland the life of a dreamer. Nevertheless I feel I see in him the beginnings of something opposite to this."[56] What Hopkins means by "the beginnings of something opposite to this" is not entirely clear. He does not go on to explain in any detail. A poet who does not live the life of a dreamer? A poet concerned not with fairyland but with the world he is so often accused of renouncing? In *Art's Undoing*, Forest Pyle understands "this" as "abandonment to unmanly and enervating luxury," as Pyle reads Keats on weakness along lines similar to my reading of Keats on beginnings.[57] Keats's figures of weakness, luxuriating indolence, and blank amazement, argues Pyle, make no ethical claims: "Keats *never presumes* that an aesthetic orientation leads to an ethical conclusion," even as the poems compel readers to revisit this disjunction over and over again.[58] I similarly find compelling Hopkins's return to the word *beginnings*, when one senses the beginnings of something opposite. "Beginning" offers Hopkins a chance to rethink Keats's relationship to what he has so often been accused of renouncing.[59]

Commitment to an apolitical Keats may be one sign that readers continue to resist the principle of beginning that Keats staked his poetry on in leaving it, from the start, to others. But by this same logic, commitment to an explicitly "political" Keats would similarly signal resistance to the principle of beginning Keats stakes his poetry on, as one risks articulating poetry and politics in all-too-knowing a fashion. Here the rethinking of politics that Keats offers, however unsatisfying it may seem, is legible: politics is always *just* beginning, just about to begin but also conditioned by the chance to begin. The instability beginnings introduce, preserve, and even pass along makes politics possible; and, for Keats, there is no instability without poetry, without poetry's untimeliness. Likely, one wants more from those one approaches for help thinking about politics. But the simple point may be all the more powerful for its simplicity. There is beginning. And so there must be politics. Only because the world is not programmable is it possible to intervene (or not).

Because one is ignorant of *all* that one does, of the full and absolute significance of what one does (such is the absence of oneself to oneself that poetry marks, preserves, and even passes along), one has a chance to begin. But to suggest that one is ignorant of *all* that one does is not to suggest that one is always ignorant. If one takes Keats to celebrate ignorance as absolute, then one has in fact controlled through negation the very instability of beginning that Keats's poetry preserves. One throws up one's hands, as if ignorance could not be helped. But in doing so one licenses whatever action feels most expedient. Such efforts to control the instability of beginnings are daily on display in contemporary democratic politics, where political leaders appear willing to perform ignorance in order to preserve power. Ignorance of this sort is nothing other than hyperbolic self-confidence in reverse, in disguise: "At the beginning of any kind of project I know what I need to know." The politics of beginning gestured at in the writing of Keats preserves and passes along a possible difference between knowledge and action, always also a sign of the very freedom to make a beginning, and so a sign, a way of acknowledging, that others are, that others precede and will come along after one. A beginning preserves the idea that others may be necessary to teach one about what one began. If, by contrast, one knows all one needs to know from the beginning, then, to put this rather bluntly, one hardly need take an interest in others at all. From the beginning there is only one, or so the so-called thinking would go. For Keats, the untimeliness of beginning always preserves the chance that one is not alone.

6. The Grammar of Romanticism: Shelley's Prepositions

With help from Keats's poems, in the preceding chapter I took up the importance of surprise to beginning, and the importance of beginning to politics. From the start of this book, I have suggested that looking round for poetry can occasion surprise as tropes and figures, the grammatical and rhetorical structures that shape poems, recur in sometimes surprising contexts. There is a chance for beginning when poetry is untimely (at least every now and again). In this final chapter I further explore the relationship between poetry, untimeliness, and politics by playing up a particular part of speech, the preposition.

Michel Serres suggests in *The Natural Contract* that belief in the human as separate, exceptional, and so sovereign has justified human possession of the nonhuman world.[1] Standing apart from the world, human beings have remade it. In response, and in an attempt to address the effects of ongoing climate catastrophe, scholars and activists have asserted the importance of various and generalized forms of entanglement, attachment, and connection. The human, but not only the human, cannot be thought except in some relationship to everything else.[2] Separate spheres must be overcome. Gaps must be dissolved. Addressing primarily the work of Bruno Latour, object-oriented critics, speculative realists, and even deep ecologists, Frédéric Neyrat argues that the principle of principles of ecology, that everything is in some way inseparable from everything else, must itself be rethought: "contrary to the madness of generalized interconnection, what we truly require is a distancing."[3] Does critical intervention depend on inseparability or its opposite?

I stage this debate about ecologies because I want readers to keep the importance of generalized interconnection in mind as we turn toward a specific grammatical part of speech, the preposition, which may seem quite tangential to these debates. But as Christopher Ricks explains, "If as a poet you are concerned above all with relations and relationships," and I would add if as a critic too, "you are bound to give special importance to those words which express relationships: prepositions."[4] Ongoing debates over the importance of relationships (and the difficulty of thinking about them) confirm for me both the importance of thinking about prepositions and, of course, the difficulty of thinking about them too. For Keats there is no beginning without one's being among others. In this concluding chapter I explore in detail the work of prepositions in poems by Percy Shelley, placing particular pressure on Shelley's use of the preposition *among*. When one is among others, is one separate from them or not?

Early chapters of *Look Round for Poetry* foreground the power of various tropes: litotes, tropes of address like apostrophe and prosopopoeia, specific metaphors (downturns and clouds, for instance). I hope these chapters demonstrate the rewards that can follow from a rhetorically inspired literary criticism. With this concluding chapter, though, I foreground the work of grammar a bit more explicitly. To my own surprise, in recent years I have been teaching a course on grammar (Grammar Survey) in place of a literary theory course that had been a regular part of my teaching rotation. At my home institution, both classes satisfy the same requirement in the English Major undergraduate curriculum. The title "Grammar Survey" predates me and I do not teach it as a survey, per se. I teach it instead as an introduction to grammatical analysis, and students spend a lot of time at the beginning of the semester diagramming sentences by way of preparation. The work can feel at times old-fashioned, even out of touch with the times. But I have found that students who were relatively comfortable with even some of the more polemical texts we read in Literary Theory have been confused and frustrated—if also inspired—by the work in Grammar Survey, especially as we linger over various parts of speech and grammatical structures. If literary theory emerges when one questions how a text means before one questions what it means, students in the grammar class have come to appreciate just how difficult is to describe with precision the grammatical structures that help make possible *how* the text means.

The title of this chapter recalls Paul de Man's *The Rhetoric of Romanticism* but with it I do not mean to suggest that grammatical concerns should replace rhetorical ones. This chapter serves as a reminder that rhetoric cannot be thought apart from grammar without eliminating the chance for surprise, the chance for beginnings, the chance for reading. In this way *Look Round for Poetry* shares a similar narrative arc with Marjorie Levinson's recent *Thinking through Poetry*. Though many meaningful differences in approach and subject matter exist between the two books, Levinson includes as a late chapter "Parsing the Frost: The Growth of a Poet's Sentence in 'Frost at Midnight,'" where she adds grammatical considerations to her discussion of the poem. Scholarship, she contends, has spent a long time studying the content of the poem and less time studying its grammar: "What we have not studied is the construction of the sentence that enacts and embodies that narrative and psychic movement."[5] And she concludes the chapter with an elaborate sentence diagram. For similar reasons, I have been inspired by Jan Mieszkowski's *Crises of the Sentence*, which offers a dramatic rethinking of modern literary theory and criticism by focusing on the sentence (and not, from Ferdinand Saussure, the sign). As Mieszkowski explains, Saussure's claim that in language there are only differences without positive terms has been crucial to the emergence of modern literary theory and criticism, and though inheritors of Saussure have acknowledged the limits of differential logics, "none goes so far as to elaborate a full-fledged theory of sentential paradigms."[6] Through careful readings of a wide range of writers, Mieszkowski shows how theory (or Theory) can still surprise by revisiting Saussure's atomic model of language. In this chapter I take up questions about grammar, the grammar of romanticism, by paying attention to the figurative power of prepositions in Shelley. When one looks round for poetry, one discovers oneself pre-positioned.

Pre-Positioning

In his *Politics*, Aristotle studies the various and best forms of partnership (κοινωνία [koinonia]: association, communion, relationship, connection) between citizens. In his 1762 *A Short Introduction to English Grammar*, Robert Lowth defines prepositions as if with an eye toward political organization: prepositions "serve to connect words with one another, and show the relation between them."[7] Politics describes connections between people; prepositions, connections between words. Building on the previous chapter, "Keats for Beginners," what can one learn about politics from prepositions? What can one learn about prepositions from politics?

Founding political documents often rely on and express the power of prepositions. For instance, and perhaps most famously, Abraham Lincoln acknowledges the importance of prepositional thinking in his Gettysburg Address, where he defends a more perfect union "of the people, by the people, for the people."[8] The powerful repetition of prepositional phrases makes the meter regular, but by repeating prepositional phrases Lincoln also foregrounds the importance of prepositions to the great task of government. Judging from Lincoln's rhetoric in the Gettysburg Address, more than one preposition may be necessary to ensure the future of the union.

In foregrounding prepositional thinking, in foregrounding his own thinking about prepositions, Lincoln extends a democratic tradition. When the authors of the *Declaration of Independence* announced their separation from England, they described the political bands that have "connected" them in terms not dissimilar to those Lowth uses to describe prepositions: every now and again, write the authors of the *Declaration*, "it becomes necessary for one people to dissolve the political bands which have connected them with another."[9] Every now and again, in other words, new and different connections between a government and a people must be fashioned. The authors of the *Declaration* would likely have found it difficult to describe the connections between one people and another without employing prepositions. The familiar story of a late eighteenth-century shift from monarchy to democracy, from a vertical model of power (metaphor) to a horizontal one (metonymy), might also be retold as a shift from one set of prepositions (above, below) to another (beside, along, among). As Kristina Mendicino suggests in "Of Rights, in other Directions—Romantic Prepositions," "the unsettling consequences of revolutionary political theory can be registered not least of all in the displacements that prepositions so often mark within a rhetoric that may otherwise appear to promote positionality and positing."[10]

A founding political document somehow composed without prepositions is difficult to imagine. And yet, individual prepositions are surprisingly difficult to define. Take the preposition *among*, for example, which plays, as we will see, a crucial role in the *Declaration*. Originally, *among* was a phrase in Old English, *on* (meaning "in") and *gemang* (meaning "mingling, assemblage, or crowd"), so in Old English *among* meant "in a crowd," which is more or less what it still means today in modern English, though the phrase has been shortened to a single word. *Among*: in the mingling or assemblage of; hence, surrounded by and associated with.[11] One notices when defining a preposition that a seemingly endless number of prepositions are required: in, of, by, with, and so on. To be "among" is to be in, of, by, with (sort of). And this trouble is not unique to the preposition *among*. Take *with*, for instance: the *OED* notes that "the prevailing senses of this prep[osition] in the earliest periods are those of opposition ('against') and of motion or rest in proximity ('towards,' 'alongside')." In the Middle English period, *with* takes over senses belonging to the Old English *mid*, denoting connection and association. To be *with* is to be against, alongside, connected to (sort of). And, predictably, this trouble defining prepositions is not unique to English. In German, for example, *unter* can mean either "under" or "among." Prepositions are meant to help us better understand the relations between words, but it seems that the longer one thinks about prepositions the less one understands about relationships.

I have not selected *among* entirely at random to explore the relationship between prepositions and politics. Despite one's difficulty securing a stable definition of *among* (or any preposition for that matter), among plays an especially important role in the *Declaration*, where government is constituted "among" men. Even if citizens are not "with" other citizens, they are necessarily "among" them, or so the *Declaration* declares. The text features numerous uses of the preposition *among* in the opening few sentences. For instance, the first sentence, which begins with a long adverbial clause, identifies two actions of the people: to dissolve and to assume. The people are able to dissolve political bands because they assume "among the powers of the earth" a separate and equal station. The second sentence also features the preposition "among": "all men are . . . endowed by their Creator with certain unalienable Rights, that among these are Life, Liberty and the pursuit of Happiness."[12] "Among" is a somewhat surprising addition in this second instance, because it suggests, however subtly, that these were not necessarily the most important rights but just a few possible ones, as if these were the rights that just happened to come to mind. The point of the phrase is to enumerate some unalienable rights, and it would seem that with "among" the drafters did not want to limit the list only to those explicitly included. The drafters of the *Declaration of the Rights of Man and the Citizen* in France took a slightly different approach. Article II of the French declaration clearly stipulates the most important rights: "The goal of any political association is the conservation of the natural and imprescriptible rights of man. These rights are liberty, property, safety and resistance against oppression."[13] More significant differences between the foundational documents for the American and French revolutions may be present in the relatively minor difference between "among these are" and "ces droits sont [these rights are]."

As I have already alluded to, "among" repeats a third time in the document's opening sentences, this time by way of defining the purpose of government: "That to secure these rights [among them Life, Liberty and the pursuit of Happiness], Governments are instituted among men." The opening of the *Declaration* repeats "among," "among," "among." In this third use, the authors might have selected a different preposition, like "by" or "between": Governments could be instituted between men, for instance. Instead, they chose to repeat "among," thus granting the preposition unique importance for modern representative government.

To approach my broad opening questions about the connection between politics and prepositions, I take up the particularly complicated example of "among": in but not really in, of but not really of, with but not really with. For help exploring "among" I turn to the poetry of Shelley, a poet famous for his attempts to think language and politics together, and a poet frequently preoccupied by this same preposition. Lines from several of Shelley's most famous poems ("Hymn to Intellectual Beauty," "Ode to the West Wind," and *The Triumph of Life*) feature the prepositions "among" and "amongst" prominently, and while Shelley may not be responding directly to the uses of "among" in the *Declaration*, Shelley's poems stage complicated questions likewise raised there: What does it mean to be "among" others? What sort of political authority (if any) follows from this particular preposition?

Unseen Amongst Us

The *OED* suggests that *amongst* is less usual than *among*, but like *among* generally implies "dispersion, intermixture, or shifting position." The opening lines from Shelley's "Hymn to Intellectual Beauty" assert the presence of some unseen Power, "Intellectual Beauty," the shadow of which floats amongst us. This Power "gives grace and truth to life's unquiet dream," and the names of God and ghosts and heaven are simply failed approximations of power.[14] The opening lines of the poem attempt to define our relationship to this Power, though it turns out that this is a particularly difficult relationship to define:

> The awful shadow of some unseen Power
> Floats though unseen amongst us,—visiting
> This various world with as inconstant wing
> As summer winds that creep from flower to flower.[15]

I quote from Donald H. Reiman and Neil Fraistat's *Norton Critical* edition of the poem, which uses "amongst." And though the 1816 version found in the Scrope Davies manuscript and the 1817 version published in the *Examiner* use "amongst," by 1819 published versions use "among" instead of "amongst." Whether one uses "amongst" or "among" the first lines of the poem assert the presence of some Power that the rest of the stanza (and even the rest of the poem) throws into question. There is something not with or even beside us but amongst us. "Amongst us," it visits each human heart and countenance. The rest of the first stanza consists of a series of similes ("like hues and harmonies," "like clouds in starlight," "like memory of music fled," "like aught that for its grace may be / Dear") that attempt to capture this Power, capture it with the minimal force of simile. As Carol Jacobs writes: "The first stanza of the 'Hymn to Intellectual Beauty' . . . is an attempt to define that elusive poetic force through a long series of similes whose terms of comparison seem peculiarly at odds with one another."[16] And, so, as Forest Pyle writes: "Our 'state' is thus one of failed likenesses."[17] The poet reaches for an adequate simile, but by piling simile upon simile he risks possible confusion. The first stanza ends with a reversal, as the poet's failure to describe Intellectual Beauty makes the mystery dearer.

But the tone of the poem switches abruptly with the beginning of the second stanza. The seeming failure of simile in the first stanza to capture this elusive poetic force leads to a desperate appeal: "Spirit of Beauty . . . where art thou gone"?[18] Merely to be among, with all of the questions that follow from that preposition, appears inadequate, as the poem rather quickly turns to the power of apostrophe to transform the relationship between poet and Power. What floats among or amongst us, visiting this various world, is soon addressed directly. The poet's direct address to the Spirit of Beauty comes just as the poet's confidence wanes, as if the power of poetic address (the power of apostrophe) could bring before the poet this Power that is so quickly disappearing, scattering into a series of similes.

   The poet's use of apostrophe suggests that this elusive power should do more than merely float amongst us. As the poet's confidence that something floats amongst us slowly dissipates, as "Hymn" announces the withdrawal of the Spirit of Beauty, the poet calls for (and attempts to initiate) a different relationship with it. The plural pronouns ("us" and "our") that open the poem are soon replaced by singular pronouns ("I" and "my") as the poet addresses the Power directly: "I vowed that I would dedicate my powers / To thee and thine . . . Thus let thy power, which like the truth / Of nature on my passive youth / Descended, to my onward life supply / Its calm."[19] Tracking the poet's use of prepositions, one sees that the Power, whose shadow passively floats "amongst" us in the poem's opening lines, is by poem's end asked (perhaps ordered) to supply its calm "to my onward life." The poet longs for a different relationship, a different set of prepositions. Through the power of apostrophe, the poet transforms this Spirit of Beauty into an inter-locutor who no longer—at least not in any simple sense—floats amongst us. Addressed directly, this spirit is transformed into something (someone) with whom the poet may speak.

My Words among Mankind

The same level of apparent dissatisfaction with *among* is not present in "Ode to the West Wind," where "among" plays a significant role in developing the poem's main idea that poetry might enable a new birth and foster political change:

> Drive my dead thoughts over the universe
> Like withered leaves to quicken a new birth!
> And, by the incantation of this verse,
>
> Scatter, as from an unextinguished hearth
> Ashes and sparks, my words among mankind![20]

Shelley does not describe his dead thoughts, his poems, as seeds, the more common metaphor; thoughts are, instead, withered leaves. The difference is great between the figures Shelley actually uses and those that David Lee Clark, for instance, imagines in his gloss to the concluding sentences of *The Defence of Poetry*, which draw on a similar set of tropes: "Just as the plowman prepares the soil for the seed, so does the poet prepare mind and heart for the reception of new ideas, and thus for change."[21] Once it had found adequate soil, a seed might germinate—an acorn become an oak. Shelley's ideas would take larger shape in the world. But a withered leaf is not a seed. And as is clear from Shelley's next lines, the poet is less interested in what will grow than in what will catch fire. The withered leaves, as Forest Pyle so carefully explores in *Art's Undoing*, are more like kindling.[22] The "incantation" of the poem will scatter ashes and sparks among the withered leaves, and one can perhaps hear the "candescent" murmuring in "incantation." Far from preparing the soil (the mind) for some seed to grow (a new idea), Shelley prepares a conflagration. Shelley is, in other words, less a farmer than an arsonist. Because he spreads kindling and not seeds, Shelley cannot know what (if anything) will grow.

Shelley uses a similar image in "To a Sky-Lark," where, among a series of similes used to describe what is most like the bird, Shelley writes: "Like a glow-worm golden / In a dell of dew, / Scattering unbeholden / Its aerial hue / Among the flowers and grass which screen it from view."[23] "Unbeholden" can mean either unseen or independent (free, not under any obligation). The glow-worm, though unseen, scatters its aerial hue, which is the most-ready interpretation; the glow-worm is not seen, but evidence of its existence is visible in the aerial hue spread among the nearby flowers and grass. But if unbeholden also means independent, then the glow-worm scatters its aerial hue, and in scattering it casts it off and sends it on its way—not unlike the poet's words scattered among mankind. In both passages, Shelley draws together scatter and the preposition "among," which returns us to the word's etymology, as in a mingling or crowd, dispersed. To be *among*, in some sense, and this seems to be the sense that Shelley gravitates toward in both poems, is to be distributed, dispelled, spread about.[24] To be among is to be scattered: not really a part of, not really separate from. Shelley's use of the verb "scatter" in "Ode" and "To a Sky-Lark" may help explain the poet's seeming dissatisfaction with "among" (or "amongst") in "Hymn," signaled by the poet's turn to apostrophe as countervailing force. "Among" introduces a split between consciousness and power. In "Ode," for instance, the poet asks the wind to scatter his words among mankind, which means that the poet must relinquish to the wind control over his words.

The concluding sentences of Shelley's *Defence* draw out some of the implications of such an insight. Scholars often read this text rightly as celebrating metaphor, but the text also shows just how rigorously Shelley thinks about metaphor, and Shelley's rigor discloses something about metaphor's unreliability. In his recent book, *Metaphor*, Denis Donoghue offers a powerful defense of metaphor's importance, a defense that can seem reminiscent of Shelley, at least readings of Shelley that foreground his idealism. Donoghue writes that "metaphor . . . expresses one's desire to be free, and to replace the given world by an imagined world of one's devising."[25] Metaphor names not only one's desire to be free but also one's capacity to be free, to imagine alternative worlds and alternative futures. Without freedom, no imagination; without imagination, no freedom. "Metaphor has the ambition to change life," suggests Donoghue, "by telling a different story about it."[26] Figurative language makes different stories possible. And Donoghue's subtle anthropomorphism (as metaphor is transformed into a being with ambition) shows off the importance of figure. One can tell a different story about metaphor by filling metaphor itself with ambition. But in Shelley's *Defence* the poet's power comes at a cost as the humanity of the poet is slowly stripped away. The *Defence*'s short, concluding sentence ("Poets are the unacknowledged legislators of the World") is probably better known than its much longer second-to-last sentence: "Poets are the hierophants of an unapprehended inspiration; the mirrors of the gigantic shadows which futurity casts upon the present; the words which express what they understand not; the trumpets which sing to battle and feel not what they inspire; the influence which is moved not, but moves."[27] While the poet is first a hierophant, a person capable of interpreting sacred mysteries, later metaphors liken the poet to objects (mirrors, words, trumpets) incapable of understanding their effects on the world. The poet is not "just" an object, as these objects are granted forms of agency (the words express but do not understand; the trumpet sings but does not feel), but the poet does not emerge from the *Defence* a hero of humanism, a fully realized, independent, and active agent. As Marc Redfield explains: "poets seem at once blind and numb, 'unacknowledged' both because the world ignores them and because they themselves lose their self-awareness—including their aesthetic sense—as they leave their mark upon the world."[28] The power of metaphor to negate the given world opens the world to change but it cannot guarantee its effects in advance. And one effect of metaphor on the poet, at least as explored by Shelley in his *Defence*, is a gradual stripping away of the poet's human agency (the ability, for instance, to know causes and effects). What makes poetry powerful, in other words, may be this unknowable gap between cause and effect, a confusion that throws into question the poet's knowing understanding. In *Imagined Sovereignties*, Kir Kuiken suggests that poets are "unacknowledged legislators" not just because their genius goes unrecognized but "because the process by which the imagination reorganizes the present and breaks with its own structure of articulation also makes poets' creative acts incomprehensible even to themselves."[29] The difference that poetry actually makes, for Shelley, is never entirely available to cognition.

The poet's words have a certain power to the extent to which he no longer has absolute power over them. Through "Ode" and "To a Sky-Lark," Shelley explores the necessary separation (the necessary powerlessness) "among" implies. To be "scattered among" is, in some sense, to be cut off from. The preposition "among" offers one way to name this gap, difference, or necessary separation between individual consciousness and poetic power. "Ode" explores a power of language divorced from individual intention: being "among" other words and the words of others. Whether the poet's words will catch fire is not up to the poet. His words, once scattered among mankind, are no longer, if ever they were, under his control. Unlike "Hymn," which turns toward apostrophe to counter the potentially destabilizing force of "among," "Ode" embraces this preposition.

As a result, "Hymn to Intellectual Beauty" and "Ode to the West Wind" move in opposing directions. "Hymn" begins with "amongst," a preposition that Shelley elsewhere links to dispersion; with the second stanza "amongst" gives way to direct address, as the poem embraces the imagined unification apostrophe makes possible. The poem, in other words, moves from the potential confusion of "among" (as it defines a relationship that seems hardly a relationship at all) toward the relative clarity of apostrophe, as the poet addresses the Power directly with the second stanza and after. Apostrophe transforms the Power into an interlocutor, someone with whom the poet might speak. "Ode," by contrast, begins with an apostrophe, "O wild West Wind, thou breath of Autumn's being," and a dream of possible unification ("Be thou me"), but moves toward scatter ("Scatter . . . my words among mankind!"). As Barbara Johnson argues of the poem, the poet claims the animating power of apostrophe even though the poem is about the poet's anxiety that he no longer has (if ever he did have) this power: the poet "is in effect saying to the wind: 'I will animate you so that you will animate, or reanimate, me.'"[30] The poet worries that he is all-too-scattered. But the poem appears to move away from apostrophe as the poem embraces its own scattering among mankind. The "incantation of . . . verse" is hardly a conversation.[31] What is at first figured as a possible conversation, as the Wind is transformed through the power of apostrophe into an interlocutor in the poem's first line, is, by this point in the poem, the negation of a conversation: "Drive my dead thoughts over the universe."[32]

With respect to "Hymn" and "Ode," then, Shelley places the preposition *among* and the power of poetic address in conflict, as one poem moves from the preposition *among* to apostrophe and the other from apostrophe to *among*. The resulting chiasmus raises questions of pressing importance: can one be among others *and* address them? Or does an effort to address another (or others) immediately move one from one sort of relationship to another, from, say a relationship determined by grammar (and the prepositions that condition the possibility of politics) to one determined by rhetoric (and the tropes that condition the possibility of understanding)? In ordinary English, one might say that one speaks with and even to another, but to speak "among others" is, in a sense, not to address them at all. To speak "among" others is to speak near them, around them, but not to them.

Among the Multitude

I have drawn out the chiastic relation between "Hymn to Intellectual Beauty" and "Ode to the West Wind" in order to develop the ways in which these poems offer competing takes on the preposition *among* and the various relationships *among* makes possible (and impossible). Like Shelley's "Hymn" and "Ode," *The Triumph of Life* prominently features the preposition *among* and so, again, offers readers a chance to think various forms of connection and relationship, even community. In *The Triumph of Life* Shelley attends to the ways *among* bears the spectral traces of a crowd, one present in the etymology of the word but absent until the preposition is paired with an object. The poem retains an important place not only in the critical reception of Shelley but also romanticism more generally, and it continues to receive critical attention as scholars attempt to think the poem's interrogation of history in the context of ongoing disaster. Recent careful and energizing readings of the poem by Jacques Khalip and Amanda Jo Goldstein, for instance, demonstrate its continued draw as Khalip reads *The Triumph of Life* in the context of disaster (a last look at the end of the world) and Goldstein focuses on possibilities for reattaching biological and rhetorical materials, even as life threatens to come apart. Both readings begin by situating the poem among some other things, as Khalip begins with the graffiti of the original manuscript: "an unfinished poem that is left strewn *among* its last thoughts and feelings"; and Goldstein reads the poem as ultimately depositing readers "in the midst of a passage from *De rerum natura* that makes figural face-exchange a mundane transaction *among* all bodies."[33] These small moments from two inspired readings testify to the strange gravity of *among* in the poem.

An unfinished fragment, the poem consists largely of a dream vision. The poet, as if in a trance, witnesses a great stream of people "hurrying to and fro."[34] Struck by the pageant, the poet-speaker wonders aloud to himself:

"And what is this?"[35] He is surprised to receive an almost immediate answer, "Life," from what he formerly thought an old root. But the root is in fact the figure of Rousseau. When Rousseau answers the poet-speaker's question, the poet-speaker discovers that what he formerly thought was "beside" the crowd is actually part of it: "That what I thought was an old root which grew / To strange distortion out of the hill side / Was indeed one of that deluded crew."[36] From early on, the poem stages a question about relationships, connections, and associations. If the root is actually part of the deluded crew, then the poem implicitly challenges the poet-speaker's belief that he is beside the public way. He only "thinks" he sits beside the road, as he announces: "Methought I sate beside a public way." The poem, in other words, raises questions about what is apart from and what is part of the crowd. By raising such questions the poem announces a concern with prepositions, one that extends from the title into the poem itself (as readers have variously interpreted the "of" in The Triumph of Life).[37] After the poet-speaker asks Rousseau for his story, Rousseau describes his encounter with a "shape all light," and in this way Shelley structures the poem around two similar encounters, one nested within the other: the poet-speaker tells of his encounter with Rousseau, Rousseau tells of his encounter with the "shape all light."

But significantly, the poem features a dramatic shift in preposition, from "amid" to "among." The poet-speaker describes the pageant using the preposition "amid." He describes how all hastened onward, "yet none seemed to know / Whither he went, or whence he came, or why / He made one of the multitude, yet so // Was borne amid the crowd."[38] The poet-speaker and Rousseau repeatedly use the preposition "amid" in early lines of the poem, up until the moment Rousseau describes the effects of his encounter with the "shape all light." The poet-speaker, listening to Rousseau, for instance, recognizes "amid" the heirs "Of Caesar's crime from him to Constantine / the Anarchs old" who spread the plague of blood.[39] Doubling, even tripling down on the poet-speaker's choice of preposition, Rousseau uses "amid" repeatedly when introducing his encounter with the "shape all light." Rousseau locates the shape in quick succession "amid the gliding waves," "amid the sun," and "amid the blaze":

> there stood
>
> Amid the sun, as he amid the blaze
> Of his own glory, on the vibrating
> Floor of the fountain, paved with flashing rays,
>
> A shape all light.[40]

In contrast to "among," "amid" implies some precision. Etymologically, "amid" means "in the middle." But the ability to locate a middle depends on one's ability to determine a whole. "Amid," therefore, communicates tremendous knowledge and power, the ability to know in advance the whole. In *Paradise Lost*, for instance, Milton uses the preposition "amid" to locate the Tree of Life in the Garden of Eden: "Out of the fertile ground he [God] caused to grow / All Trees of noblest kind for sight, smell, taste; / And all amid them stood the tree of life, / High eminent, blooming ambrosial fruit / Of vegetable gold."[41] Because God knows the whole, he can cause the Tree of Life to grow amid all others, as if precisely in the middle.[42]

But after the encounter with the "shape all light," and to describe the effects of the encounter, Rousseau switches from the preposition "amid" to the preposition "among." Just as the poet-speaker poses a series of questions to Rousseau about the pageant he sees, so too does Rousseau pose to the "shape all light" a series of questions about history, self-knowledge, and power. After telling of his encounter with the "shape all light," Rousseau describes himself not "amid the crowd" but "among the multitude":

> I among the multitude
> Was swept; me sweetest flowers delayed not long,
> Me not the shadow nor the solitude,
>
> Me not the falling stream's Lethean song,
> Me, not the phantom of that early form
> Which moved upon its motion,—but among
>
> The thickest billows of the living storm
> I plunged.[43]

If there is a before and after the encounter with the "shape all light" in the poem, it appears, at least within the prepositional logic of the poem, to be the difference between "amid" and "among." Among the multitude, Rousseau is swept. Among the thickest billows, Rousseau plunges. First in describing his passivity and then in describing his activity, Rousseau uses the same preposition: in the many of the many, in the crowd of the crowd. After the encounter with the "shape all light," Rousseau's ability to locate himself precisely fails and gives way. Unlike Milton's God in *Paradise Lost*, in other words, Shelley's Rousseau no longer knows (or pretends to know) the midpoint. Rousseau describes himself swept away, in a living storm: in a network of relations and differences, disseminated, scattered.

By revising the poet-speaker's earlier formulation ("amid the crowd"), Shelley returns readers to the poem's opening questions about self-knowledge and power. When the poet-speaker first encounters the "great stream of people," he believes that those "amid the crowd" do not know where they came from, where they are going, or even why they are there. In a sense, Rousseau's story about his encounter with the "shape all light" confirms the poet's initial impression. Rousseau's encounter does not bring enlightenment or understanding. Instead, the shape "blot[s] / The thoughts of him who gaze[s]"; as Rousseau looks, "soon / All that was seemed as if it had been not."[44] Of this shape, Rousseau asks: "Shew whence I came, and where I am, and why."[45] But instead of providing answers to his questions, the shape offers Rousseau a cup. Drinking from the cup, Rousseau discovers: "suddenly my brain became as sand."[46] The sibilance at the end and beginning of the word "as" and "sand," respectively, blurs the boundaries between them in such a way that, paradoxically, their blurred proximity allows them to be parsed differently ("as and"), which corresponds to the dissolution of Rousseau's consciousness. At this point, "among" takes over from "amid." Like Shelley's "Ode," where words are scattered among mankind and so split off from conscious will, *The Triumph of Life* stages the opposition of power and consciousness. And like "Ode," *The Triumph of Life* figures the potential opposition of power and consciousness through "among," as the preposition signals and describes the effect of an encounter with a "shape all light." To be among the multitude is to have one's memory in some way blotted, to discover one's brain sand. The early appearances of "amid" in *The Triumph of Life* seem, in retrospect, a defense against the poem's ultimate suggestion that we may be "among" the multitude from the beginning and not know it.

At the beginning of this chapter I mentioned that my title alludes to de Man's *The Rhetoric of Romanticism* and my reading of Shelley's poem owes much, in particular, to de Man's chapter "Shelley Disfigured." With Shelley's prepositions in mind, I turn briefly now to the conclusion of de Man's essay. Shelley's attention to prepositions may make legible de Man's own use of them. If theory is to retain the potential to surprise, we need to read theory with attention to its own literariness. In his provocative reading of *The Triumph of Life* de Man suggests that the "shape all light" is a catachresis, an abuse of metaphor, because a shape all light can hardly take a shape. De Man's conclusions are as potentially shocking today as they were when his essay was first published: the poem, he writes, "warns us that nothing, whether deed, word, thought, or text, ever happens in relation, positive or negative, to anything that precedes, follows, or exists elsewhere, but only as a random event whose power, like the power of death, is due to the randomness of its occurrence." "It also warns us," de Man continues, "why and how these events then have to be reintegrated in a historical and aesthetic system of recuperation."[47] I have focused on *The Triumph of Life*'s sustained interrogation of prepositions, as the poem subtly shifts from "amid" to "among"; but one might use Shelley's thinking about prepositions to re-write de Man's sentences. The poem warns that there are no prepositions; it also warns that prepositions are necessary. And indeed, de Man's own prose bears out this point, as one cannot write de Man's sentences without prepositions: nothing happens *in* relation *to* anything else but only *as* a random event. When it comes to relationships, prepositions are a necessary reminder that we cannot get away from them so easily, as de Man's writing demonstrates. It may not be possible to think even the absence of connection without prepositions, without various forms of grammatical relationship.[48]

Inter Homines Esse

With "Hymn to Intellectual Beauty," "Ode to the West Wind," and *The Triumph of Life* Shelley demonstrates rigorous engagement with the logic of prepositions. By focusing on some instances of *among* in Shelley's poems, I have drawn out Shelley's simultaneous commitment to association and disassociation (articulation and disarticulation). To be among others (mankind, the multitude) is also—always possibly—to be separated from others (with but not entirely with). In a crowd or assembly, *among* names a with-without-with that is neither association nor disassociation.[49]

I began with the frequent appearance of "among" in the *Declaration of Independence*, but *among* and *amongst* appear more generally in political theory. John Locke explicitly builds his model of the social contract in *The Second Treatise of Government* (1689) on the preposition *amongst*. When the authors of the *Declaration* foreground the preposition "among," they may have in mind Locke's *Second Treatise*, where he writes: "The only way whereby any one devests himself of his Natural Liberty, and puts on the bonds of Civil Society is by agreeing with other Men to joyn and unite into a Community, for their comfortable, safe and peaceable living one amongst another."[50] Locke wants to think of our being "among" others as a free choice and not as a conditioning possibility for being. For Locke, the individual puts on the bonds of Civil Society and thus individuals form community. One is among or amongst others because one so chooses, and in this way individual liberty precedes community. The individual gives up something (some liberty), but in giving it up proves it was his (proves it was "natural"). Divestment is proof, in retrospect, of possession. And in this way "among" (one's amongness among others) is in fact no existential threat to the individual, but one way in which individuality is guarded and guaranteed. Like the authors of the *Declaration*, Locke posits a separation (a natural liberty) that precedes coming together.

But if one begins with Aristotle, then Locke's story can seem a defense against the possibility that individuality emerges from togetherness. Locke's language in the *Second Treatise* in fact reverses Aristotle's language in *Politics*, where Aristotle famously suggests in the opening paragraphs that "the city-state is prior in nature to the household and to each of us individually."[51] Locke's story has been so powerfully successful in the United States, for instance, that Aristotle now seems almost unconventional. Aristotle suggests that the city-state is not a logical result of individuals coming together; as a natural growth, the city-state must, in some minimal way, be present from the start. As a natural growth, the city-state precedes the individual. To allegorize, one could say that, for Aristotle, prepositions (connections, relations, differences) precede nouns. Individuals are pre-positioned.

Hannah Arendt, when she takes up the human condition in her book by the same name, turns toward the importance of *among* (translating the Latin *inter*) to the Romans. She writes: "While all aspects of the human condition are somehow related to politics, this plurality is specifically *the* condition—not only the *conditio sine qua non*, but the *conditio per quam*—of all political life. Thus the language of the Romans, perhaps the most political people we have known, used the words 'to live' and 'to be among men' (*inter homines esse*) or 'to die' and 'to cease to be among men' (*inter homines esse desinere*) as synonyms."[52] Arendt follows Aristotle into the language of the Romans: we begin not as sovereign individuals, but as always already among others, among the multitude.

We are left with two competing stories: either the individual emerges from "among" others only as an effect of community, or the individual precedes the community (thus community emerges from out of a collection of individuals). And these stories disguise underlying theories of language: language is either a system of differences or a collection of names; reference is either an effect of language or its conditioning possibility. Just as Saussure dramatically transformed conventional notions of language, it likewise goes without saying today that if amongness conditions the possibility of individuality, then prevailing ideals of sovereignty need to be rethought.[53] Shelley investigates the very same prepositions ("amongst" and "among") that ground politics for Locke and the authors of the *Declaration*. Shelley shows how prepositions like *among* and *amongst* scatter to the winds even as they inaugurate democratic political theory. For this reason, and remembering that *among* enters modern English as "in a crowd," it is perhaps no surprise that the crowd should generate such worry in the nineteenth century and after.[54] Our amongness among others has not ceased to signify.

Prepositional Romanticism

As "Hymn to Intellectual Beauty" and "Ode to the West Wind" set *among* and poetic address in tension, *The Triumph of Life* sets *among* and knowledge in tension; one can be among others, but it is not clear that one can know oneself among them. To be among the multitude is to discover oneself blotted, one's mind always possibly turned to sand, as Rousseau's mind is turned to sand after the encounter with the "shape all light." To be among others also is not necessarily to address them; to discover oneself among others is to discover others (and even oneself as other) as always possibly unaddressable. The conversation between the poet-speaker and Rousseau results in a series of unanswered (and perhaps unanswerable) questions. The poem breaks off, a fragment. In this way, *The Triumph of Life* offers a version of the problem with which "Ode to the West Wind" concludes, as the poem marks the apparent tension between language, action, and self-knowledge. The poet of "Ode to the West Wind" longs for his words to be scattered "among mankind"; words may have power, but only if, only once, only because the actions of words are blotted in advance, unknowably unanticipated. *The Triumph of Life* allegorizes a similar dilemma, a dilemma it likewise associates with the preposition *among*. To be among others, it seems, always possibly risks one's ability to guarantee one's speech, to know for sure that what one says is what one means. One risks one's ability to speak in part because one's existence among others always also includes one's existence among words that are never fully, entirely, or absolutely one's own.[55]

A poet committed to thinking poetry and politics together is also a poet committed to thinking prepositions rigorously. Shelley's preoccupation with the preposition "among"—with its accompanying push toward separation and possible muteness—is matched only by his desire for association. A reading of Shelley that follows the pressure Shelley's poems put on prepositions results in a series of complicated questions: Is to be among others in some sense to be mute, to be muted? Do our efforts to address others (say for the purposes of political organization) deny our being among them?[56] If yes, then Shelley poses tremendous challenges to prevailing forms of political action. There is politics because one always finds oneself among others and this being-among-others conditions the possibility of the human, even as it conditions the possibility of muteness, of a failure of (and to) address. There is politics because there is always this threat to communication, a threat that Shelley's poems repeatedly mark with the preposition *among*.

In drawing our attention to the preposition *among* in Shelley I have not tried to make the argument that among is the most important preposition *in* Shelley. As I suggested at the start of this chapter, prepositions are in general difficult to define and almost impossible to define without recourse to other prepositions. To pick just one may not, strictly speaking, be possible. In closing, I want to be careful not to celebrate *among* alone, for if my attention to *among* inspires further work on prepositions, then I will consider this chapter a success. But I have chosen *among* in part because it resonates so powerfully across political theory and because it even gives us a way to understand various and current attempts to think about the importance of assemblage. As literary critics attempt to think about competing critical and postcritical models, it may be that various methodological differences are conveyed by and through differences in prepositions, those words that attempt to mark, trace, and even perform various connections and produce possible disconnections.

By way of conclusion, though, I would like to point to one of the ways Shelley's questions about prepositions, in particular the preposition *among*, and related questions about political speech recur today. The First Amendment of the Bill of Rights separates into two distinct clauses: freedom of speech and freedom of assembly. I have already mentioned that the *OED* defines one meaning of *among* as "in an assemblage," so that the freedom of assembly can also be interpreted as the freedom to be among others. In her recent *Notes toward a Performative Theory of Assembly*, Judith Butler asserts that assembly itself is a performative speech act, as those gathered say, in effect, we are not disposable. "Gathering," writes Butler, "signifies in excess of what is said."[57] For Butler, assembly does not negate speech but makes a different sort of speech possible. In an early chapter she reflects on her career and explains how a book like *Gender Trouble* fits with her more recent work: "Now I am working the question of alliances, among various minorities or populations deemed disposable; more specifically, I am concerned with how precarity—that middle term and, in some ways, that mediating term—might operate, or is operating, as a site of alliance among groups of people who do not otherwise find much in common."[58] Butler suggests that one can be among others without being with them, and while assembling is a speech act it is not entirely or absolutely one's own. Not only because Butler repeats the preposition *among* several times in the quotation above but also because she works to articulate the difficult hope of assembly for life and politics, a chance for amongness that does not depend on the withness of what is deemed "common," Butler extends Shelley's engagement with *among*. For Shelley, the question is what sort of speech is possible *among* others. Butler takes up Shelley's question, one he did not answer, either because he died before completing *The Triumph of Life* or because the answer would not allow itself to be thought (at least by him), by exploring the power of assembly, of gathering, of being among others, one necessary response to the increasing emergency of our times.

Conclusion

The preceding chapter, which traced the appearance of the preposition *among* through several of Percy Shelley's poems, concluded at something of an impasse. To be among others is to be with them but not entirely with them, separate but not entirely separate. Given this impasse, I return to and rephrase the opening question of *Look Round for Poetry*: what does it mean to read oneself among poems, to discover that poetry is all around one, and what difference can such a reading make? If Apple's iCloud now seems a literary inheritor of Wordsworthian romanticism after "I Wandered Lonely as an iCloud," and if a vote for the dead, discussed in "On the Poetry of Posthumous Election," now seems not only a political but also a poetical act, then *Look Round for Poetry* will have succeeded. In the advertisement to *Lyrical Ballads*, Wordsworth worries that readers will open the book expecting to find poetry and, not finding it there, look elsewhere for it. Anticipating readerly dissatisfaction, Wordsworth offers *Lyrical Ballads* in hopes of transforming what might count as poetry. In *Look Round for Poetry* I discover in Wordsworth's idiom—this imagined reader looking round for poetry—a methodological charge, one I am tempted to call lyrical: looking round for poetry makes possible reading among poems. And reading among poems foregrounds reading's own untimeliness. One always reads with but not only with one's times.

In placing myself in the position of Wordsworth's imagined reader, I have tried to discover in Wordsworth's language a chance for future critical encounters. *Look Round for Poetry* exploits the difference between poems and what is round them, even as it challenges the knowability of that difference. Are we among that which is around us? I hope this book inspires readers to look round for poetry and discover it at work in sometimes surprising contexts. Because trope and figure are themselves aspects of poetry's content as well as form, readerly attention to poetry's language is also readerly attention to language's effects. Poetry interrogates the positing power of language—the power of language, more colloquially put, to give shape to worlds, to that which is all around one. When I say that I hope this book inspires readers to look round for poetry, I mean that I hope it inspires them not only to notice the workings of trope and figure but also to begin to work like poets. Looking round for poetry is a creative project, a readerly project. It is also a social one. As I have worked to show in my last two chapters, the chance for reading is not dissimilar from the chance for social life, our being among others: to acknowledge the ways poems are pre-positioned is also to acknowledge the ways readers are determined.[1]

Scarcely a week goes by without an opinion piece stridently asserting the uselessness of a humanities degree, and often these pieces single out English (shorthand for the humanities in general and literature more specifically). These opinion pieces are often then countered by defenses of the humanities, of the English major, of the study of literature—showing that students do get jobs and do have skills valued by employers. Given that the number of English degrees awarded per year makes up a very small percentage of the total number of bachelor's degrees awarded in all fields, one wonders why so much time is spent by authors of such opinion pieces warning students (and parents of students) away, as William McGurn recently did in his piece for *The Wall Street Journal*, "Is Majoring in English Worth It?"[2] Arguments about literature's uselessness (drawn from the discourse of the aesthetic) are older than the major, of course, but the energy required continually to bash the study of literature makes of the 3 percent who make the choice something other than a paper tiger. What risk does *The Wall Street Journal* perceive?

In closing, I want to suggest that these repeated attempts to criticize literary study take seriously and recognize the power of literary study. One only bashes so publicly that which one finds valuable in some way. To learn to look round for poetry—and find it given-to-be read around one—is to become aware of the ways poetry's linguistic power is fundamental to (and in some ways indistinguishable from) political and social power. If this is true, then harping on the uselessness of literary study is one way one might keep the power of literary study for oneself and away from others.

In "The Suppression of Rhetoric in the Nineteenth Century," Hayden White argues that the rise of literature after romanticism, paradoxically, helped strengthen political arguments that advanced practical literacy over literary instruction.[3] As literature was increasingly identified with the work of genius, it became possible to call literature unteachable. In an increasingly utilitarian world, that which is unteachable is also useless. Literacy is useful, literature useless. Literature's defenders secured for it a high cultural station, suggests White, but only by embracing an aesthetic ideology that divorced literature from rhetoric and poetics. The rise of literature in the nineteenth century occurs, in other words, at the expense of instruction in literature as language capable of shaping worlds. What matters is literacy, not the literary. Across the nineteenth century, institutions of higher education advance basic literacy over literary instruction, especially in the United States where the passage of the Morrill Land Grant Acts of 1862 and 1890 developed an idea of the public university dedicated to basic literacy as a component of higher education in practical, mechanical arts.

In other words, those committed to practical literacy seized the opportunity. Literature's rise was made possible by its narrowed definition, one that could be deemed irrelevant to broader educational goals focused on increasing a student's basic literacy. An education in literacy produces people who can understand the messages conveyed to them. An education in literature produces people who can shape the world around them. With the passage of the Morrill Land Grant Acts, awareness of the power of the literary to shape worlds became increasingly reserved for the few, as the universities created in the United States through these acts privileged (and largely still privilege) the practicality of literacy over the (so-called) impracticality of the literary. In recent years this cultural belief in practicality has helped move large numbers of students toward market-oriented fields of study, with poor learning outcomes. In 2010, sociologists Richard Arum and Josipa Roksa argued that student learning had declined since the 1990s: "If the purpose of a college education is for students to learn, academe is failing."[4] Arum and Roksa found that forty-five percent of students did not demonstrate any significant improvement in learning during the first two years of college, and thirty-six percent of students did not demonstrate any significant improvement in learning over the four years of college. These findings where shocking, but as Christopher Newfield notes in *The Great Mistake*, when one digs into the data one sees that student learning varies widely by major. The problem, argues Newfield, is that "structural changes [are] moving students from the liberal arts and sciences, where students learn well, to market-oriented fields where they [do] not."[5] Students in less market-oriented majors "showed about double the average improvement."[6] Newfield suggests that this limited learning is a feature, not a bug of the public university system: "We have here an answer to the mystery of why public college teaching isn't as good as it could be. The answer is that it is exactly as good as it needs to be to produce masses of *post-middle-class workers* with the commodity version of 'high skill' that entitles them to low wage."[7]

Attacks on literary instruction have broadened to attacks on the humanities, especially at public universities, but all with the same end: to reserve for the few advanced knowledge of the workings of trope and figure—the work, that is, of poems, of stories, of language at its most critical and self-aware. Despite his undergraduate degree in business, the former president of the United States, Donald J. Trump, was primarily a storyteller-in-chief. His election was proof of the power of stories. And as if on cue, and continuing a centuries-long strategy, his administration worked assiduously to limit the future of literary (as opposed to literate, market-oriented) education. I situate this book—which could not have been written without the support of a public university—in the context of this centuries-long political and ideological struggle to limit literary education by way of explaining my continued commitment to poetry as trope and figure. When one looks round for poetry and reads poetic understatement by the light of market-oriented demands for more, when one takes the downturned brow as an occasion to explore the figural logic of economic catastrophe, one senses again language's power to posit and trope. There is power in this version of poetry. And it's a reason we still might need Romantic poems (every now and again).

Acknowledgments

This book began as a series of chapters and it has taken a while for the ideas to coalesce into a proper book, one that tries for a narrative. The chapters would never have been written, let alone published as a book, without a lot of help and encouragement from valued friends and colleagues.

Cameron Bushnell, Erin Goss, Mike LeMahieu, and Elizabeth Rivlin read every word over many years of meetings in person and online. The book has benefited enormously from their close attention and timely interventions. I thank them as well for their profound generosity and good company. Walt Hunter and Lee Morrissey read a very, very early draft and helped me to begin to pull some loose threads together. Walt (again) and Erin (again) read a late version all the way through, one last time. I cannot thank them enough for their patience, intelligence, and wise counsel. Conversations at Clemson over ideas related to this book have been intellectually sustaining, and I thank Susanna Ashton, Maria Bose, Nic Brown, David Coombs, Megan Eatman, Jonathan Beecher Field, Jordan Frith, Gabe Hankins, Maya Hislop, Matt Hooley, Tharon Howard, Andy Lemons, Kim Manganelli, Dominic Mastroianni, Keith Morris, Angela Naimou, Aga Skrodzka, Michelle Smith, Will Stockton, Rhondda Thomas, Michelle Ty, and Jillian Weise.

No academic writing is possible without a community that extends far beyond one's home institution. I would like to thank numerous friends and colleagues at other institutions whose targeted interventions and gentle asides have helped guide and sustain me: Ian Balfour, Geoffrey Bennington, Timothy Campbell, Cathy Caruth, Cynthia Chase, David Clark, David Collings, Jonathan Culler, Anne-Lise François, Amanda Jo Goldstein, Kevis Goodman, Lily Gurton-Wachter, Sara Guyer, Daniel Hoffman-Schwartz, Tony Jarrells, Jacques Khalip, Amelia Klein, Kir Kuiken, Celeste Langan, Jacques Lezra, Eric Lindstom, Elissa Marder, Kristina Mendicino, Jan Mieszkowski, Jonathan Mulrooney, Anahid Nersessian, Suzie A. Park, Forest Pyle, Marc Redfield, Emily Rohrbach, Adam Rosenthal, Jonathan Sachs, Lauren Schachter, Taylor Schey, Zachary Sng, Dan Stout, Emily Sun, Karen Swann, Orrin N. C. Wang, Andrew Warren, C. C. Wharram, Deborah Elise White, and Joshua Wilner.

Portions of the book were presented at annual meetings of the American Comparative Literature Association, the North American Society for the Study of Romanticism, the Modern Language Association, and the International Conference on Romanticism. Conversations at these conferences have shaped the book and kept me going. Portions were also presented at the University of Wisconsin, the University of Pennsylvania, the University of Chicago, Eastern Illinois University, the Washington Area Romanticists Group at the University of Maryland, the University of South Carolina, and the University of Vermont. I thank the organizers of those events for inviting me and audiences for their thoughtful engagements.

I feel tremendously honored to get to work closely with Sara Guyer on Lit Z. I thank Sara for her friendship and for numerous conversations about this book, the importance of reading, and the future of the humanities (and so much else). I would also like to thank Tom Lay, whose dedication to the series and to publishing rigorous academic work has been an inspiration. My thanks to Jennifer Manley Rogers for her expert copyediting. My sincerest gratitude to Jonathan Culler (again) and the anonymous reader for Fordham University Press for their careful reading of the manuscript and considered and helpful suggestions for revision. The book was immeasurably improved by these reports.

The very idea of my writing a book would not have been possible without my family. My parents, Pamela and John, have been a constant source of support. My sister, Sarah, and my nieces, Abigail and Annabelle, have helped me to laugh at myself more than once. Most importantly, this book and so much else in my life would not be possible without Erin (again and again), whose love and laugh I cannot measure, and Finnegan, whose enthusiasms make everything surprising and fun. Thank you for making a life together with me.

Chapter 1 was originally published in *New Literary History* 49.3 (Summer 2018). Some portions of chapter 3 appeared in my essay "Material Excursions," published in a special issue of *Romantic Praxis* edited by Sara Guyer and Celeste Langan. A version of chapter 4 appeared as "Dead Men Running" in *diacritics* 42.4 (2014). Chapter 5 was originally published in a special issue of *Studies in Romanticism* 50 (Summer 2011) on Keats and politics edited by Emily Rohrbach and Emily Sun. Much of chapter 6 appeared as "Shelley, Among Other Things" in a special issue of *MLN* 133.5 (December 2018) edited by Kristina Mendicino and Jan Mieszkowski. I thank these journals for permission to reproduce previously published material.

★ ★ ★

Lucille Clifton, "jasper texas 1998" from *The Collected Poems of Lucille Clifton*. Copyright © 2000 by Lucille Clifton. Reprinted with the permission of The Permissions Company, Inc., on behalf of BOA Editions Ltd., www.boaeditions.org.

Notes

Introduction

1. In *Dying Modern: A Meditation on Elegy* (Durham, NC: Duke University Press, 2013), Diana Fuss suggests that poems featuring prosopopoeia (in which the dead address the living directly) are becoming more common. See pages 44–77.

2. Barbara Johnson, *Persons and Things* (Cambridge, MA: Harvard University Press, 2008), 14.

3. Yohei Igarashi, *The Connected Condition: Romanticism and the Dream of Communication* (Palo Alto, CA: Stanford University Press, 2019). In *Loving Literature*, Deidre Shauna Lynch argues that our relationship to literature is transformed during the eighteenth and nineteenth centuries as literary texts become objects of love and affection and so, figuratively speaking, are turned into beings one can love. We learn to love literature by granting books faces, by turning them into animate beings. Deidre Shauna Lynch, *Loving Literature: A Cultural History* (Chicago, IL: University of Chicago Press, 2015).

4. Stephanie Burt, *Don't Read Poetry: A Book about How to Read Poems* (New York: Basic Books, 2019), 6. See also Ben Lerner, *The Hatred of Poetry* (New York: FSG, 2016).

5. For a related discussion of attention, see Lucy Alford, *Forms of Poetic Attention* (New York: Columbia University Press, 2020). For more historically minded reflections, see Natalie Phillips, *Distraction: Problems of Attention in Eighteenth-Century Literature* (Baltimore, MD: Johns Hopkins University Press, 2016); Lily Gurton-Wachter, *Watchwords: Romanticism and the Poetics of Attention* (Palo Alto, CA: Stanford University Press, 2016); and Margaret Koehler, *Poetry of Attention in the Eighteenth Century* (New York: Palgrave Macmillan, 2012).

6. Charles Bernstein, *Attack of the Difficult Poems: Essays and Inventions* (Chicago, IL: University of Chicago Press, 2011), 30.

7. Jonathan Culler, *The Literary in Theory* (Palo Alto, CA: Stanford University Press, 2007), 2, 3.

8. Johnson, *Persons and Things*, 18, 19.

9. William Wordsworth, *The Major Works including* The Prelude, ed. Stephen Gill (Oxford, UK: Oxford University Press, 2008), 591.

10. Wordsworth, *The Major Works,* 591.

11. On slogans, see Jan Mieszkowski, *Crises of the Sentence* (Chicago, IL: University of Chicago Press, 2019), especially chapter 1, "Slogans and Other One-Liners."

12. Rei Terada, *Looking Away: Phenomenality and Dissatisfaction, Kant to Adorno* (Cambridge, MA: Harvard University Press, 2009). My title may also recall Slavoj Žižek's *Looking Awry: An Introduction to Jacques Lacan through Popular Culture* (Cambridge, MA: MIT Press, 1992). For Žižek, looking awry "renders visible aspects that would otherwise remain unnoticed" (3).

13. Wordsworth, *The Major Works*, 297, lines 12–13.

14. Wordsworth, *The Major Works*, 129, lines 9–10.

15. See for instance Virginia Jackson and Yopie Prins, eds., *The Lyric Theory Reader: A Critical Anthology* (Baltimore, MD: Johns Hopkins University Press, 2014), 2–4.

16. See Mary Poovey, "The Model System of Contemporary Literary Criticism," *Critical Inquiry* 27, no. 3 (Spring 2001): 408–38.

17. In poetry criticism today, "experimental" has become a strange genre term. Only some versions of poetry are considered "experimental," and often the term is used to describe poets and poems that self-consciously depart from standard conventions of grammar, syntax, typography, etc. But Robert Mitchell argues that Romantic writers embraced the idea of the experiment in order to "channel the revolutionary energies unfolding around them to make possible new, and more equitable, social and political forms of life." As the Romantic lyric becomes paradigmatic of poetry in general, it is increasingly considered conventional and un-experimental, less capable, that is, of inducing surprise. Robert Mitchell, *Experimental Life: Vitalism in Romantic Science and Literature* (Baltimore, MD: Johns Hopkins University Press, 2013), 4.

18. For a related line of thought, see Rei Terada, "Looking at the Stars Forever," *Studies in Romanticism* 50, no. 2 (Summer 2011): 275–309.

19. I allude to a line from Wallace Stevens' "An Ordinary Evening in New Haven": "in the intricate evasions of as." See Wallace Stevens, *The Collected Poems* (Vintage, 1990), 486. For attention to *as* in Wallace Stevens, see Harold Bloom, *Wallace Stevens: The Poems of Our Climate* (Ithaca, NY: Cornell University Press, 1977), 332. For fuller discussion, see David Letzler, "The Problem of *Of*, the Evasions of *As*, and Other Grammatical Curiosities in Stevens' 'An Ordinary Evening in New Haven,'" *Wallace Stevens Journal* 36, no. 2 (Fall 2012): 206–24. See also Charles Altieri, *Wallace Stevens and the Demands of Modernity: Toward a Phenomenology of Value* (Ithaca, NY: Cornell University Press, 2013). On the importance of analogy across scientific and literary discourses of the Romantic period, see Devin Griffiths, *The Age of Analogy: Science and Literature Between the Darwins* (Baltimore, MD: Johns Hopkins University Press, 2016).

20. Marjorie Levinson, *Thinking through Poetry: Field Reports on Romantic Lyric* (Oxford, UK: Oxford University Press, 2019), 23–24. For the Benjamin quote, see Walter Benjamin, *The Arcades Project*, trans. Howard Eiland and Kevin McLaughlin (Cambridge, MA: Harvard University Press, 1999), 462.

21. Maureen N. McLane, "Romanticism, or Now: Learning to Read in Postmodern," *Modern Philology* 105, no. 1 (August 2007): 124.

22. Bruce Holsinger and Andrew Stauffer, "Romanticism, Now and Then: An Introduction," *New Literary History* 49, no. 4 (Autumn 2018): v–xi.

23. See James Chandler, *England in 1819: The Politics of Literary Culture and the Case of Romantic Historicism* (Chicago, IL: University of Chicago Press, 1998), xiv.

24. Cynthia Chase, ed., *Romanticism* (New York: Longman, 1993), 1.

25. Ted Underwood, *Why Literary Periods Mattered: Historical Contrast and the Prestige of Literary Studies* (Palo Alto, CA: Stanford University Press, 2013).

26. Chandler, *England in 1819*, 4–5.

27. Paul de Man, *The Rhetoric of Romanticism* (New York: Columbia University Press, 1984), 50. See also Marc Redfield, *The Politics of Aesthetics: Nationalism, Gender, Romanticism* (Palo Alto, CA: Stanford University Press, 2003), 31.

28. Anahid Nersessian, *Utopia, Limited: Romanticism and Adjustment* (Cambridge, MA: Harvard University Press, 2015), 22.

29. Rei Terada, *Looking Away*, 51.

30. Anne-Lise François, *Open Secrets: The Literature of Uncounted Experience* (Palo Alto, CA: Stanford University Press, 2007), 209.

31. Jacques Khalip, *Last Things: Disastrous Form from Kant to Hujar* (New York: Fordham University Press, 2018). See also David L. Clark and Jacques Khalip, eds., *Minimal Romanticism* (Romantic Praxis Series, May 2016).

32. For a similar argument about the lyric, see also Rei Terada, "After the Critique of Lyric," *PMLA* 123, no. 1 (January 2008): 195–200. For a wider discussion relating to romanticism and forms of "letting be," see Eric Lindstrom, *Romantic Fiat: Demystification and Enchantment in Lyric Poetry* (New York: Palgrave Macmillan, 2011).

33. M. H. Abrams, *The Correspondent Breeze: Essays on English Romanticism* (New York: W. W. Norton & Company, 1984), 76–108.

34. Anahid Nersessian, *The Calamity Form: On Poetry and Social Life* (Chicago, IL: University of Chicago Press, 2020), 21.

35. Karen Swann, *Lives of the Dead Poets: Keats, Shelley, Coleridge* (New York: Fordham University Press, 2019), 135.

36. Holsinger and Stauffer, "Romanticism, Now & Then: An Introduction," vi. Such a timely untimeliness would risk the end of history. See, for instance, Jerome Christensen, *Romanticism at the End of History* (Baltimore, MD: Johns Hopkins University Press, 2004).

37. As Deborah Elise White writes: "Romanticism dares to (dis)articulate its own ends." Deborah Elise White, *Romantic Returns: Superstition, Imagination, History* (Palo Alto, CA: Stanford University Press, 2000), 6.

38. Jacques Khalip and Forest Pyle, "Introduction: The Present Darkness of Romanticism," in *Constellations of a Contemporary Romanticism* (New York: Fordham University Press, 2016), 6, 8.

39. Rita Felski, *The Limits of Critique* (Chicago, IL: University of Chicago Press, 2015), 11.

40. And maybe also, among others, Fredric Jameson's "Always historicize!" Fredric Jameson, *The Political Unconscious: Narrative as a Socially Symbolic Act* (Ithaca, NY: Cornell University Press, 1981), 9. I remain indebted to Jerome Christensen's rejoinder to Jameson in *Romanticism at the End of History*: "Until there is justice, all historicization is premature. Until there is justice, the timely slogan of Romantic politics will not be 'always historicize,' but 'now and then anachronize'" (41).

41. On the history of rhetorical moves that conceal the work of rhetoric, figure specifically, see Ian Balfour, "Figures in Excess and the Matter of Inversion in the Discourse of the Sublime," *ELH* 84, no. 2 (Summer 2017): 315–37.

42. Caroline Levine, *Forms: Whole, Rhythm, Hierarchy, Network* (Princeton, NJ: Princeton University Press, 2015), 2.

43. Levine, *Forms*, xii

44. Wordsworth, *The Major Works*, 131.

45. Paul de Man, *The Rhetoric of Romanticism* (New York: Columbia University Press, 1984), 122.

46. De Man, *The Rhetoric of Romanticism*, ix. My thanks to Zachary Sng and Susan

Bernstein for organizing the ACLA seminar at which I presented an early version of this material.

47. Orrin N. C. Wang, *Romantic Sobriety: Sensation, Revolution, Commodification, History* (Baltimore, MD: Johns Hopkins University Press, 2011), 5.

48. As Geoffrey Hartman suggests in *Beyond Formalism: Literary Essays, 1958–1970* (New Haven, CT: Yale University Press, 1970), what literary study needs is "a hundred percent of formalism and a hundred percent of critical intuition" (56).

49. On resonance, see Wai Chee Dimock, "A Theory of Resonance," *PMLA* 112, no. 5 (1997): 1060–71.

50. Robert Lowth, *A Short Introduction to English Grammar* (Mension, UK: The Scolar Press Limited, 1969), 91.

51. Barbara Johnson, *A World of Difference* (Baltimore, MD: Johns Hopkins University Press, 1987), 16.

1. Understating Poetry

1. Virginia Jackson and Yopie Prins, eds. *The Lyric Theory Reader: A Critical Anthology* (Baltimore, MD: Johns Hopkins University Press, 2013), 7.

2. Charles Baudelaire, *Œuvres complètes*, ed. Claude Pichois (Paris: Gallimard, 1976), vol. 2, 164–65.

3. Jonathan Culler, *Theory of the Lyric* (Cambridge, MA: Harvard University Press, 2015), 212. See also page 38 for Culler's earlier gloss on Baudelaire's argument.

4. Culler, *Theory*, 233.

5. Culler, *Theory*, 38.

6. Aristotle, *On Rhetoric*, trans. George A. Kennedy (Oxford, UK: Oxford University Press, 1991), 253

7. Quintilian, *The Orator's Education*, ed. and trans. Donald A. Russell, Loeb Classical Library (Cambridge, MA: Harvard University Press, 2001), 469.

8. Quintilian, *Orator's*, 469.

9. George Puttenham, *The Arte of English Poesie*, ed. Frank Whigham and Wayne A. Rebhorn (Ithaca, NY: Cornell University Press, 2007), 276. The author of the *Rhetorica ad Herennium* defines hyperbole as "a manner of speech exaggerating the truth, whether for the sake of magnifying or minimizing something." *Rhetorica ad Herennium* (Cambridge, MA: Loeb Classical Library, 1989), 341. For an extensive and illuminating discussion of hyperbole, see Christopher D. Johnson, *Hyperboles: The Rhetoric of Excess in Baroque Literature and Thought* (Cambridge, MA: Harvard University Press, 2010).

10. Puttenham, *Arte*, 277.

11. *The Norton Anthology of Poetry*, 5th ed., ed. Margaret Ferguson, Mary Jo Salter, and Jon Stallworthy (New York: W. W. Norton & Company, 2005), 267. Hereinafter abbreviated as *NAP*. One might connect Shakespeare's response to hyperbole with recent interest in the power of description. See for instance "Description Across Disciplines," *Representations* 135 (Summer 2016), ed. Sharon Marcus, Heather Love, and Stephen Best.

12. On further figures of excess and their relationship to the discourse of the sublime, a discourse as committed to reining in excess as developing it, see Ian Balfour, "Figures in Excess and the Matter of Inversion in the Discourse of the Sublime," *ELH*

84, no. 2 (Summer 2017): 315–37. On the question of excess and sexual difference, see Ian Balfour, "Torso: (The) Sublime Sex, Beautiful Bodies, and the Matter of the Text," *Eighteenth-Century Studies* 39, no. 3 (Spring 2008): 323–36.

13. See for instance Kevin McLaughlin, *Poetic Force: Poetry after Kant* (Palo Alto, CA: Stanford University Press, 2014).

14. I use lyric here in part because Baudelaire singles out the term. I have tried to indicate in my title ("Understating Poetry") the ways the association of lyric with hyperbole may limit the discussion of poetry more generally and exclude from discussion the importance, for instance, of litotes.

15. See for instance Anne-Lise François, *Open Secrets: The Literature of Uncounted Experience* (Palo Alto, CA: Stanford University Press, 2007), especially her discussion of "lyric inconsequence" as a response to various and ongoing demands for relentless activity.

16. Lee M. Hollander, "Litotes in Old Norse," *PMLA* 53, no. 1 (March 1938), 1. Hollander draws his authority from Carl Weyman, "Studien über die Figur der Litotes," *Jahrbücher für classische Philologie*, fünfzehnter Supplementband (1887), 457.

17. Puttenham, *Arte*, 268–69.

18. Chaim Perelman and Lucie Olbrechts-Tyteca, *The New Rhetoric* (South Bend, IN: University of Notre Dame Press, 1991), 291–92.

19. See Martin Shovel, "Litotes: The Most Common Rhetorical Device You've Never Heard Of," *The Guardian*, March 26, 2015.

20. J. R. Bergmann, "Veiled Morality: Notes on Discretion in Psychiatry," in *Talk at Work: Interaction in Institutional Settings*, ed. Paul Drew and John Heritage (Cambridge, UK: Cambridge University Press, 1993), 141.

21. George Orwell, *The Orwell Reader*, ed. Richard H. Rovere (New York: Harcourt, 1984), 365.

22. *NAP*, 4. "ne gefeah hé þaére faéhðe," which might also be translated as "this feud he did not enjoy" or "he got no satisfaction from this feud."

23. *NAP*, 579.

24. *NAP*, 410.

25. *NAP*, 410.

26. *Rhetorica ad Herennium*, 355.

27. *NAP*, 410.

28. *NAP*, 414.

29. *NAP*, 414.

30. *NAP*, 414.

31. *NAP*, 675.

32. Richard Wendorf, *William Collins and Eighteenth-Century English Poetry* (Minneapolis, MN: University of Minnesota Press, 1981), 188.

33. Geoffrey Hartman situates Collins in relationship to the epiphanic: "By addressing in epiphanic terms a subject intrinsically nonepiphanic, and adjusting his style subtly to it, Collins opens the way to a new, if still uneasy, nature-poetry." Geoffrey Hartman, *The Fate of Reading* (Chicago, IL: University of Chicago Press, 1975), 138–39.

34. *NAP*, 676.

35. *NAP*, 1655.

36. Alexander Pope, *The Major Works*, ed. Pat Rogers (Oxford, UK: Oxford University Press, 1993), 231.

37. See Barbara Johnson, *The Feminist Difference* (Cambridge, MA: Harvard University Press, 1998), 91–101.

38. Marianne Moore, "A Modest Expert: *North & South*," in *Elizabeth Bishop and Her Art*, ed. Lloyd Schwartz and Sybil Estess (Ann Arbor, MI: University of Michigan Press, 1983), 177.

39. *NAP*, 465.

40. *NAP*, 465.

41. *NAP*, 465.

42. *NAP*, 465.

43. On the rhetoric of modesty in women's writing, see Patricia Pender, *Early Modern Women's Writing and the Rhetoric of Modesty* (New York: Palgrave Macmillan, 2012).

44. *NAP*, 719.

45. *NAP*, 719.

46. John Crowe Ransom, "William Wordsworth: Notes toward an Understanding of Poetry," *The Kenyon Review* 12, no. 3 (Summer, 1950), 507. Many thanks to Christopher Rovee for this reference.

47. Anahid Nersessian, *Utopia, Limited: Romanticism and Adjustment* (Cambridge, MA: Harvard University Press, 2015), 12. For various critical attempts that similarly question the association of romanticism with excess, and excess with freedom, see for instance Anne-Lise François, *Open Secrets: The Literature of Uncounted Experience* (Palo Alto, CA: Stanford University Press, 2007); Jacques Khalip, *Anonymous Life: Romanticism and Dispossession* (Palo Alto, CA: Stanford University Press, 2008); Rei Terada, *Looking Away: Phenomenality and Dissatisfaction, Kant to Adorno* (Cambridge, MA: Harvard University Press, 2009); Orrin N. C. Wang, *Romantic Sobriety: Sensation, Revolution, Commodification, History* (Baltimore, MD: Johns Hopkins University Press, 2011), and David L. Clark and Jacques Khalip, eds. *Minimal Romanticism* (Romantic Praxis Series, May 2016).

48. *NAP*, 806.

49. *NAP*, 806.

50. *NAP*, 806.

51. *NAP*, 806.

52. *NAP*, 765. The quoted lines are 23–24, 31–32, 80–81, and 155. For an excellent discussion of litotes and Romantic syntax, with specific attention to Wordsworth's "Tintern Abbey," see Andrew Elfenbein, *Romanticism and the Rise of English* (Palo Alto, CA: Stanford University Press, 2009), 45–56. Elfenbein places Wordsworth's use of double negatives in relation to eighteenth-century grammarians who labored to correct English syntax by eliminating formulations like "I cannot by no means allow him."

53. *NAP*, 785.

54. John Jones, *The Egotistical Sublime* (London: Chatto and Windus, 1954), 204.

55. Johnson, *Hyperboles*, 9.

56. *NAP*, 992, and *NAP*, 1471.

57. For a review of various new formalisms, see "What Is New Formalism?" in Marjorie Levinson, *Thinking through Poetry: Field Reports on Romantic Lyric* (Oxford, UK:

Oxford University Press, 2018): 140–68. On historical poetics, see Yopie Prins, "What Is Historical Poetics?" *Modern Language Quarterly* 77, no. 1 (2016): 13–40.

58. Immanuel Kant, *Critique of Judgment*, trans. Werner S. Pluhar (Indianapolis, IN: Hackett, 1987), 190. See also Jan Mieszkowski, *Labors of Imagination: Aesthetics and Political Economy from Kant to Althusser* (Fordham University Press, 2006), 8.

59. Friedrich Schlegel, *Philosophical Fragments*, trans. Peter Firchow (Minneapolis, MN: University of Minnesota Press, 1991), 31.

60. On the crisis of infinity, see Rachel Feder, "The Poetic Limit: Mathematics, Aesthetics, and the Crisis of Infinity," *ELH* 81, no. 1 (Spring 2014): 167–95.

61. Culler, *Theory*, 260.

62. Paul de Man, *Blindness and Insight: Essays in the Rhetoric of Contemporary Criticism* (Minneapolis, MN: University of Minnesota Press, 1983), 215.

63. Marjorie Levinson, *Wordsworth's Great Period Poems* (Cambridge, UK: Cambridge University Press, 1984), 24–25.

64. On "not nothing," see Rei Terada, *Looking Away: Phenomenality and Dissatisfaction, Kant to Adorno* (Cambridge, MA: Harvard University Press, 2009), 18.

65. *NAP*, 768.

66. *NAP*, 768.

67. *NAP*, 768.

68. Theodor W. Adorno, *Negative Dialectics*, trans. E. B. Ashton (New York: Bloomsbury, 2007), 159–60.

69. On Adorno, see Jacques Khalip, *Anonymous Life: Romanticism and Dispossession* (Palo Alto, CA: Stanford University Press, 2008), 175.

70. *NAP*, 217.

71. Oscar Wilde, "The Decay of Lying," in *The Artist as Critic: Critical Writings of Oscar Wilde*, ed. Richard Ellmann (Chicago, IL: University of Chicago Press, 1982), 302. See also Johnson, *Hyperboles*, 1.

72. Jacques Derrida, "Passions: 'An Oblique Offering,'" in *Derrida: A Critical Reader*, ed. David Wood (Oxford, UK: Blackwell, 1992), 28.

73. Charles Baudelaire, *The Painter of Modern Life and Other Essays*, trans. Jonathan Mayne (London: Phaidon Press, 1995), 13 (translation modified). Charles Baudelaire, *Œuvres complètes*, vol. 2, 695. Michel Foucault comments on this passage in "What Is Enlightenment?" See Michel Foucault, *The Foucault Reader*, ed. Paul Rabinow (New York: Penguin, 1991), 40.

74. See for instance Rei Terada, *Looking Away*, 50–51.

2. The Poetics of Downturns

1. Jonathan Culler, *Theory of the Lyric* (Cambridge, MA: Harvard University Press, 2015), 190.

2. Jonathan Culler, *Theory*, 229.

3. Barbara Johnson, *Persons and Things* (Cambridge, MA: Harvard University Press, 2008), 9. For more on Wordsworth and apostrophe, see among others Mary Jacobus, "Apostrophe and Lyric Voice in *The Prelude*," in *Lyric Poetry: Beyond New Criticism*, ed. Chavia Hošek and Patricia Parker (Ithaca, NY: Cornell University Press, 1985), 167–81;

Sara Guyer, *Romanticism After Auschwitz* (Palo Alto, CA: Stanford University Press, 2007), especially "The Rhetoric of Wakefulness," 141–59; and Daniel Hoffman-Schwartz, "'Rapt Auditors!': Burke and the Revision of Rhetorical Violence in Wordsworth's *The Prelude*," *European Romantic Review* 30, no. 3 (2019): 297–306.

4. Barbara Johnson, *A World of Difference* (Baltimore, MD: Johns Hopkins University Press, 1987), 198.

5. Virginia Jackson, "Historical Poetics and the Dream of Interpretation: A Response to Paul Fry," *Modern Language Quarterly* 81, no. 3 (September 2020): 289–318, 307.

6. Anahid Nersessian, *The Calamity Form: On Poetry and Social Life* (Chicago, IL: University of Chicago Press, 2020), 129–69. My book shares with *The Calamity Form* a commitment to rhetorical tropes, though obviously in this chapter I stress the term catastrophe over calamity.

7. Amanda Jo Goldstein, *Sweet Science: Romantic Materialism and the New Logics of Life* (Chicago, IL: University of Chicago Press, 2017). Goldstein concludes with a "Romantic Marx." For an extended reading of Lucretius, Marx, and materialism, see Jacques Lezra, *On the Nature of Marx's Things: Translating as Necrophilology* (New York: Fordham University Press, 2018). On the relationship between catastrophe, Lucretius, and Epicurean materialism, see Gerard Passannante, *Catastrophizing: Materialism and the Making of Disaster* (Chicago, IL: University of Chicago Press, 2019). Passannante suggests that "the sudden turn of an atom from the vertical line of its descent through the abyss" is both the beginning of the world and a prophecy of its end (10).

8. Jonathan Sachs, *The Poetics of Decline in British Romanticism* (Cambridge, UK: Cambridge University Press, 2018), 4. In this context, Anne McCarthy's focus on suspension, neither a figure for falling nor rising, resonates powerfully. See Anne McCarthy, *Awful Parenthesis: Suspension and the Sublime in Romantic and Victorian Poetry* (Toronto: University of Toronto Press, 2018). See also McCarthy's wonderful essay, "Reading the Red Bull Sublime," *PMLA* 132, no. 3 (2017): 543–57, where she discusses the importance of the descent to an aesthetic tradition that so often foregrounds elevation.

9. Hannah Arendt, *The Human Condition*, 2nd ed. (Chicago, IL: University of Chicago Press, 1998), 6.

10. See Susan Sontag, *On Photography* (New York: Picador, 1973) and *Regarding the Pain of Others* (New York: Picador, 2003).

11. John Keats, *Complete Poems*, ed. Jack Stillinger (Cambridge, MA: Harvard University Press, 1978), 163. See also Anne-Lise François, "'The Feel of Not to Feel it,' or the Pleasures of Enduring Form," in *A Companion to Romantic Poetry*, ed. Charles Mahoney (Oxford, UK: Blackwell Publishing, 2012): 443–66.

12. I foreground *catastrophe* but much scholarship in romanticism in recent years has foregrounded related concepts. On *disaster*, see, for instance, Jacques Khalip and David Collings, eds., *Romanticism and Disaster*, Romantic Circles Praxis Series (2012) http://romantic-circles.org/praxis/disaster/index.html. See also Jacques Khalip, *Last Things: Disastrous Form from Kant to Hujar* (New York: Fordham University Press, 2018) and David Collings, *Disastrous Subjectivities: Romanticism, Modernity, and the Real* (Toronto: University of Toronto Press, 2019). On romanticism and *apocalypse*, see Chris Washington, *Romantic Revelations: Visions of Post-Apocalyptic Life and Hope in the Anthropocene* (Toronto: University of Toronto Press, 2019). On romanticism and extinction, see Marc

Redfield, "Wordsworth's Dream of Extinction," *Qui Parle* 21, no. 1 (Spring/Summer 2013): 61–68. On romanticism and *calamity*, see Nersessian, *The Calamity Form*. For a thorough reading of catastrophe that extends beyond romanticism, with particular attention to Black environmental writing, see Sonya Posmentier, *Cultivation and Catastrophe: The Lyric Ecology of Modern Black Literature* (Baltimore, MD: Johns Hopkins University Press, 2020). For a related reading of economic downturns in American Literature, see Dan Sinykin, *American Literature and the Long Downturn: Neoliberal Apocalypse* (Oxford, UK: Oxford University Press, 2020).

13. Jonathan Mulrooney, "How Keats Falls," *Studies in Romanticism* 50, no. 2 (Summer 2011): 251–73. For more on the difficulty of referring to falling, see Cathy Caruth, *Unclaimed Experience: Trauma, Narrative, and History* (Baltimore, MD: Johns Hopkins University Press, 1996), 76–93.

14. See Passannante, *Catastrophizing*, 9. Scott J. Juengel makes a similar point about the figural quality of *catastrophe* in "The Early Novel and Catastrophe," *Novel: A Forum on Fiction* 42, no. 3 (2009): 443–50, 443.

15. William Wordsworth, *The Poems*, volume 2, ed. John O. Hayden (New Haven, CT: Yale University Press, 1977), 114, lines 779–81.

16. William Wordsworth, *The Major Works including* The Prelude, ed. Stephen Gill (Oxford, UK: Oxford University Press, 2008), 30, lines 21–29. Future references to line numbers in this poem will be made parenthetically.

17. Geoffrey Hartman, *The Unremarkable Wordsworth*, "Inscriptions and Romantic Nature Poetry" (Minneapolis, MN: University of Minnesota Press, 1987), 31–33.

18. Thomas De Quincey, *Reminiscences of the English Lake Poets* (London: J. M. Dent, 1961), 122. Quoted in Lily Gurton-Wachter, *Watchwords: Romanticism and the Poetics of Attention* (Palo Alto, CA: Stanford University Press, 2016), 85.

19. Gurton-Wachter, *Watchwords*, 86.

20. In this way Gurton-Wachter participates in a broader effort among scholars of romanticism to shift attention away from revolution to war, as the operative term. Key texts here include Mary Favret, *War at a Distance: Romanticism and the Making of Modern Wartime* (Princeton, NJ: Princeton University Press, 2009); Jan Mieszkowski, *Watching War* (Palo Alto, CA: Stanford University Press, 2012); Jeffrey Cox, *Romanticism in the Shadow of War: Literary Culture in the Napoleonic War Years* (Cambridge, UK: Cambridge University Press, 2014). See also Neil Ramsey and Joshua Gooch, "Romanticism and War," a special issue of *Romanticism* 24, no. 3 (October 2018).

21. Wordsworth, *The Major Works*, 44, lines 6–8.

22. William Wordsworth, *Lyrical Ballads, and Other Poems, 1797–1800*, ed. James Butler and Karen Green (Ithaca, NY: Cornell University Press, 1992), 276.

23. Wordsworth, *The Major Works*, 45, line 23.

24. William Wordsworth, *The Prelude, 1799, 1805, 1850*, ed. Jonathan Wordsworth, M. H. Abrams, and Stephen Gill (New York: W. W. Norton & Company, Norton Critical Edition, 1979), 458, lines 29–32.

25. Wordsworth, *The Prelude*, 460. 1805, book 13, lines 39–42.

26. Wordsworth, *The Prelude*, 461. 1850, book 14, lines 38–41.

27. Geoffrey Hartman, *Wordsworth's Poetry, 1787–1814* (New Haven, CT: Yale University Press, 1971), 65.

28. See Joshua Wilner, "'Self-Displacing Vision': Snowdon and the Dialectic of the Senses," *The Wordsworth Circle* 31, no. 1 (Winter 2006): 27–30, 27. See also Hartman, *Wordsworth's Poetry, 1787–1814*, 17 and 65.

29. Wordsworth, *The Prelude*, 460. 1805, book 13, line 52.

30. Geoff Colvin, *The Upside of the Downturn: Ten Management Strategies to Prevail in the Recession and Thrive in the Aftermath* (New York: Portfolio, 2009), 4.

31. Wordsworth, *The Major Works*, 48, line 105; 40, line 377.

32. Wordsworth, *The Major Works*, 36, line 217; 39, line 333.

33. Emily Sun, *Succeeding King Lear: Literature, Exposure, and the Possibility of Politics* (New York: Fordham University Press, 2010), 108–23.

34. Wordsworth, *The Major Works*, 51, lines 44–51. Future references to the poem in this paragraph will be made parenthetically by line number.

35. *The Fenwick Notes of William Wordsworth*, ed. Jared Curtis (London: Bristol Classical Press, 1993), 56.

36. Philip Connell, *Romanticism, Economics and the Question of "Culture"* (Oxford, UK: Oxford University Press, 2005), 21.

37. For more on the history of the prospect poem, see Helen Deutsch, "Elegies in Country Churchyards: The Prospect Poem in and around the Eighteenth Century," in *The Oxford Handbook of the Elegy*, ed. Karen Weisman (Oxford, UK: Oxford University Press, 2010), 187–205; and David Fairer, *English Poetry of the Eighteenth Century, 1700–1789* (New York: Routledge, 2014), especially 192–214. For a rereading of the genre in the context of ecological arguments, see Jonathan Kramnick, *Paper Minds: Literature and the Ecology of Consciousness* (Chicago, IL: University of Chicago Press, 2018), 79–85.

38. Joseph Addison and Sir Richard Steele, *The Spectator*, ed. Donald F. Bond, 5 vols. (Oxford, UK: Clarendon Press, 1965): vol. 3, 538. For a fuller discussion of this passage, see Kevis Goodman, *Georgic Modernity and British Romanticism: Poetry and the Mediation of History* (Cambridge, UK: Cambridge University Press, 2004), 36.

39. In *Forms of a World*, Walt Hunter explores what he terms the No-Prospect poem, drawing a line of literary inheritance from eighteenth-century and Romantic examples of the prospect poem to contemporary poets like J. H. Prynne, Kofi Awoonor, Natasha Trethewey, and Juliana Spahr, who examine the prospects for precarious subjectivities "shaped by twentieth-century ideologies of modernization and neoliberalism." Walt Hunter, *Forms of a World: Contemporary Poetry and the Making of Globalization* (New York: Fordham University Press, 2019), 100.

40. John Barrell, *English Literature in History, 1730–80: An Equal, Wide Survey* (New York: St. Martin's Press, 1983), 17–28.

41. See for instance Cleanth Brooks, "Wordsworth and Human Suffering," in *From Sensibility to Romanticism: Essays Presented to Frederick A. Pottle* (Oxford, UK: Oxford University Press, 1965), 373–87; David Simpson, *Wordsworth's Historical Imagination: The Poetry of Displacement* (London: Methuen, 1987); Gary Harrison, *Wordsworth's Vagrant Muse: Poetry, Poverty, and Power* (Detroit, MI: Wayne State University Press, 1994); David Collings, *Wordsworthian Errancies: The Poetics of Cultural Dismemberment* (Baltimore, MD: Johns Hopkins University Press, 1994), 100–117; Alex Dick, "Poverty, Charity, Poetry: The Unproductive Labors of the 'Old Cumberland Beggar,'" *Studies in Romanticism* 39,

no. 3 (2000), 365–96; David Chandler, "Wordsworth versus Malthus: The Political Context(s) of 'The Old Cumberland Beggar,'" *The Charles Lamb Bulletin* 155 (July 2001), 72–85; David Simpson, *Wordsworth, Commodification, and Social Concern: The Poetics of Modernity* (Cambridge, UK: Cambridge University Press, 2009); and Eric Reid Lindstrom, *Romantic Fiat: Demystification and Enchantment in Lyric Poetry* (New York: Palgrave Macmillan, 2011).

42. Wordsworth, *The Major Works*, 51–52, lines 79–86. Future references to the poem in this paragraph will be made parenthetically by line number.

43. David Simpson, "Criticism, Politics, and Style in Wordsworth's Poetry," *Critical Inquiry* 11, no. 1 (September 1984): 52–81, 54.

44. Harrison, *Wordsworth's Vagrant Muse*, 141.

45. Lindstrom, *Romantic Fiat*, 102.

46. Plato, *The Republic*, ed. G. R. F. Ferrari, trans. Tom Griffith (Cambridge, UK: Cambridge University Press, 2012), 267 (8.555). For more on this particular passage, see also Jacques Derrida, *Rogues: Two Essays on Reason*, trans. Pascale-Anne Brault and Michael Naas (Palo Alto, CA: Stanford University Press, 2005), 22.

47. Plato, *The Republic*, 305 (9.586).

48. Dante Alighieri, *The Divine Comedy of Dante Alighieri*, trans. Allen Mandelbaum (Berkeley, CA: University of California Press, 1982), 166, lines 40–42; 166, line 52; 166, lines 71–72; 170, lines 118–120. In the original, lines 40–42 read: "*Seguendo lui, portava la mia fronte / come colui che l'ha di pensier carca, / che fa di sé un mezzo arco di ponte*" (167).

49. John Milton, *The Major Works including* Paradise Lost, ed. Stephen Orgel and Jonathan Goldberg (Oxford, UK: Oxford University Press, 2008), 63, line 739.

50. Milton, *The Major Works*, 63, line 723.

51. Milton, *The Major Works*, 64, lines 768–79.

52. Milton returns to the figure in *Paradise Lost*, describing Mammon thusly: "even in heaven his looks and thoughts / Were always downward bent." Milton, *The Major Works*, 372, lines 680–681. For a related discussion of charity, see Lee Morrissey, "'Charity,' Social Control and the History of English Literary Criticism," in *Print and Power in France and England, 1500–1800*, ed. Adrian Armstrong and David Adams (New York: Routledge, 2016), 61–76.

53. Wordsworth, *Major Works*, 51, lines 67–70.

54. See Rei Terada, *Looking Away: Phenomenality and Dissatisfaction, Kant to Adorno* (Cambridge, MA: Harvard University Press, 2009), especially the postscript, pages 199–204.

55. Forest Pyle, *Art's Undoing: In the Wake of a Radical Aestheticism* (New York: Fordham University Press, 2014), 22.

56. Kevis Goodman, *Pathologies of Motion: Medicine, Aesthetics, Poetics* (New Haven, CT: Yale University Press, forthcoming).

57. John Maynard Keynes, *The Essential Keynes*, ed. Robert Skidelsky (New York: Penguin, 2016), 234.

58. Anna Kornbluh, *Realizing Capital: Financial and Psychic Economies in Victorian Form* (New York: Fordham University Press, 2014), 25.

59. Anahid Nersessian, *Utopia, Limited: Romanticism and Adjustment* (Cambridge, MA: Harvard University Press, 2015), 46.

60. "Downturn, Start Up: The Effects of Recessions on Entrepreneurs and Managers Run Deep," *The Economist*, January 7, 2012.

3. I Wandered Lonely as an iCloud

1. Jonathan Goldberg and Madhavi Menon, "Queering History," *PMLA* 120, no. 5 (Oct. 2005): 1608–1617, 1609.

2. For a helpful summary of similar critical trends, see Rita Felski, "Context Stinks!," *New Literary History* 42, no. 4 (Autumn 2011): 573–91.

3. Ted Underwood, *Why Literary Periods Mattered: Historical Contrast and the Prestige of English Studies* (Palo Alto, CA: Stanford University Press, 2013), 3.

4. James Chandler, *England in 1819: The Politics of Literary Culture and the Case of Romantic Historicism* (Chicago, IL: University of Chicago Press, 1998), 107.

5. Cynthia Chase, "Introduction," in *Romanticism*, ed. Cynthia Chase (New York: Longman, 1993), 1.

6. In *Modernity's Mist: British Romanticism and the Poetics of Anticipation* (New York: Fordham University Press, 2016), Emily Rohrbach discovers in romanticism's various historicisms a future anterior, an opening to what is not yet known about the past and the present. My play on "fits" follows Barbara Johnson's reading of Wordsworth in "Strange Fits: Poe and Wordsworth on the Nature of Poetic Language." See Barbara Johnson, *A World of Difference* (Baltimore, MD: Johns Hopkins University Press, 1987), 89–99. See also Adela Pinch, *Strange Fits of Passion: Epistemologies of Emotion, Hume to Austen* (Palo Alto, CA: Stanford University Press, 1997).

7. William Wordsworth, *The Prelude, 1799, 1805, 1850*, ed. Jonathan Wordsworth, M. H. Abrams, and Stephen Gill (New York: W. W. Norton & Company, 1979), 42; Percy Bysshe Shelley, *Shelley's Poetry and Prose*, ed. Donald H. Reiman and Neil Fraistat (New York: W. W. Norton & Company, 2002), 489.

8. For more on this questioning potential in Romantic poems, see Susan J. Wolfson, *The Questioning Presence: Wordsworth, Keats, and the Interrogative Mode in Romantic Poetry* (Ithaca, NY: Cornell University Press, 1986).

9. Lynn Hunt, "Against Presentism," Perspectives on History (May 2002). https://www.historians.org/publications-and-directories/perspectives-on-history/may-2002/against-presentism.

10. Jerome McGann, *The Romantic Ideology: A Critical Investigation* (Chicago, IL: University of Chicago Press, 1983), 1.

11. Anahid Nersessian, *Utopia, Limited: Romanticism and Adjustment* (Cambridge, MA: Harvard University Press, 2015). The genre of Romantic writing that Nersessian calls "Rcsm" "strives for a gentling of our imaginative and appetitive powers," 24.

12. J. Hillis Miller, "Anachronistic Reading," *Derrida Today* 3, no. 1 (May 2010): 75–91, 76.

13. Natalie Melas, "Untimeliness, or Négritude and the Poetics of Contramodernity," *South Atlantic Quarterly* 108, no. 3 (Summer 2009): 563–80, 565.

14. Marjorie Levinson, *Thinking Through Poetry: Field Reports on Romantic Lyric* (Oxford, UK: Oxford University Press, 2019), 169. Levinson summarizes six variant readings of the poem. The poem is about the transformation of sensation into thought; about

mediated access to the real; about the rupture of narcissistic closure; about the artist's anxiety over dwindling raw materials; about political representation (how a crowd might be transformed into a political body); about colonial development (which explains the poem's frequent appearance in colonial education). On the poem's use in colonial education, see Gauri Viswanathan, *Masks of Conquest: Literary Study and British Rule in India* (New York: Columbia University Press, 1989); see also Karen Welberry, "Colonial and Postcolonial Deployment of 'Daffodils,'" *Kunapipi* 19, no. 1 (1997): 32–44.

15. Levinson, *Thinking Through Poetry*, 172.

16. William Wordsworth, *The Major Works including* The Prelude, ed. Stephen Gill (Oxford, UK: Oxford University Press, 2008), 303–4.

17. See Mary Jacobus, *Romantic Things: A Tree, A Rock, A Cloud* (Chicago, IL: University of Chicago Press, 2012); Marjorie Levinson, *Thinking Through Poetry: Field Reports on Romantic Lyric*, especially chapter 7, "Of Being Numerous"; and Anahid Nersessian, *The Calamity Form: On Poetry and Social Life* (Chicago, IL: University of Chicago Press, 2020), especially chapter 4, "Apostrophe: Clouds." For a broader historical understanding of similar Romantic metaphors drawn from the atmosphere, not only clouds but also winds, mists, and breezes, see Thomas H. Ford, *Wordsworth and the Poetics of Air* (Cambridge, UK: Cambridge University Press, 2018). Ford's conclusion, "Romantic Poetry after Climate Change," situates these early metaphors in our contemporary context (and predicament), showing how climate change "changes language at the level of its material mediation," 200.

18. On the importance of print technology to the emergence of romanticism, see for instance Kevin McLaughlin, *Paperwork: Fiction and Mass Mediacy in the Paper Age* (Philadelphia, PA: University of Pennsylvania Press, 2005); Andrew Piper, *Dreaming in Books: The Making of the Bibliographic Imagination in the Romantic Age* (Chicago, IL: University of Chicago Press, 2009); Christina Lupton, *Knowing Books: The Consciousness of Mediation in Eighteenth-Century Britain* (Philadelphia, PA: University of Pennsylvania Press, 2011); Deidre Shauna Lynch, *Loving Literature: A Cultural History* (Chicago, IL: University of Chicago Press, 2015); The Multigraph Collective, *Interacting with Print: Elements of Reading in the Era of Print Saturation* (Chicago, IL: University of Chicago Press, 2017).

19. Quoted in Celeste Langan and Maureen N. McLane, "The Medium of Romantic Poetry," in *The Cambridge Companion to British Romantic Poetry*, ed. James Chandler and Maureen N. McLane (Cambridge, UK: Cambridge University Press, 2008), 239–62, 239.

20. Langan and McLane, "The Medium of Romantic Poetry," 245. In recent monographs, Andrew Burkett and Yohei Igarashi have continued to develop a Romantic media theory. In *Romantic Mediation*, Burkett focuses on how Romantic writers express various flexible conceptions of media and mediation before the concept of media "became distilled later in the nineteenth century into its modern sense as the notion of the technological channel of communication." Andrew Burkett, *Romantic Mediation: Media Theory and British Romanticism* (Albany, NY: SUNY Press, 2016), 3. In *The Connected Condition*, Igarashi discovers the origins of modern communication fantasies in Romantic texts, before the emergence of electronic media technologies in the later nineteenth

century. Yohei Igarashi, *The Connected Condition: Romanticism and the Dream of Communication* (Palo Alto, CA: Stanford University Press, 2019). On the relationship between romanticism and questions about media and mediation, see also Zachary Sng, *Middling Romanticism: Reading in the Gaps from Kant to Ashbery* (New York: Fordham University Press, 2020). On the relationship between media and forms of nonknowing, see Orrin N. C. Wang, *Techno-Magism: Media, Mediation, and the Cut of Romanticism* (New York: Fordham University Press, 2022).

21. Cited in Vincent Mosco, *To the Cloud: Big Data in a Turbulent World* (New York: Routledge, 2014), 16.

22. Eric Schmidt and Jonathan Rosenberg, *How Google Works* (New York: Grand Central, 2014), 11. See also John Durham Peters, *The Marvelous Clouds: Toward a Philosophy of Elemental Media* (Chicago, IL: University of Chicago Press, 2015), especially the seventh chapter, "God and Google."

23. Quoted in Antonio Regalado, "Who Coined 'Cloud Computing'?" *MIT Technology Review* (October 31, 2011). https://www.technologyreview.com/2011/10/31/257406/who-coined-cloud-computing/

24. Peters, *The Marvelous Clouds*, 332.

25. Jerome McGann, *The Romantic Ideology: A Critical Investigation* (Chicago, IL: University of Chicago Press, 1983), 1.

26. C. L. R. James, *The Black Jacobins: Toussaint L'Ouverture and the San Domingo Revolution,* 2nd ed. (New York: Vintage Books, 1989), xi.

27. There has been such wonderful work on these questions in recent years that it is difficult to include references to all, but Saree Makdisi's *Romantic Imperialism: Universal Empire and the Culture of Modernity* (Cambridge, UK: Cambridge University Press, 1998), reshaped the field. See also Andrew Warren's more recent exploration of orientalism in *The Orient and the Young Romantics* (Cambridge, UK: Cambridge University Press, 2014). On romanticism, nationalism, and globalization, see Evan Gottlieb, *Romantic Globalism: British Literature and the Modern World Order, 1750–1830* (Columbus, OH: The Ohio State University Press, 2014). On romanticism's uneven resistance to colonial power, see Manu Samriti Chander, *Brown Romantics: Poetry and Nationalism in the Global Nineteenth Century* (Lewisburg, PA: Bucknell University Press, 2017).

28. Kenneth Goldsmith, *Uncreative Writing: Managing Language in the Digital Age* (New York: Columbia University Press, 2011), 2.

29. Goldsmith, *Uncreative Writing*, 1.

30. Charles Olson, *Selected Writings*, ed. Robert Creeley (New York: New Directions, 1964), 24. Also quoted in Craig Dworkin and Kenneth Goldsmith, eds., *Against Expression: An Anthology of Conceptual Writing* (Evanston, IL: Northwestern University Press, 2011), xliii.

31. Dworkin and Goldsmith, *Against Expression*, xliii.

32. Dworkin, introduction to the *UbuWeb Anthology of Conceptual Writing*, http://www.ubu.com/concept.

33. Goldsmith, *Uncreative Writing*, 61.

34. Dworkin and Goldsmith, *Against Expression*, xliii.

35. Dworkin and Goldsmith, *Against Expression*, 289.

36. Dworkin and Goldsmith, *Against Expression*, 290.

37. See Eric Lindstrom, "What Wordsworth Planted," which offers an interesting contrast with Dworkin's use of "supplanted" in his description of how the spontaneous overflow of emotion is supplanted by meticulous procedure in nonexpressive poetry and poetics. Eric Lindstrom, "What Wordsworth Planted," *Romanticism and Victorianism on the Net* 56 (November 2009). https://www.erudit.org/en/journals/ravon/2009-n56 -ravon1503285/1001093ar/.

38. Goldsmith, *Uncreative Writing*, 1.

39. William Wordsworth, *The Major Works*, 599.

40. John Keats, *Letters of John Keats*, ed. Robert Gittings (Oxford, UK: Oxford University Press, 1970), 157.

41. Contemporary poet Christian Bök provocatively suggests that in the future poetry will be written by machines for other machines to read (see Goldsmith, *Uncreative Writing*, 11).

42. Diane Coole and Samantha Frost, eds., *New Materialisms: Ontology, Agency, and Politics* (Durham, NC: Duke University Press, 2010), 11.

43. *The Fenwick Notes of William Wordsworth*, ed. Jared Curtis (London: Bristol Classical Press, 1993), 61.

44. Bruno Latour, *Pandora's Hope: Essays on the Reality of Science Studies* (Cambridge, UK: Harvard University Press, 1999), 1.

45. Latour, *Pandora's Hope*, 8. With my description of critique as running out of steam, I allude to Latour's well-known essay "Why Has Critique Run Out of Steam? From Matters of Fact to Matters of Concern," *Critical Inquiry* 30, no. 2 (Winter 2004): 225–48. Latour's essay is dedicated to Graham Harman, whose own object-oriented ontology owes much to Latour's criticisms of Kant in *Pandora's Hope*. "Why Has Critique Run Out of Steam?" also helped give rise to various post-critical approaches to literary study, as helpfully framed by Rita Felski in *The Limits of Critique* (Chicago, IL: University of Chicago Press, 2015).

46. Coole and Frost, *New Materialisms*, 3.

47. Amanda Jo Goldstein, *Sweet Science: Romantic Materialism and the New Logics of Life* (Chicago, IL: University of Chicago Press, 2017), 25.

48. For more on this point, see Orrin N. C. Wang, *Romantic Sobriety: Sensation, Revolution, Commodification, History* (Baltimore, MD: Johns Hopkins University Press, 2011), 92.

49. Paul de Man, *Aesthetic Ideology* (Minneapolis, MN: University of Minnesota Press, 1996), 132.

50. De Man, *Aesthetic Ideology*, 132.

51. Geoffrey Hartman, *Beyond Formalism: Literary Essays, 1958–1970* (New Haven, CT: Yale University Press, 1970). For a dedicated exploration of how Romantic texts engage speculative realism and object-oriented ontologies, see Evan Gottlieb, *Romantic Realities: Speculative Realism and British Romanticism* (Edinburgh, UK: Edinburgh University Press, 2016).

52. Coole and Frost, *New Materialisms*, 11.

53. Jacobus, *Romantic Things*, 6.

54. See Nersessian, *The Calamity Form*, 129–68.

55. Levinson, *Thinking through Poetry*, 172.

56. I have already mentioned Celeste Langan's work on media, but her work on vagrancy has also been integral to the conceptualization of this chapter. See Celeste Langan, *Romantic Vagrancy: Wordsworth and the Right to Wander* (Cambridge, UK: Cambridge University Press, 1995).

57. David Simpson, *Wordsworth, Commodification, and Social Concern* (Cambridge, UK: Cambridge University Press, 2009), 168.

58. Simpson, *Wordsworth*, 173.

59. Henry David Thoreau, *Collected Essays and Poems* (New York: Library of America, 2001), 227. I do not linger over Thoreau's reference to suicide. For more careful study of suicide and its broader philosophical implications, see Jared Stark, *A Death of One's Own: Literature, Law and the Right to Die* (Evanston, IL: Northwestern University Press, 2018). On the figure of suicide in Romantic texts, see Deanna P. Koretsky, *Death Rights: Romantic Suicide, Race, and the Bounds of Liberalism* (Albany, NY: SUNY Press, 2021).

60. Luc Boltanski and Eve Chiapello, *The New Spirit of Capitalism*, trans. Gregory Elliott (New York: Verso, 2005), 468.

61. Alan Liu, *The Laws of Cool: Knowledge Work and the Culture of Information* (Chicago, IL: University of Chicago Press, 2004), 292.

62. Liu, *Laws*, 293–94.

63. Tung-Hui Hu, *A Prehistory of the Cloud* (Cambridge, MA: MIT Press, 2016), ix.

64. Since the initial launch of iCloud, Apple has revised the language used to describe it. The language quoted above is from December of 2011. For the current language, see http://www.apple.com/icloud/. For the original language, now see http://ihackthatifone.com/apple-intros-icloud/.

65. See, for instance, Derek Thompson, "A World Without Work," *The Atlantic* (July/August 2015).

66. See for instance Denis Donoghue, *Metaphor* (Cambridge, MA: Harvard University Press, 2014), 34. I allude to I. A. Richards's definition of metaphor, which Donoghue quotes on page 1.

4. On the Poetry of Posthumous Election

1. For a short history of posthumous elections and a discussion of the legal arguments for and against Jean Carnahan's appointment, see Michael G. Adams, "Missouri Compromise: Did the Posthumous Election of Mel Carnahan and Subsequent Appointment of Jean Carnahan Compromise Federal or State Law?" *Northern Kentucky Law Review* 29, no. 3 (2002): 433–54.

2. Jean Carnahan lost in a special election in 2002.

3. The requirements to serve in the Senate, as elaborated in the Constitution, do not by law pertain to running for election or being elected. Joe Biden was not yet thirty years old when he won election to the Senate; he was sworn in only after his thirtieth birthday.

4. Valerie Richardson, "Missouri's Carnahan is first with posthumous Senate win; Opponent honors vote, but others may raise challenge," *The Washington Times* (Washington, DC), November 9, 2000.

5. Percy Bysshe Shelley, *Shelley's Poetry and Prose*, ed. Donald H. Reiman and Neil Fraistat, 2nd ed. (New York: W. W. Norton & Company, 2002), 298, 300 (lines 1 and 57).

6. Shelley, *Shelley's Poetry and Prose*, 301, line 1.

7. Diana Fuss, *Dying Modern: A Mediation on Elegy* (Durham, NC: Duke University Press, 2013), 46.

8. Nicholas Roe, *John Keats and the Culture of Dissent* (Oxford, UK: Oxford University Press, 1997).

9. Manu Samriti Chander, *Brown Romantics: Poetry and Nationalism in the Global Nineteenth Century* (Lewisburg, PA: Bucknell University Press, 2017), 3.

10. *Toronto Star*, "Ashcroft is Pro-Life, but Voters were Pro-Dead," January 21, 2001.

11. Immanuel Kant, *Political Writings*, ed. H. S. Reiss (Cambridge, UK: Cambridge University Press, 1970).

12. Sigmund Freud, *Beyond the Pleasure Principle*, ed. James Strachey (New York: W.W. Norton & Company, 1990), 38.

13. Though I do not take it up in this context, my formulation recalls Bruno Latour's parliament of things. See Bruno Latour, *We Have Never Been Modern*, trans. Catherine Porter (Cambridge, MA: Harvard University Press, 1993), especially pp. 142–45.

14. For more on "the politics of politics," see Geoffrey Bennington, *Scatter I: The Politics of Politics in Foucault, Heidegger, and Derrida* (New York: Fordham University Press, 2016).

15. Russ Castronovo, *Necro Citizenship: Death, Eroticism, and the Public Sphere in the Nineteenth-Century United States* (Durham, NC: Duke University Press, 2001), 4.

16. Castronovo, *Necro Citizenship*, 4.

17. Jacques Rancière, *Disagreement: Politics and Philosophy*, trans. Julie Rose (Minneapolis, MN: University of Minnesota Press, 1998).

18. François offers "recessive action" as an alternative to "overly narrow definitions of action as production . . . associated with Western modernity's ideology of improvement." Anne-Lise François, *Open Secrets: Literature and Uncounted Experience* (Palo Alto, CA: Stanford University Press, 2008), 33.

19. On the de-democratization of democracy, see Wendy Brown, "We Are All Democrats Now," in *Democracy in What State?* (New York: Columbia University Press, 2011), 44. Along with the other essays collected in *Democracy in What State?* see also Jacques Rancière, *Hatred of Democracy*, trans. Steve Corcoran (New York: Verso, 2006).

20. See Plato, *The Republic*, trans. Tom Griffith (Cambridge, UK: Cambridge University Press, 2012), 320–22.

21. See Jonathan Lamb, *The Things Things Say* (Princeton, NJ: Princeton University Press, 2011); Tobias Menely, *The Animal Claim: Sensibility and the Creaturely Voice* (Chicago, IL: University of Chicago Press, 2015); Heather Keenleyside, *Animals and Other People: Literary Forms and Living Beings in the Long Eighteenth Century* (Philadelphia, PA: University of Pennsylvania Press, 2016). On speaking objects and other thing-poems, see also Christopher Flint, "Speaking Objects: The Circulation of Stories in Eighteenth Century Prose Fiction," *PMLA* 113, no. 2 (1998), 212–26; and Barbara Benedict, "Encounters with the Object: Advertisements, Time and Literary Discourse in the Early 18th-Century Thing-Poem," *Eighteenth-Century Studies* 40, no. 2 (2007): 193–207.

22. Monique Allewaert, *Ariel's Ecology: Personhood and Colonialism in the American Tropics, 1760–1820* (Minneapolis, MN: University of Minnesota Press, 2013); Angela Naimou, *Salvage Work: U.S. and Caribbean Literatures amid the Debris of Legal Personhood* (New York: Fordham University Press, 2015).

23. Michel Foucault, *"Society Must Be Defended": Lectures at the Collège de France 1975–1976* (New York: Picador, 2003), 240.

24. Alastair Hunt and Matthias Rudolf, "Introduction: The Romantic Rhetoric of Life," in "Romanticism and Biopolitics," a special issue of Romantic Circles Praxis Series (December 2012). https://romantic-circles.org/praxis/biopolitics/HTML/praxis .2012.hunt-rudolf. The importance of biopolitics has renewed interest in Romantic notions of "life." See, for instance, Denise Gigante, *Life: Organic Form and Romanticism* (New Haven, CT: Yale University Press, 2009). On biopolitics and animal life, see Ron Broglio, *Beasts of Burden: Biopolitics, Labor, and Animal Life in British Romanticism* (Albany, NY: SUNY Press, 2017). For a recent rethinking of romanticism and biopolitics, see Robert Mitchell, *Infectious Liberty: Biopolitics between Romanticism and Liberalism* (New York: Fordham University Press, 2021). On romanticism and sovereignty, see Kir Kuiken, *Imagined Sovereignties: Toward a New Political Romanticism* (New York: Fordham University Press, 2014).

25. Sara Guyer, *Reading with John Clare: Biopoetics, Sovereignty, Romanticism* (New York: Fordham University Press, 2015), 24.

26. Paul de Man, *The Rhetoric of Romanticism* (New York: Columbia University Press, 1984), 55.

27. Barbara Johnson, *Persons and Things* (Cambridge, MA: Harvard University Press, 2008), 14.

28. John Milton, *The Major Works including* Paradise Lost, ed. Stephen Orgel and Jonathan Goldberg (Oxford, UK: Oxford University Press, 2008), 20.

29. De Man, *The Rhetoric of Romanticism*, 78.

30. See R. Clifton Spargo, *The Ethics of Mourning: Grief and Responsibility in Elegiac Literature* (Baltimore, MD: Johns Hopkins University Press, 2004).

31. Fuss, *Dying Modern*, 71.

32. Randall Jarrell, *Little Friend, Little Friend* (New York: Dial Press, 1945), 15–16.

33. Fuss, *Dying Modern*, 63.

34. Lucille Clifton, *The Collected Poems of Lucille Clifton 1965–2010* (Rochester, NY: BOA Editions, 2012), 552.

35. For short discussions of the poem, see Hilary Holladay, *Wild Blessings: The Poetry of Lucille Clifton* (Baton Rouge, LA: Louisiana State University Press, 2004), 59; and Mary Jane Lupton, *Lucille Clifton: Her Life and Letters* (Westport, CT: Praeger, 2006), 77–79.

36. Brian Norman, *Dead Women Talking: Figures of Injustice in American Literature* (Baltimore, MD: Johns Hopkins University Press, 2012), 1.

37. Richard Wright, "Between the World and Me," in *Against Forgetting: Twentieth-Century Poetry of Witness*, ed. Carolyn Forché (New York: W. W. Norton & Company, 1993), 633–634.

38. See Johnson, *Persons and Things*, 18–22.

39. On related figures that demonstrate the continued importance of Romantic poetry to the rhetoric of survival, making possible reconceptualizations of life and death, see Sara Guyer, *Romanticism after Auschwitz* (Palo Alto, CA: Stanford University Press, 2007).

40. Achille Mbembe, *Necropolitics*, trans. Steven Corcoran (Durham, NC: Duke Uni-

versity Press, 2019), 92. On questions of race and biopolitics, especially the ways bio-
political discourse associated with Michel Foucault and Giorgio Agamben leaves aside
the importance of race, see Alexander G. Weheliye, *Habeas Viscus: Racializing Assemblages,
Biopolitics, and Black Feminist Theories of the Human* (Durham, NC: Duke University
Press, 2014). On related questions of race and social death, see also Orlando Patterson,
Slavery and Social Death (Cambridge, MA: Harvard University Press, 1982) and Sharon
Patricia Holland, *Raising the Dead: Readings of Death and (Black) Subjectivity* (Durham,
NC: Duke University Press, 2000).

41. *Toronto Star*, "Ashcroft is Pro-Life, but Voters were Pro-Dead," January 21, 2001.

42. Lauren Berlant, *Cruel Optimism* (Durham, NC: Duke University Press, 2011), 213.

43. Mbembe, *Necropolitics*, 92.

5. Keats for Beginners

1. Achille Mbembe, *Necropolitics* (Durham, NC: Duke University Press, 2019), 6.

2. Gerard Manley Hopkins, *A Hopkins Reader*, ed. John Pick (New York: Doubleday,
1966), 230.

3. Hannah Arendt, *The Human Condition*, 2nd ed. (Chicago, IL: University of Chicago Press, 1998), 9.

4. Donald J. Trump, *Great Again: How to Fix Our Crippled America* (New York:
Threshold Editions, 2016), 16.

5. Stopford A. Brooke, *Studies in Poetry* (London, 1907), 204. See also Nicholas Roe,
John Keats and the Culture of Dissent (Oxford, UK: Oxford University Press, 1997), 12.
The reading of Keats as indifferent to politics continues, as P. M. S. Dawson argues in
"Poetry in an Age of Revolution," where Keats is described as "the most apolitical of
the great Romantic poets." P. M. S. Dawson, "Poetry in an Age of Revolution," in *The
Cambridge Companion to British Romanticism*, ed. Stuart Curran (Cambridge, UK: Cam-
bridge University Press, 1993), 49.

6. Jerome McGann, *The Romantic Ideology: A Critical Investigation* (Chicago, IL: University of Chicago Press, 1983), 1.

7. Of Keats's poem "To Autumn" in particular, McGann writes: "[The poem] is an
attempt to 'escape' the period which provides the poem with its context, and to offer
its readers the same opportunity of refreshment." Jerome McGann, "Keats and the Historical Method in Criticism," *Modern Language Notes* 94, no. 5 (1979): 1023.

8. In recent decades the sense of Keats as uninterested in history and politics has
been questioned. See for instance the special issue of *Studies in Romanticism* 25 (Summer
1986), ed. Susan Wolfson; Marjorie Levinson's path-breaking *Keats's Life of Allegory: The
Origins of a Style* (London: Basil Blackwell, 1988), where she explores the threat Keats
posed to an idea of the literary gentleman. The political attacks on Keats published
in *Blackwell's Edinburgh Magazine* aligned Keats with the Cockney school of poetry;
in portraying Keats as immature and unworldly, these attacks defended conservative
cultural values against Cockney politics. The dominant reading of Keats as apolitical
emerges, then, with political attacks against Keats. See also Nicholas Roe, ed., *Keats and
History* (Cambridge, UK: Cambridge University Press, 1995); Nicholas Roe, *John Keats
and the Culture of Dissent* (Oxford, UK: Oxford University Press, 1997); and Jeffrey N.

Cox, *Poetry and Politics in the Cockney School: Keats, Shelley, Hunt and Their Circle* (Cambridge, UK: Cambridge University Press, 2004). The history of criticism on Keats and politics is nicely summarized by Roe in the opening pages of *John Keats and the Culture of Dissent*, esp. 3–7. Roe finds in Keats a powerful political voice for reform. Instead of viewing Keats as turning away from politics, Roe attends to Keats's eloquence as a representative voice of the culture of dissent.

9. Robert Gittings, ed., *The Letters of John Keats* (Oxford, UK: Oxford University Press, 1970), 398. See also Stanley Plumly, *Posthumous Keats: A Personal Biography* (New York: W. W. Norton & Company, 2008).

10. John Keats, *Complete Poems*, ed. Jack Stillinger (Cambridge, MA: Harvard University Press, 1978). The poem is found on pages 361–73. The quoted lines are 142–43. Keats links poetry to survival, to a death "felt" if not fully experienced. See also Brendan Corcoran, "Keats's Death: Toward a Posthumous Poetics," *Studies in Romanticism* 48, no. 2 (Summer 2009).

11. Andrew Bennett, *Romantic Poetry and the Culture of Posterity* (Cambridge, UK: Cambridge University Press, 1998), 143. Jonathan Mulrooney gentles and simultaneously complicates this reading of Keats in "How Keats Falls," *Studies in Romanticism* 50, no. 2 (Summer 2011): 251–73: "We live, like Keats, because we are already dying. Dying, but not dead" (269).

12. See Susan Wolfson, "Keats enters History," in *Keats and History*.

13. Karen Swann, *Lives of the Dead Poets: Keats, Shelley, Coleridge* (New York: Fordham University Press, 2019), 5.

14. Swann, *Lives of the Dead Poets*, 31.

15. In offering a new account of Keats's relationship to politics Nicholas Roe powerfully reverses the more familiar story of Keats's total indifference. But in what ways does such a reversal leave intact the definition of politics brought to bear on Keats's poems, a definition of politics that Keats may be interrogating? As Roe explains his purpose: "I have . . . sought to show how Keats's poems responded to and negotiated with contemporary history, rather than presenting an aesthetic resort in which to 'escape' or 'evade' the world" (*John Keats and the Culture of Dissent*, 266). Keats's poems are not divorced from contemporary politics. Keats is a poet deeply invested in the political struggles of his day. But in redeeming Keats from New Historicist criticisms and demonstrating the numerous ways in which Keats engaged with contemporary politics, Roe repeats and reconfirms the opposition between history on the one hand and poetry on the other, an opposition that privileges the real-world power of politics to change history over the comparatively weak power of poetry, which merely responds to history. With the help of Roe's subtle personification, poetry responds to history but the reverse does not seem the case. Poetry is not something to which history and contemporary politics respond.

16. On the figure of the return in Romantic writing, see Deborah Elise White, *Romantic Returns: Superstition, Imagination, History* (Palo Alto, CA: Stanford University Press, 2000).

17. Lawrence Lipking, *The Life of the Poet: Beginning and Ending Poetic Careers* (Chicago, IL: University of Chicago Press, 1981), 4. See also Helen Vendler, *Coming of Age as a Poet: Milton, Keats, Eliot, Plath* (Cambridge, MA: Harvard University Press, 2003).

18. One need not turn to his letters for Keats's thinking about belatedness fully to emerge, as Charles Rzepka has recently shown. While many readers of "On First Looking into Chapman's Homer" take the reference to Cortez (and not Balboa) as a mistake, Rzepka argues that the inclusion of Cortez helps underscore "the poignant theme, announced in the very title of [the] sonnet, of the belatedness of the poet's own sublime ambitions" (39). Like Keats, who only encounters Homer after Chapman, Cortez looks on the Pacific only after Balboa already had done so before him. In Rzepka's reading, the poem is more about indebtedness and belated repetition than the power of origination. Charles J. Rzepka, "'Cortez: Or Balboa, or Somebody like That': Form, Fact, and Forgetting in Keats's 'Chapman's Homer' Sonnet," *Keats-Shelley Journal* 51 (2002): 35–75.

19. Keats, *Letters*, 12.

20. Helen Vendler, "The Experiential Beginnings of Keats's Odes," *Studies in Romanticism* 12, no. 3 (Summer 1973). For an extended reading of Vendler's essay, see Christopher R. Miller, "'Fine Suddenness': Keats's Sense of a Beginning," in *Surprise: The Poetics of the Unexpected from Milton to Austen* (Ithaca, NY: Cornell University Press, 2015).

21. Keats, *Letters*, 291–92.

22. Vendler, "Experiential Beginnings," 606.

23. Keats, *Letters*, 12.

24. When Keats introduces *Endymion* with regret in the published prefatory remarks, he finds *Endymion* full of inexperience and immaturity. The published poem is offered as "a feverish attempt, rather than a deed accomplished" (*Complete Poems*, 64). The very presence of the prefatory remarks announces that *Endymion* is "finished" (in that it has been published), but Keats simultaneously implies with the remarks that he has not yet properly begun to write the poem. I thank Chuck Rzepka for this important insight.

25. See Cathy Caruth, *Unclaimed Experience: Trauma, Narrative, History* (Baltimore, MD: Johns Hopkins University Press, 1996).

26. Emily Rohrbach, *Modernity's Mist: British Romanticism and the Poetics of Anticipation* (New York: Fordham University Press, 2016), 5. William H. Galperin, *The History of Missed Opportunities: British Romanticism and the Emergence of the Everyday* (Palo Alto, CA: Stanford University Press, 2017).

27. Vendler, "Experiential Beginnings," 591–92.

28. Keats, *Complete Poems*, 44, lines 270–71.

29. Keats, *Complete Poems*, 40, lines 96–97.

30. Keats, *Complete Poems*, 46, lines 358–59.

31. Keats, *Collected Poems*, 47, lines 397–404.

32. Because a "father" is always possibly absent at the moment of conception of "his" child, the name "father" must be claimed. See also related discussions of the "Blessed Babe" passage from Book II of William Wordsworth's *The Prelude* in which the mute child claims manifest kindred with "an earthly soul." What the passage shows, however, are the ways in which language promises filial preservation even as it relentlessly undoes its own claims. See Paul de Man, *Rhetoric of Romanticism* (New York: Columbia University Press, 1984), 90–91; and Cathy Caruth, *Empirical Truths and Critical Fictions* (Baltimore, MD: Johns Hopkins University Press, 1991), 44–57.

33. See also Marc Redfield, *The Politics of Aesthetics: Nationalism, Gender, Romanticism* (Palo Alto, CA: Stanford University Press, 2003): "By making legible the fact that poetic

words do not understand what they express, or feel what they inspire, poetry . . . opens aesthetics to the contingency of history, and the constitutive uncertainty of futurity" (171).

34. Hannah Arendt, *On Revolution* (New York; Penguin, 1990), 21.

35. Arendt, *On Revolution*, 44.

36. In this way, a beginning has the status of an event or what Paul de Man somewhat enigmatically calls history; something happens with "the materiality of actual history." Paul de Man, *The Rhetoric of Romanticism*, 262.

37. Arendt, *The Human Condition*, 177–78.

38. For a related discussion of beginnings in psychoanalysis and in the writing of Hannah Arendt, see Cathy Caruth, *Literature in the Ashes of History* (Baltimore, MD: Johns Hopkins University Press, 2013), especially pages 8 and 48–51.

39. Arendt, *The Human Condition*, 177.

40. Arendt, *The Human Condition*, 177.

41. As Arendt's quote also shows, a beginning is the chance to say something a second time. Key to the principle of beginning is "another way of saying," the chance to say something "another way," to say another way what has been said. In this way, a beginning (and the freedom to begin) is linked to metaphor, to figure, to speaking "other ways" or "otherwise"—in other words, to poetry.

42. Arendt, *The Human Condition*, 192.

43. Jacques Rancière, *The Politics of Aesthetics*, trans. Gabriel Rockhill (New York: Continuum, 2004), 13.

44. Keats, *Complete Poems*, 65, lines 23 and 34–39.

45. Keats, *Complete Poems*, 65–66, lines 39–40.

46. Keats returns to his first volume and yet, as Karen Swann has suggested, Keats's project "of image-making begins . . . with the poem [*Endymion*]." Karen Swann, "Endymion's Beautiful Dreamers," in *The Cambridge Companion to Keats*, ed. Susan J. Wolfson (Cambridge, UK: Cambridge University Press, 2001), 21. See also Levinson, *Keats's Life of Allegory*: "'Romantic retirement' gains a whole new dimension with Keats. Imagine the solitude of a young man in a seaside rooming house in April, a borrowed picture of Shakespeare his only companion: a man with nothing to do for a set period of time but write the pastoral epic which would, literally, *make* him" (7).

47. See William Keach, "Cockney Couplets: Keats and the Politics of Style," *Studies in Romanticism* 25, no. 2 (Summer 1986): 182–96.

48. G. M. Matthews, ed. *John Keats: The Critical Heritage* (Routledge & Kegan Paul, 1971), 104.

49. Matthews, *John Keats: The Critical Heritage*, 112.

50. As Robert Creeley once told Burton Hatlen, "Oh yes, the sentence, that's what we call it when we put someone in jail."

51. Matthews, *John Keats: The Critical Heritage*, 105.

52. For a different reading of the trace in Keats, one sensitive to the structure of the trace in the writing of Jacques Derrida, see Karen Swann's *Lives of the Dead Poets*, especially the first chapter, "Tracing Keats" (29–52).

53. One can certainly cite many examples of such moments in the body of criticism surrounding Keats, and examples are not limited to it. But Keats's poems do seem particularly effective in this regard. William Keach begins his essay "Cockney Couplets:

Keats and the Politics of Style" with a similar echo: "The focus of this paper—Keats's couplet writing in the Poems of 1817 and in *Endymion* of 1818—may seem less than inviting if you take the *dim* view of this poetry that still prevails" (182, my emphasis). The "music of the name" *Endymion* reverberates across the dash with the "dim" view of Keats's poetry that prevails.

54. In her article on Keats's experiential beginnings, Helen Vendler discusses Keats's major odes with the exception of "Ode to Psyche" and "Ode on Indolence." In his response to Vendler's essay, Christopher R. Miller discusses "Ode to Psyche" at some length. "Ode on Indolence," however, remains absent from these discussions that privilege what can be experienced as a beginning.

55. Keats, *Complete Poems*, 284, lines 11–12.

56. *A Hopkins Reader*, 237.

57. Forest Pyle, *Art's Undoing: In the Wake of a Radical Aestheticism* (New York: Fordham University Press, 2014), 72.

58. Pyle, *Art's Undoing*, 68. I also have in mind arguments from Robert Kaufman and Emily See. See Robert Kaufman, "Negatively Capable Dialectics: Keats, Vendler, Adorno, and the Theory of the Avant-Garde," *Critical Inquiry* 27, no. 2 (Winter 2001): 354–84; and Emily Sun, "Facing Keats with Winnicott: On the New Therapeutics of Poetry," *Studies in Romanticism* 46, no. 1 (Spring 2007): 57–75.

59. See also Daniel P. Watkins, *Keats's Poetry and the Politics of the Imagination* (London and Toronto: Fairleigh Dickinson University Press, 1989). Watkins argues that Keats's poetry is political "from the beginning" (22), as if beginning itself conditioned the possibility of Keats's political poetry.

6. The Grammar of Romanticism: Shelley's Prepositions

1. Michel Serres, *The Natural Contract*, trans. Elizabeth MacArthur and William Paulson (Ann Arbor, MI: University of Michigan Press, 1995).

2. Timothy Morton offers a compelling account of what he calls the entangling mesh in *The Ecological Thought* (Cambridge, MA: Harvard University Press, 2012). On the figure of entanglement, see also Andrew Warren, " 'Incomprehensible Contextures': Laurence Sterne and David Hume on Entanglement," *Studies in English Literature* 59, no. 3 (Summer 2019): 581–603.

3. Frédéric Neyrat, *The Unconstructable Earth: An Ecology of Separation*, trans. Drew S. Burk (New York: Fordham University Press, 2018), 14.

4. Christopher Ricks, "William Wordsworth 2: 'A Sinking Inward into Ourselves from Thought to Thought,'" in *The Force of Poetry* (Oxford University Press, 1984): 117–34, 120. See also John Hollander, "Of *of*: The Poetics of a Preposition," in *The Work of Poetry* (New York: Columbia University Press, 1997), 96–110. For a related discussion of the preposition *along* in Wordsworth, see Anne-Lise François, "Passing Impasse," *Comparative Literature* 72, no. 2 (2020): 240–57.

5. Marjorie Levinson, *Thinking through Poetry: Field Reports on Romantic Lyric* (Oxford, UK: Oxford University Press, 2018), 236.

6. Jan Mieszkowski, *Crises of the Sentence* (Chicago, IL: University of Chicago Press, 2019), 23.

7. Robert Lowth, *A Short Introduction to English Grammar* (Mension, UK: The Scolar Press Limited, 1969), 91.

8. Abraham Lincoln, *Lincoln Speeches*, ed. Allen C. Guelzo (New York: Penguin, 2012), 149.

9. Richard Beeman, ed., *Declaration of Independence and the United States Constitution* (New York: Penguin, 2012), 1.

10. Kristina Mendicino, "Of Rights, in Other Directions—Romantic Prepositions," *MLN* 133, no. 5 (December 2018): 1143–52, 1146. An early version of my chapter appeared in this special issue of *MLN* as "Shelley, among Other Things," and I thank Kristina for her helpful and inspired suggestions. Other essays in the issue by Jan Mieszkowski, Lauren Schachter, Kristina Mendicino, and Zachary Sng have greatly influenced my understanding of prepositions.

11. For an in-depth discussion of *among* see Seth Lindstromberg, *English Prepositions Explained: Revised Edition* (Amsterdam: John Benjamins, 2010); Andrea Tyler, *The Semantics of English Prepositions: Spatial Scenes, Embodied Meaning, and Cognition* (Cambridge, UK: Cambridge University Press, 2003); Elizabeth O'Dowd, *Prepositions and Particles in English* (Oxford, UK: Oxford University Press, 1998); C. Zelinsky-Wibbelt, *Semantics of Prepositions* (Berlin: Mouton de Gruyter, 1993).

12. Beeman, ed., *Declaration of Independence and the United States Constitution*, 2.

13. "Le but de toute association politique est la conservation des droits naturels et imprescriptibles de l'Homme. Ces droits sont la liberté, la propriété, la sûreté, et la résistance à l'oppression" (Baron F. M. Van Asbeck, ed., *The Universal Declaration of Human Rights and Its Predecessors (1679–1948)* (Leiden, NL: E. J. Brill, 1949), 49.

14. On the power of names, see Adam Rosenthal, "The Gift of the Name in Shelley's 'Hymn to Intellectual Beauty,'" *Studies in Romanticism* 55, no. 1 (Spring 2016): 29–50.

15. Percy Bysshe Shelley, *Shelley's Poetry and Prose*, 2nd ed., ed. Donald H. Reiman and Neil Fraistat (New York: W. W. Norton & Company, 2002), 93, lines 1–4.

16. Carol Jacobs, "On Looking at Shelley's Medusa," *Yale French Studies* 69 (1985), 171. See also William Keach, *Shelley's Style* (New York: Methuen, 1984): "What is most arresting about the stanza is the way in which its entire figurative progression enacts the vanishing of an impalpable 'Power' named in the first three lines" (120).

17. Forest Pyle, *Art's Undoing: In the Wake of a Radical Aestheticism* (New York: Fordham University Press, 2014), 33.

18. Shelley, *Shelley's Poetry and Prose*, 94, lines 13 and 15.

19. Shelley, *Shelley's Poetry and Prose*, 95, lines 61–62 and 78–81.

20. Shelley, *Shelley's Poetry and Prose*, 300–1, lines 63–67.

21. P. B. Shelley, *Shelley's Prose, or The Trumpet of a Prophecy*, ed. David Lee Clark (Albuquerque, NM: University of New Mexico Press, 1954), 297.

22. Forest Pyle, *Art's Undoing*, 47. On kindling, especially as communion, see also Deborah Elise White, *Romantic Returns: Superstition, Imagination, History* (Palo Alto, CA: Stanford University Press, 2000), 133–41.

23. Shelley, *Shelley's Poetry and Prose*, 305, lines 46–50.

24. For a fuller discussion of scatter and scattering and its political implications, see Geoffrey Bennington, *Scatter 1* (New York: Fordham University Press, 2016).

25. Denis Donoghue, *Metaphor* (Cambridge, MA: Harvard University Press, 2014), 86.

26. Donoghue, *Metaphor*, 95.

27. Shelley, *Shelley's Poetry and Prose*, 535.

28. Marc Redfield, *The Politics of Aesthetics: Nationalism, Gender, Romanticism* (Palo Alto, CA: Stanford University Press, 2003), 170.

29. Kir Kuiken, *Imagined Sovereignties: Toward a New Political Romanticism* (New York: Fordham University Press, 2014), 207.

30. Barbara Johnson, *A World of Difference* (Baltimore, MD: Johns Hopkins University Press, 1987), 188.

31. Shelley, *Shelley's Poetry and Prose*, 300, line 65.

32. Shelley, *Shelley's Poetry and Prose*, 300, line 63.

33. Jacques Khalip, *Last Things: Disastrous Form from Kant to Hujar* (New York: Fordham University Press, 2018), 75. Amanda Jo Goldstein, *Sweet Science: Romantic Materialism and the New Logics of Life* (Chicago, IL: University of Chicago Press, 2017), 138. As a testament to the poem's continued force, *Romantic Circles* recently published a Praxis volume, *The Futures of Shelley's Triumph* (October 2019), ed. Joel Faflak, that features many sensitive readings of the poem by Khalip, Elizabeth Fay, Forest Pyle, Chris Washington, and Orrin N. C. Wang. For background and fuller elaboration, see also Faflak, "The Difficult Education of Shelley's 'The Triumph of Life,'" *Keats-Shelley Journal* 58 (2009), 53–78. See also the concluding section of Pyle's "'A Light More Dread Than Obscurity': Spelling and Kindling in Percy Bysshe Shelley," in *Art's Undoing*, 57–66, and the third chapter of Pyle's earlier *The Ideology of Imagination: Subject and Society in the Discourse of Romanticism* (Palo Alto, CA: Stanford University Press, 1995). See also the second chapter of Orrin N. C. Wang's *Fantastic Modernity: Dialectical Readings in Romanticism and Theory* (Baltimore, MD: Johns Hopkins University Pres, 1996).

34. Shelley, *Shelley's Poetry and Prose*, 485, line 45.

35. Shelley, *Shelley's Poetry and Prose*, 489, line 177.

36. Shelley, *Shelley's Poetry and Prose*, 489, lines 182–84.

37. As Paul de Man wonders in *The Rhetoric of Romanticism*: is the poem about the triumph of life or the triumph over life? On "of," see David Letzler, "The Problem of *Of*, the Evasions of *As*, and Other Grammatical Curiosities in Stevens' 'An Ordinary Evening in New Haven,'" *Wallace Stevens Journal* 36, no. 2 (Fall 2012): 206–24.

38. Shelley, *Shelley's Poetry and Prose*, 485, lines 47–50.

39. Shelley, *Shelley's Poetry and Prose*, 492, lines 284–85.

40. Shelley, *Shelley's Poetry and Prose*, 494, lines 347–52.

41. John Milton, *The Major Works including* Paradise Lost, ed. Stephen Orgel and Jonathan Goldberg (Oxford, UK: Oxford University Press, 2008), 426 (Book IV, lines 216–20).

42. For fuller discussion of middles and the middle, see Zachary Sng, *Middling Romanticism: Reading in the Gaps, from Kant to Ashbery* (New York: Fordham University Press, 2020). See in particular Sng's opening discussion of the etymological ties between middles, media, and mediation. On media, see Orrin N. C. Wang, *Techno-Magism: Media, Mediation, and the Cut of Romanticism* (New York: Fordham University Press, 2022). On mediation, see Kevis Goodman, *Georgic Modernity and British Romanticism: Poetry and the Mediation of History* (Cambridge, UK: Cambridge University Press, 2004), as well as her forthcoming *Pathologies of Motion*.

43. Shelley, *Shelley's Poetry and Prose*, 497, lines 460–67.

44. Shelley, *Shelley's Poetry and Prose*, 495, lines 385–86.

45. Shelley, *Shelley's Poetry and Prose*, 495, line 398.

46. Shelley, *Shelley's Poetry and Prose*, 496, line 405.

47. Paul de Man, *The Rhetoric of Romanticism* (New York: Columbia University Press, 1984), 122.

48. One might draw a line from de Man's reading of Shelley's *The Triumph of Life* to his discussion of Yeats's "Among School Children" in the opening chapter of *Allegories of Reading* (New Haven, CT: Yale University Press, 1979). While de Man never discusses the preposition "among" in any detail, some of his most famous (perhaps most infamous) interpretations involve readings of poems that figure it.

49. For more on "with-without-with," see Werner Hamacher's reading of Heidegger in *Premises: Essays on Philosophy and Literature from Kant to Celan*, trans. Peter Fenves (Palo Alto, CA: Stanford University Press, 1999), 37.

50. John Locke, *Two Treatises of Government*, ed. Peter Laslett (Cambridge, UK: Cambridge University Press, 1988), 330–31. The Academy at Dijon takes up the question of *among* when in 1754 they famously asked: "what is the origin of inequality among [*parmi*] men?" to which Rousseau responded with his second discourse.

51. Aristotle, *Politics*, trans. H. Rackham (Cambridge, MA: Harvard University Press [Loeb Classical Library], 1998), 11. "kaí próteron dé tí fýsei pólis í oikía kaí ékastos imón estin" (I.i.12). Aristotle uses "before" (próteron).

52. Hannah Arendt, *The Human Condition*, 2nd ed. (Chicago, IL: University of Chicago Press, 1998), 7–8. On *inter* see also Geoffrey Bennington, "Inter," in *Post-Theory: New Directions in Criticism*, ed. Martin McQuillan (Edinburgh, UK: Edinburgh University Press, 1999).

53. For a valuable rethinking of sovereignty along these lines, see Kuiken's *Imagined Sovereignties*: "Romanticism . . . bears witness to a sovereignty that ceases to be itself the moment it is created" (8).

54. See Walter Benjamin, *Illuminations: Essays and Reflections*, ed. Hannah Arendt (New York: Schocken Books, 1969): "The crowd—no subject was more entitled to the attention of nineteenth century writers" (166). On the relationship between crowds and bodies, see Erin M. Goss, *Revealing Bodies: Anatomy, Allegory, and the Grounds of Knowledge in the Eighteenth Century* (Lewisburg, PA: Bucknell University Press, 2013), 36–38.

55. For more on this aspect of Shelley's writing, see Stuart Peterfreund, *Shelley among Others: The Play of the Intertext and the Idea of Language* (Baltimore, MD: Johns Hopkins University Press, 2002). Peterfreund does not foreground the question of prepositions quite as explicitly as I do in this chapter, but Peterfreund's study was important to my conceptualization of the question. For a related discussion of the ways Romantic texts test the limits of the individual and develop ideas of corporate or collective personhood, see Daniel M. Stout, *Corporate Romanticism: Liberalism, Justice, and the Novel* (New York: Fordham University Press, 2017). For a discussion of how aesthetic discourse both founds and challenges Romantic notions of the individual, see Frances Ferguson, *Solitude and the Sublime: Romanticism and the Aesthetics of Individuation* (New York: Routledge, 1992).

56. See Jacques Khalip, *Anonymous Life: Romanticism and Dispossession* (Palo Alto, CA:

Stanford University Press, 2008). We often equate romanticism with the development of the expressive, bourgeois individual, but as Khalip writes: "There can be no self without selves, no sense of the one without the many, of the individual outside the group" (6). For this reason, as Khalip discovers in the writing of William Hazlitt, the self "is but a particular of the more general 'ourselves,' lost in a crowd of other selves" (6).

57. Judith Butler, *Notes toward a Performative Theory of Assembly* (Cambridge, MA: Harvard University Press, 2015), 8.

58. Butler, *Notes*, 27.

Conclusion

1. On the double meaning of "determination," see Raymond Williams, *Marxism and Literature* (Oxford, UK: Oxford University Press, 1977), 83–89. For a discussion of Williams and how poetry mediates history, especially the very idea of the "here and now," see Kevis Goodman, *Georgic Modernity and British Romanticism: Poetry and the Mediation of History* (Cambridge, UK: Cambridge University Press, 2004), 6–8.

2. William McGurn, "Is Majoring in English Worth It?" *The Wall Street Journal*, September 9, 2019.

3. Hayden White, "The Suppression of Rhetoric in the Nineteenth Century," in *The Fiction of Narrative: Essays on History, Literature, and Theory, 1957–2007* (Baltimore, MD: Johns Hopkins University Press, 2010): 293–303.

4. Richard Arum and Josipa Roksa, *Academically Adrift: Limited Learning on College Campuses* (Chicago, IL: University of Chicago Press, 2010), 35–36.

5. Christopher Newfield, *The Great Mistake: How We Wrecked Public Universities and How We Can Fix Them* (Baltimore, MD: Johns Hopkins University Press, 2016), 261.

6. Newfield, *Great Mistake*, 261.

7. Newfield, *Great Mistake*, 300–1.

Bibliography

Abrams, M. H. *The Correspondent Breeze: Essays on English Romanticism*. New York: W. W. Norton & Company, 1984.

Adams, Michael G. "Missouri Compromise: Did the Posthumous Election of Mel Carnahan and Subsequent Appointment of Jean Carnahan Compromise Federal or State Law?" *Northern Kentucky Law Review* 29, no. 3 (2002): 433–54.

Addison, Joseph, and Sir Richard Steele. *The Spectator*. Edited by Donald F. Bond. 5 volumes. Oxford, UK: Clarendon Press, 1965.

Adorno, Theodor W. *Negative Dialectics*. Translated by E. B. Ashton. New York: Bloomsbury, 2007.

Alford, Lucy. *Forms of Poetic Attention*. New York: Columbia University Press, 2020.

Alighieri, Dante. *The Divine Comedy of Dante Alighieri*. Translated by Allen Mandelbaum. Berkeley, CA: University of California Press, 1982.

Allewaert, Monique. *Ariel's Ecology: Personhood and Colonialism in the American Tropics, 1760–1820*. Minneapolis, MN: University of Minnesota Press, 2013.

Altieri, Charles. *Wallace Stevens and the Demands of Modernity: Toward a Phenomenology of Value*. Ithaca, NY: Cornell University Press, 2013.

Arendt, Hannah. *The Human Condition*. 2nd ed. Chicago, IL: University of Chicago Press, 1998.

———. *On Revolution*. New York: Penguin, 1990.

Aristotle. *On Rhetoric*. Translated by George A. Kennedy. Oxford, UK: Oxford University Press, 1991.

———. *Politics*. Translated by H. Rackham. Loeb Classical Library. Cambridge, MA: Harvard University Press, 1932.

Arum, Richard, and Josipa Roksa. *Academically Adrift: Limited Learning on College Campuses*. Chicago, IL: University of Chicago Press, 2010.

"Ashcroft Is Pro-Life, but Voters Were Pro-Dead." *Toronto Star*. January 21, 2001.

Balfour, Ian. "Figures in Excess and the Matter of Inversion in the Discourse of the Sublime." *ELH* 84, no. 2 (Summer 2017): 315–37.

———. "Torso: (The) Sublime Sex, Beautiful Bodies, and the Matter of the Text." *Eighteenth-Century Studies* 39, no. 3 (Spring 2008): 323–36.

Barrell, John. *English Literature in History, 1730–80: An Equal, Wide Survey*. New York: St. Martin's Press, 1983.

Baudelaire, Charles. *Œuvres complètes*. Edited by Claude Pichois. Volume 2. Paris: Gallimard, 1976.

———. *The Painter of Modern Life and Other Essays*. Translated by Jonathan Mayne. London: Phaidon Press, 1995.

Beeman, Richard, ed. *Declaration of Independence and the United States Constitution*. New York: Penguin, 2012.

Benedict, Barbara. "Encounters with the Object: Advertisements, Time and Literary Discourse in the Early 18th-Century Thing-Poem." *Eighteenth-Century Studies* 40, no. 2 (2007): 193–207.

Benjamin, Walter. *The Arcades Project.* Translated by Howard Eiland and Kevin McLaughlin. Cambridge, MA: Harvard University Press, 1999.

———. *Illuminations: Essays and Reflections.* Edited by Hannah Arendt. New York: Schocken Books, 1969.

Bennett, Andrew. *Romantic Poetry and the Culture of Posterity.* Cambridge, UK: Cambridge University Press, 1998.

Bennington, Geoffrey. "Inter." In *Post-Theory: New Directions in Criticism*, edited by Martin McQuillan, 103–19. Edinburgh, UK: Edinburgh University Press, 1999.

———. *Scatter I: The Politics of Politics in Foucault, Heidegger, and Derrida.* New York: Fordham University Press, 2016.

Bergmann, J. R. "Veiled Morality: Notes on Discretion in Psychiatry." In *Talk at Work: Interaction in Institutional Settings*, edited by Paul Drew and John Heritage, 137–62. Cambridge, UK: Cambridge University Press, 1993.

Berlant, Lauren. *Cruel Optimism.* Durham, NC: Duke University Press, 2011.

Bernstein, Charles. *Attack of the Difficult Poems: Essays and Inventions.* Chicago, IL: University of Chicago Press, 2011.

Bloom, Harold. *Wallace Stevens: The Poems of Our Climate.* Ithaca, NY: Cornell University Press, 1977.

Boltanski, Luc, and Eve Chiapello, *The New Spirit of Capitalism.* Translated by Gregory Elliott. New York: Verso, 2005.

Broglio, Ron. *Beasts of Burden: Biopolitics, Labor, and Animal Life in British Romanticism.* Albany, NY: SUNY Press, 2017.

Brooke, Stopford A. *Studies in Poetry.* London: Duckworth and Company, 1907.

Brooks, Cleanth. "Wordsworth and Human Suffering." In *From Sensibility to Romanticism: Essays Presented to Frederick A. Pottle*, edited by Frederick W. Hilles and Harold Bloom, 373–87. New York: Oxford University Press, 1965.

Brown, Wendy. "We Are All Democrats Now." In *Democracy in What State?*, 44–57. New York: Columbia University Press, 2011.

Burkett, Andrew. *Romantic Mediation: Media Theory and British Romanticism.* Albany, NY: SUNY Press, 2016.

Burt, Stephanie. *Don't Read Poetry: A Book about How to Read Poems.* New York: Basic Books, 2019.

Butler, Judith. *Notes Toward a Performative Theory of Assembly.* Cambridge, MA: Harvard University Press, 2015.

Caruth, Cathy. *Empirical Truths and Critical Fictions.* Baltimore, MD: Johns Hopkins University Press, 1991.

———. *Literature in the Ashes of History.* Baltimore, MD: Johns Hopkins University Press, 2013.

———. *Unclaimed Experience: Trauma, Narrative, and History.* Baltimore, MD: Johns Hopkins University Press, 1996.

Castronovo, Russ. *Necro Citizenship: Death, Eroticism, and the Public Sphere in the Nineteenth-Century United States.* Durham, NC: Duke University Press, 2001.

Chander, Manu Samriti. *Brown Romantics: Poetry and Nationalism in the Global Nineteenth Century*. Lewisburg, PA: Bucknell University Press, 2017.

Chandler, David. "Wordsworth versus Malthus: The Political Context(s) of 'The Old Cumberland Beggar.'" *The Charles Lamb Bulletin* 155 (July 2001): 72–85.

Chandler, James. *England in 1819: The Politics of Literary Culture and the Case of Romantic Historicism*. Chicago, IL: University of Chicago Press, 1998.

Chase, Cynthia, ed. *Romanticism*. New York: Longman, 1993.

Christensen, Jerome. *Romanticism at the End of History*. Baltimore, MD: Johns Hopkins University Press, 2004.

Clark, David L., and Jacques Khalip, eds. *Minimal Romanticism*. Romantic Praxis Series, 2016. https://romantic-circles.org/praxis/brevity.

Clifton, Lucille. *The Collected Poems of Lucille Clifton 1965–2010*. Edited by Kevin Young and Michael S. Glaser. Rochester, NY: BOA Editions, 2012.

Collings, David. *Disastrous Subjectivities: Romanticism, Modernity, and the Real*. Toronto: University of Toronto Press, 2019.

———. *Wordsworthian Errancies: The Poetics of Cultural Dismemberment*. Baltimore, MD: Johns Hopkins University Press, 1994.

Colvin, Geoff. *The Upside of the Downturn: Ten Management Strategies to Prevail in the Recession and Thrive in the Aftermath*. New York: Portfolio, 2009.

Connell, Philip. *Romanticism, Economics and the Question of "Culture."* New York: Oxford University Press, 2005.

Coole, Diane, and Samantha Frost, eds. *New Materialisms: Ontology, Agency, and Politics*. Durham, NC: Duke University Press, 2010.

Corcoran, Brendan. "Keats's Death: Toward a Posthumous Poetics," *Studies in Romanticism* 48, no. 2 (Summer 2009): 321–48.

Cox, Jeffrey N. *Poetry and Politics in the Cockney School: Keats, Shelley, Hunt and Their Circle*. Cambridge, UK: Cambridge University Press, 2004.

———. *Romanticism in the Shadow of War: Literary Culture in the Napoleonic War Years*. Cambridge, UK: Cambridge University Press, 2014.

Culler, Jonathan. *The Literary in Theory*. Palo Alto, CA: Stanford University Press, 2007.

———. *Theory of the Lyric*. Cambridge, MA: Harvard University Press, 2015.

Dawson, P. M. S. "Poetry in an Age of Revolution." In *The Cambridge Companion to British Romanticism*, edited by Stuart Curran, 48–73. Cambridge, UK: Cambridge University Press, 1993.

De Man, Paul. *Aesthetic Ideology*. Minneapolis, MN: University of Minnesota Press, 1996.

———. *Allegories of Reading*. New Haven, CT: Yale University Press, 1979.

———. *Blindness and Insight: Essays in the Rhetoric of Contemporary Criticism*. Minneapolis, MN: University of Minnesota Press, 1983.

———. *The Rhetoric of Romanticism*. New York: Columbia University Press, 1984.

De Quincey, Thomas. *Reminiscences of the English Lake Poets*. London: J. M. Dent, 1961.

Derrida, Jacques. *The Death Penalty, Volume 1*. Translated by Peggy Kamuf. Chicago, IL: University of Chicago Press, 2014.

———. "Passions: 'An Oblique Offering.'" In *Derrida: A Critical Reader*, edited by David Wood, 5–35. Oxford, UK: Blackwell, 1992.

———. *Rogues: Two Essays on Reason.* Translated by Pascale-Anne Brault and Michael Naas. Palo Alto, CA: Stanford University Press, 2005.

Deutsch, Helen. "Elegies in Country Churchyards: The Prospect Poem in and around the Eighteenth Century." In *The Oxford Handbook of the Elegy*, edited by Karen Weisman, 187–205. Oxford, UK: Oxford University Press, 2010.

Dick, Alex. "Poverty, Charity, Poetry: The Unproductive Labors of the 'Old Cumberland Beggar.'" *Studies in Romanticism* 39, no. 3 (2000): 365–96.

Dimock, Wai Chee. "A Theory of Resonance." *PMLA* 112, no. 5 (1997): 1060–71.

Donoghue, Denis. *Metaphor.* Cambridge, MA: Harvard University Press, 2014.

"Downturn, Start Up: The Effects of Recessions on Entrepreneurs and Managers Run Deep." *The Economist.* January 7, 2012.

Dworkin, Craig, and Kenneth Goldsmith, eds. *Against Expression: An Anthology of Conceptual Writing.* Evanston, IL: Northwestern University Press, 2011.

Elfenbein, Andrew. *Romanticism and the Rise of English.* Palo Alto, CA: Stanford University Press, 2009.

Faflak, Joel. "The Difficult Education of Shelley's 'The Triumph of Life.'" *Keats-Shelley Journal* 58 (2009): 53–78.

———, ed. *The Futures of Shelley's* Triumph. Romantic Circles Praxis Series. October 2019. https://romantic-circles.org/praxis/triumph.

Fairer, David. *English Poetry of the Eighteenth Century 1700–1789.* New York: Routledge, 2014.

Favret, Mary. *War at a Distance: Romanticism and the Making of Modern Wartime.* Princeton, NJ: Princeton University Press, 2009.

Feder, Rachel. "The Poetic Limit: Mathematics, Aesthetics, and the Crisis of Infinity." *ELH* 81, no. 1 (Spring 2014): 167–195.

Felski, Rita. "Context Stinks!" *New Literary History* 42, no. 4 (Autumn 2011): 573–91.

———. *The Limits of Critique.* Chicago, IL: University of Chicago Press, 2015.

Ferguson, Frances. *Solitude and the Sublime: Romanticism and the Aesthetics of Individuation.* New York: Routledge, 1992.

Ferguson, Margaret, Mary Jo Salter, and Jon Stallworthy, eds. *The Norton Anthology of Poetry*, 5th edition. New York: W. W. Norton & Company, 2005.

Flint, Christopher. "Speaking Objects: The Circulation of Stories in Eighteenth-Century Prose Fiction." *PMLA* 113, no. 2 (March 1998): 212–26.

Ford, Thomas H. *Wordsworth and the Poetics of Air.* Cambridge, UK: Cambridge University Press, 2018.

Foucault, Michel. *"Society Must Be Defended": Lectures at the Collège de France 1975–1976.* New York: Picador, 2003.

———. "What Is Enlightenment." In *The Foucault Reader*, edited by Paul Rabinow, 32–50. New York: Pantheon, 1984.

François, Anne-Lise. "'The Feel of Not to Feel It,' or the Pleasures of Enduring Form." In *A Companion to Romantic Poetry*, edited by Charles Mahoney, 443–66. Oxford, UK: Blackwell Publishing, 2012.

———. *Open Secrets: The Literature of Uncounted Experience.* Palo Alto, CA: Stanford University Press, 2007.

———. "Passing Impasse." *Comparative Literature* 72, no. 2 (2020): 240–57.

Freud, Sigmund. *Beyond the Pleasure Principle*. Edited by James Strachey. New York: W. W. Norton & Company, 1990.

Fuss, Diana. *Dying Modern: A Meditation on Elegy*. Durham, NC: Duke University Press, 2013.

Galperin, William H. *The History of Missed Opportunities: British Romanticism and the Emergence of the Everyday*. Palo Alto, CA: Stanford University Press, 2017.

Gigante, Denise. *Life: Organic Form and Romanticism*. New Haven, CT: Yale University Press, 2009.

Goldberg, Jonathan, and Madhavi Menon. "Queering History." *PMLA* 120, no .5 (Oct. 2005): 1608–17.

Goldsmith, Kenneth. *Uncreative Writing: Managing Language in the Digital Age*. New York: Columbia University Press, 2011.

Goldstein, Amanda Jo. *Sweet Science: Romantic Materialism and the New Logics of Life*. Chicago, IL: University of Chicago Press, 2017.

Goodman, Kevis. *Georgic Modernity and British Romanticism: Poetry and the Mediation of History*. Cambridge, UK: Cambridge University Press, 2004.

———. *Pathologies of Motion: Medicine, Aesthetics, Poetics*. New Haven, CT: Yale University Press, forthcoming.

Goss, Erin M. *Revealing Bodies: Anatomy, Allegory, and the Grounds of Knowledge in the Eighteenth Century*. Lewisburg, PA: Bucknell University Press, 2013.

Gottlieb, Evan. *Romantic Globalism: British Literature and the Modern World Order, 1750–1830*. Columbus, OH: The Ohio State University Press, 2014.

———. *Romantic Realities: Speculative Realism and British Romanticism*. Edinburgh, UK: Edinburgh University Press, 2016.

Griffiths, Devin. *The Age of Analogy: Science and Literature Between the Darwins*. Baltimore, MD: Johns Hopkins University Press, 2016.

Gurton-Wachter, Lily. *Watchwords: Romanticism and the Poetics of Attention*. Palo Alto, CA: Stanford University Press, 2016.

Guyer, Sara. *Reading with John Clare: Biopoetics, Sovereignty, Romanticism*. New York: Fordham University Press, 2015.

———. *Romanticism After Auschwitz*. Palo Alto, CA: Stanford University Press, 2007.

Hamacher, Werner. *Premises: Essays on Philosophy and Literature from Kant to Celan*. Translated by Peter Fenves. Palo Alto, CA: Stanford University Press, 1999.

Harrison, Gary. *Wordsworth's Vagrant Muse: Poetry, Poverty, and Power*. Detroit, MI: Wayne State University Press, 1994.

Hartman, Geoffrey. *Beyond Formalism: Literary Essays, 1958–1970*. New Haven, CT: Yale University Press, 1970.

———. *The Fate of Reading*. Chicago, IL: University of Chicago Press, 1975.

———. *The Unremarkable Wordsworth*. Minneapolis, MN: University of Minnesota Press, 1987.

———. *Wordsworth's Poetry, 1787–1814*. New Haven, CT: Yale University Press, 1971.

Hoffman-Schwartz, Daniel. "'Rapt Auditors!': Burke and the Revision of Rhetorical Violence in Wordsworth's *The Prelude*." *European Romantic Review* 30, no. 3 (2019): 297–306.

Holladay, Hilary. *Wild Blessings: The Poetry of Lucille Clifton*. Baton Rouge, LA: Louisiana State University Press, 2004.

Holland, Sharon Patricia. *Raising the Dead: Readings of Death and (Black) Subjectivity*. Durham, NC: Duke University Press, 2000.

Hollander, John. "Of *of*: The Poetics of a Preposition." In *The Work of Poetry*, 96–110. New York: Columbia University Press, 1997.

Hollander, Lee M. "Litotes in Old Norse." *PMLA* 53, no. 1 (March, 1938): 1–33.

Holsinger, Bruce, and Andrew Stauffer, "Romanticism, Now & Then: An Introduction." *New Literary History* 49, no. 4 (Autumn 2018): v–xi.

Hopkins, Gerard Manley. *A Hopkins Reader*. Edited by John Pick. New York: Doubleday, 1966.

Hu, Tung-Hui. *A Prehistory of the Cloud*. Cambridge, MA: MIT Press, 2016.

Hunt, Alastair, and Matthias Rudolf, "Introduction: The Romantic Rhetoric of Life." In *Romanticism and Biopolitics*, edited by Alastair Hunt and Matthias Rudolf. Romantic Circles Praxis Series (December 2012). https://romantic-circles.org/praxis/bio politics/HTML/praxis.2012.hunt-rudolf.html.

Hunt, Lynn. "Against Presentism." Perspectives on History (May, 2002). https://www .historians.org/publications-and-directories/perspectives-on-history/may-2002 /against-presentism.

Hunter, Walt. *Forms of a World: Contemporary Poetry and the Making of Globalization*. New York: Fordham University Press, 2019.

Igarashi, Yohei. *The Connected Condition: Romanticism and the Dream of Communication*. Palo Alto, CA: Stanford University Press, 2019.

Jackson, Virginia. "Historical Poetics and the Dream of Interpretation: A Response to Paul Fry." *Modern Language Quarterly* 81, no. 3 (September 2020): 289–318.

Jackson, Virginia, and Yopie Prins, eds. *The Lyric Theory Reader: A Critical Anthology*. Baltimore, MD: Johns Hopkins University Press, 2014.

Jacobs, Carol. "On Looking at Shelley's Medusa." *Yale French Studies* 69 (1985):163–79.

Jacobus, Mary. "Apostrophe and Lyric Voice in *The Prelude*." In *Lyric Poetry: Beyond New Criticism*, edited by Chavia Hošek and Patricia Parker, 167–81. Ithaca, NY: Cornell University Press, 1985.

———. *Romantic Things: A Tree, A Rock, A Cloud*. Chicago, IL: University of Chicago Press, 2012.

James, C. L. R. *The Black Jacobins: Toussaint L'Ouverture and the San Domingo Revolution*. 2nd edition. New York: Vintage Books, 1989.

Jameson, Fredric. *The Political Unconscious: Narrative as a Socially Symbolic Act*. Ithaca, NY: Cornell University Press, 1981.

Jarrell, Randall. *Little Friend, Little Friend*. New York: Dial Press, 1945.

Johnson, Barbara. *The Critical Difference: Essays in the Contemporary Rhetoric of Reading*. Baltimore, MD: Johns Hopkins University Press, 1985.

———. *The Feminist Difference*. Cambridge, MA: Harvard University Press, 1998.

———. *Persons and Things*. Cambridge, MA: Harvard University Press, 2008.

———. *A World of Difference*. Baltimore, MD: Johns Hopkins University Press, 1987.

Johnson, Christopher D. *Hyperboles: The Rhetoric of Excess in Baroque Literature and Thought*. Cambridge, MA: Harvard University Press, 2010.

Jones, John. *The Egotistical Sublime*. London: Chatto and Windus, 1954.

Juengel, Scott J. "The Early Novel and Catastrophe." *Novel: A Forum on Fiction* 42, no. 3 (2009): 443–50.

Kant, Immanuel. *Critique of Judgment*. Translated by Werner S. Pluhar. Indianapolis, IN: Hackett, 1987.

———. *Political Writings*. Edited by H. S. Reiss. Cambridge, UK: Cambridge University Press, 1970.

Kaufman, Robert. "Negatively Capable Dialectics: Keats, Vendler, Adorno, and the Theory of the Avant-Garde." *Critical Inquiry* 27, no. 2 (Winter 2001): 354–84.

Keach, William. "Cockney Couplets: Keats and the Politics of Style." *Studies in Romanticism* 25, no. 2 (Summer 1986): 182–96.

———. *Shelley's Style*. New York: Methuen, 1984.

Keats, John. *Complete Poems*. Edited by Jack Stillinger. Cambridge, MA: Harvard University Press, 1978.

———. *The Letters of John Keats*. Edited by Robert Gittings. Oxford: Oxford University Press, 1970.

Keenleyside, Heather. *Animals and Other People: Literary Forms and Living Beings in the Long Eighteenth Century*. Philadelphia, PA: University of Pennsylvania Press, 2016.

Keynes, John Maynard. *The Essential Keynes*. Edited by Robert Skideslky. New York: Penguin, 2016.

Khalip, Jacques. *Anonymous Life: Romanticism and Dispossession*. Palo Alto, CA: Stanford University Press, 2008.

———. *Last Things: Disastrous Form from Kant to Hujar*. New York: Fordham University Press, 2018.

Khalip, Jacques, and David Collings, eds. *Romanticism and Disaster*. Romantic Circles Praxis Series (2012). https://romantic-circles.org/praxis/disaster/index.html.

Khalip, Jacques, and Forest Pyle. "Introduction: The Present Darkness of Romanticism." In *Constellations of a Contemporary Romanticism*, edited by Jacques Khalip and Forest Pyle, 1–16. New York: Fordham University Press, 2016.

Koehler, Margaret. *Poetry of Attention in the Eighteenth Century*. New York: Palgrave Macmillan, 2012.

Koretsky, Deanna P. *Death Rights: Romantic Suicide, Race, and the Bounds of Liberalism*. Albany, NY: SUNY Press, 2021.

Kornbluh, Anna. *Realizing Capital: Financial and Psychic Economies in Victorian Form*. New York: Fordham University Press, 2014.

Kramnick, Jonathan. *Paper Minds: Literature and the Ecology of Consciousness*. Chicago, IL: University of Chicago Press, 2018.

Kuiken, Kir. *Imagined Sovereignties: Toward a New Political Romanticism*. New York: Fordham University Press, 2014.

Lamb, Jonathan. *The Things Things Say*. Princeton, NJ: Princeton University Press, 2011.

Langan, Celeste. *Romantic Vagrancy: Wordsworth and the Right to Wander*. Cambridge, UK: Cambridge University Press, 1995.

Langan, Celeste, and Maureen N. McLane. "The Medium of Romantic Poetry." In *The Cambridge Companion to British Romantic Poetry*, edited by James Chandler and Maureen N. McLane, 239–62. Cambridge, UK: Cambridge University Press, 2008.

Latour, Bruno. *Pandora's Hope: Essays on the Reality of Science Studies*. Cambridge, MA: Harvard University Press, 1999.

———. *We Have Never Been Modern*. Translated by Catherine Porter. Cambridge, MA: Harvard University Press, 1993.

———. "Why Has Critique Run Out of Steam? From Matters of Fact to Matters of Concern." *Critical Inquiry* 30, no. 2 (Winter 2004): 225–48.

Lerner, Ben. *The Hatred of Poetry*. New York: Farrar, Straus and Giroux, 2016.

Letzler, David. "The Problem of *Of*, the Evasions of *As*, and Other Grammatical Curiosities in Stevens' 'An Ordinary Evening in New Haven.'" *Wallace Stevens Journal* 36, no. 2 (Fall 2012): 206–24.

Levine, Caroline. *Forms: Whole, Rhythm, Hierarchy, Network*. Princeton, NJ: Princeton University Press, 2015.

Levinson, Marjorie. *Keats's Life of Allegory: The Origins of a Style*. Oxford, UK: Basil Blackwell, 1988.

———. *Thinking through Poetry: Field Reports on Romantic Lyric*. Oxford, UK: Oxford University Press, 2019.

———. *Wordsworth's Great Period Poems*. Cambridge, UK: Cambridge University Press, 1984.

Lezra, Jacques. *On the Nature of Marx's Things: Translating as Necrophilology*. New York: Fordham University Press, 2018.

Lincoln, Abraham. *Lincoln Speeches*. Edited by Allen C. Guelzo. New York: Penguin, 2012.

Lindstrom, Eric. *Romantic Fiat: Demystification and Enchantment in Lyric Poetry*. New York: Palgrave Macmillan, 2011.

———. "What Wordsworth Planted." *Romanticism and Victorianism on the Net* 56 (November 2009). https://www.erudit.org/en/journals/ravon/2009-n56-ravon1503285/1001093ar/.

Lindstromberg, Seth. *English Prepositions Explained: Revised Edition*. Amsterdam: John Benjamins, 2010.

Lipking, Lawrence. *The Life of the Poet: Beginning and Ending Poetic Careers*. Chicago, IL: The University of Chicago Press, 1981.

Liu, Alan. *The Laws of Cool: Knowledge Work and the Culture of Information*. Chicago, IL: University of Chicago Press, 2004

Locke, John. *Two Treatises of Government*. Edited by Peter Laslett. Cambridge, UK: Cambridge University Press, 1988.

Lowth, Robert. *A Short Introduction to English Grammar* (1762). Reprint. Mension, UK: The Scolar Press Limited, 1969.

Lupton, Christina. *Knowing Books: The Consciousness of Mediation in Eighteenth-Century Britain*. Philadelphia, PA: University of Pennsylvania Press, 2011.

Lupton, Mary Jane. *Lucille Clifton: Her Life and Letters*. Westport, CT: Praeger, 2006.

Lynch, Deidre Shauna. *Loving Literature: A Cultural History*. Chicago, IL: University of Chicago Press, 2015.

Makdisi, Saree. *Romantic Imperialism: Universal Empire and the Culture of Modernity*. Cambridge, UK: Cambridge University Press, 1998.

Marcus, Sharon, Heather Love, and Stephen Best, eds. "Description Across Disciplines." A special issue of *Representations* 135 (Summer 2016).

Matthews, G. M., ed. *John Keats: The Critical Heritage*. London: Routledge & Kegan Paul, 1971.

Mbembe, Achille. *Necropolitics*. Durham, NC: Duke University Press, 2019.

McCarthy, Anne. *Awful Parenthesis: Suspension and the Sublime in Romantic and Victorian Poetry*. Toronto: University of Toronto Press, 2018.

———. "Reading the Red Bull Sublime." *PMLA* 132, no. 3 (2017): 543–57.

McGann, Jerome. "Keats and the Historical Method in Criticism." *Modern Language Notes* 94, no. 5 (1979): 988–1032.

———. *The Romantic Ideology: A Critical Investigation*. Chicago, IL: University of Chicago Press, 1983.

McGurn, William. "Is Majoring in English Worth It?" *The Wall Street Journal*. September 9, 2019.

McLaughlin, Kevin. *Paperwork: Fiction and Mass Mediacy in the Paper Age*. Philadelphia, PA: University of Pennsylvania Press, 2005.

———. *Poetic Force: Poetry after Kant*. Palo Alto, CA: Stanford University Press, 2014.

McLane, Maureen N. "Romanticism, or Now: Learning to Read in Postmodern." *Modern Philology* 105, no. 1 (August 2007): 118–56.

Melas, Natalie. "Untimeliness, or Négritude and the Poetics of Contramodernity." *South Atlantic Quarterly* 108, no. 3 (Summer 2009): 563–80.

Mendicino, Kristina. "Of Rights, in Other Directions—Romantic Prepositions." *MLN* 133, no. 5 (December 2018): 1143–52.

Menely, Tobias. *The Animal Claim: Sensibility and the Creaturely Voice*. Chicago, IL: University of Chicago Press, 2015.

Mieszkowski, Jan. *Crises of the Sentence*. Chicago, IL: University of Chicago Press, 2019.

———. *Labors of Imagination: Aesthetics and Political Economy from Kant to Althusser*. New York: Fordham University Press, 2006.

———. *Watching War*. Palo Alto, CA: Stanford University Press, 2012.

Miller, Christopher R. *Surprise: The Poetics of the Unexpected from Milton to Austen*. Ithaca, NY: Cornell University Press, 2015.

Miller, J. Hillis. "Anachronistic Reading." *Derrida Today* 3, no. 1 (May 2010): 75–91.

Milton, John. *The Major Works including* Paradise Lost. Edited by Stephen Orgel and Jonathan Goldberg. Oxford, UK: Oxford University Press, 2008.

Mitchell, Robert. *Experimental Life: Vitalism in Romantic Science and Literature*. Baltimore, MD: Johns Hopkins University Press, 2013.

———. *Infectious Liberty: Biopolitics between Romanticism and Liberalism*. New York: Fordham University Press, 2021.

Moore, Marianne. "A Modest Expert: *North & South*." In *Elizabeth Bishop and Her Art*, edited by Lloyd Schwartz and Sybil Estess, 177–79. Ann Arbor, MI: University of Michigan Press, 1983.

Morrissey, Lee. "'Charity,' Social Control and the History of English Literary Criticism." In *Print and Power in France and England, 1500–1800*, edited by Adrian Armstrong and David Adams, 61–76. New York: Routledge, 2016.

Morton, Timothy. *The Ecological Thought*. Cambridge, MA: Harvard University Press, 2012.

Mosco, Vincent. *To the Cloud: Big Data in a Turbulent World*. New York: Routledge, 2014.

Mulrooney, Jonathan. "How Keats Falls." *Studies in Romanticism* 50, no. 2 (Summer 2011): 251–73.

Multigraph Collective, The. *Interacting with Print: Elements of Reading in the Era of Print Saturation*. Chicago, IL: University of Chicago Press, 2017.

Naimou, Angela. *Salvage Work: U.S. and Caribbean Literatures amid the Debris of Legal Personhood*. New York: Fordham University Press, 2015.

Nersessian, Anahid. *The Calamity Form: On Poetry and Social Life*. Chicago, IL: University of Chicago Press, 2020.

———. *Utopia, Limited: Romanticism and Adjustment*. Cambridge, MA: Harvard University Press, 2015.

Newfield, Christopher. *The Great Mistake: How We Wrecked Public Universities and How We Can Fix Them*. Baltimore, MD: Johns Hopkins University Press, 2016.

Neyrat, Frédéric. *The Unconstructable Earth: An Ecology of Separation*. Translated by Drew S. Burk. New York: Fordham University Press, 2018.

Norman, Brian. *Dead Women Talking: Figures of Injustice in American Literature*. Baltimore, MD: Johns Hopkins University Press, 2012.

O'Dowd, Elizabeth. *Prepositions and Particles in English*. Oxford, UK: Oxford University Press, 1998.

Olson, Charles. *Selected Writings*. Edited by Robert Creeley. New York: New Directions, 1964.

Orwell, George. *The Orwell Reader*. Edited by Richard H. Rovere. New York: Harcourt, 1984.

Passannante, Gerard. *Catastrophizing: Materialism and the Making of Disaster*. Chicago, IL: University of Chicago Press, 2019.

Patterson, Orlando. *Slavery and Social Death*. Cambridge, MA: Harvard University Press, 1982.

Pender, Patricia. *Early Modern Women's Writing and the Rhetoric of Modesty*. New York: Palgrave Macmillan, 2012.

Perelman, Chaim, and Lucie Olbrechts-Tyteca. *The New Rhetoric: A Treatise on Argumentation*. South Bend, IN: University of Notre Dame Press, 1969.

Peterfreund, Stuart. *Shelley among Others: The Play of the Intertext and the Idea of Language*. Baltimore, MD: Johns Hopkins University Press, 2002.

Peters, John Durham. *The Marvelous Clouds: Toward a Philosophy of Elemental Media*. Chicago, IL: University of Chicago Press, 2015.

Phillips, Natalie. *Distraction: Problems of Attention in Eighteenth-Century Literature*. Baltimore, MD: Johns Hopkins University Press, 2016.

Pinch, Adela. *Strange Fits of Passion: Epistemologies of Emotion, Hume to Austen*. Palo Alto, CA: Stanford University Press, 1997.

Piper, Andrew. *Dreaming in Books: The Making of the Bibliographic Imagination in the Romantic Age*. Chicago, IL: University of Chicago Press, 2009.

Plato. *The Republic*. Edited by G. R. F. Ferrari. Translated by Tom Griffith. Cambridge, UK: Cambridge University Press, 2012.

Plumly, Stanley. *Posthumous Keats: A Personal Biography*. New York: W. W. Norton & Company, 2008.

Poovey, Mary. "The Model System of Contemporary Literary Criticism." *Critical Inquiry* 27, no. 3 (Spring 2001): 408–38.

Pope, Alexander. *The Major Works*. Oxford, UK: Oxford University Press, 1993.

Posmentier, Sonya. *Cultivation and Catastrophe: The Lyric Ecology of Modern Black Litera-*
ture. Baltimore, MD: Johns Hopkins University Press, 2020.

Prins, Yopie. "What Is Historical Poetics?" *Modern Language Quarterly* 77, no. 1 (2016):
13–40.

Puttenham, George. *The Arte of English Poesie*. Edited by Frank Whigham and Wayne A.
Rebhorn. Ithaca, NY: Cornell University Press, 2007.

Pyle, Forest. *Art's Undoing: In the Wake of a Radical Aestheticism*. New York: Fordham
University Press, 2014.

———. *The Ideology of Imagination: Subject and Society in the Discourse of Romanticism*.
Palo Alto, CA: Stanford University Press, 1995.

Quintilian. *The Orator's Education*. Edited and translated by Donald A. Russell. Loeb
Classical Library. Cambridge, MA: Harvard University Press, 2001.

Ramsey, Neil, and Joshua Gooch. "Romanticism and War." A special issue of *Romanti-*
cism 24, no. 3 (October, 2018).

Rancière, Jacques. *Disagreement: Politics and Philosophy*. Translated by Julie Rose. Minneapolis, MN: University of Minnesota Press, 1998.

———. *Hatred of Democracy*. Translated by Steve Corcoran. New York: Verso, 2006.

———. *The Politics of Aesthetics*. Translated by Gabriel Rockhill. New York: Continuum,
2004.

Ransom, John Crowe. "William Wordsworth: Notes toward an Understanding of
Poetry." *The Kenyon Review* 12, no. 3 (Summer, 1950): 498–519.

Redfield, Marc. *The Politics of Aesthetics: Nationalism, Gender, Romanticism*. Palo Alto, CA:
Stanford University Press, 2003.

———. "Wordsworth's Dream of Extinction." *Qui Parle* 21, no. 1 (Spring/Summer
2013): 61–68.

Regalado, Antonio. "Who Coined 'Cloud Computing'?" *MIT Technology Review* (October 31, 2011). https://www.technologyreview.com/2011/10/31/257406/who
-coined-cloud-computing/.

Rhetorica ad Herennium. Loeb Classical Library. Cambridge, MA: Harvard University
Press, 1989.

Richardson, Valerie. "Missouri's Carnahan is first with posthumous Senate win; Opponent honors vote, but others may raise challenge." *The Washington Times* (Washington, DC), November 9, 2000.

Ricks, Christopher. "William Wordsworth 2: 'A Sinking Inward into Ourselves from
Thought to Thought.'" In *The Force of Poetry*, 117–34. Oxford, UK: Oxford University Press, 1984.

Roe, Nicholas. *John Keats and the Culture of Dissent*. Oxford, UK: Oxford University
Press, 1997.

———, ed. *Keats and History*. Cambridge, UK: Cambridge University Press, 1995.

Rohrbach, Emily. *Modernity's Mist: British Romanticism and the Poetics of Anticipation*. New
York: Fordham University Press, 2016.

Rosenthal, Adam. "The Gift of the Name in Shelley's 'Hymn to Intellectual Beauty.'"
Studies in Romanticism 55, no. 1 (Spring 2016): 29–50.

Rzepka, Charles J. "'Cortez: Or Balboa, or Somebody Like That': Form, Fact, and Forgetting in Keats's 'Chapman's Homer' Sonnet." *Keats-Shelley Journal* 51 (2002): 35–75.

Sachs, Jonathan. *The Poetics of Decline in British Romanticism*. Cambridge, UK: Cambridge University Press, 2018.

Schlegel, Friedrich. *Philosophical Fragments*. Translated by Peter Firchow. Minneapolis, MN: University of Minnesota Press, 1991.

Schmidt, Eric, and Jonathan Rosenberg. *How Google Works*. New York: Grand Central, 2014.

Serres, Michel. *The Natural Contract*. Translated by Elizabeth MacArthur and William Paulson. Ann Arbor, MI: University of Michigan Press, 1995.

Shelley, Percy Bysshe. *Shelley's Poetry and Prose*. 2nd edition. Edited by Donald H. Reiman and Neil Fraistat. New York: W. W. Norton & Company, 2002.

———. *Shelley's Prose, or The Trumpet of a Prophecy*. Edited by David Lee Clark. Albuquerque, NM: University of New Mexico Press, 1954.

Shovel, Martin. "Litotes: The Most Common Rhetorical Device You've Never Heard Of." *The Guardian*, March 26, 2015.

Simpson, David. "Criticism, Politics, and Style in Wordsworth's Poetry." *Critical Inquiry* 11, no. 1 (September 1984): 52–81.

———. *Wordsworth, Commodification, and Social Concern: The Poetics of Modernity*. Cambridge, UK: Cambridge University Press, 2009.

———. *Wordsworth's Historical Imagination: The Poetry of Displacement*. London: Methuen, 1987.

Sinykin, Dan. *American Literature and the Long Downturn: Neoliberal Apocalypse*. Oxford, UK: Oxford University Press, 2020.

Sng, Zachary. *Middling Romanticism: Reading in the Gaps from Kant to Ashbery*. New York: Fordham University Press, 2020.

Sontag, Susan. *On Photography*. New York: Picador, 1973.

———. *Regarding the Pain of Others*. New York: Picador, 2003.

Spargo, R. Clifton. *The Ethics of Mourning: Grief and Responsibility in Elegiac Literature*. Baltimore, MD: Johns Hopkins University Press, 2004.

Stark, Jared. *A Death of One's Own: Literature, Law and the Right to Die*. Evanston, IL: Northwestern University Press, 2018.

Stevens, Wallace. *The Collected Poems*. New York: Vintage, 1990.

Stout, Daniel M. *Corporate Romanticism: Liberalism, Justice, and the Novel*. New York: Fordham University Press, 2017.

Sun, Emily. "Facing Keats with Winnicott: On the New Therapeutics of Poetry." *Studies in Romanticism* 46, no. 1 (Spring 2007): 57–75.

———. *Succeeding King Lear: Literature, Exposure, and the Possibility of Politics*. New York: Fordham University Press, 2010.

Swann, Karen. "Endymion's Beautiful Dreamers." In *The Cambridge Companion to Keats*, edited by Susan J. Wolfson, 20–36. Cambridge, UK: Cambridge University Press, 2001.

———. *Lives of the Dead Poets: Keats, Shelley, Coleridge*. New York: Fordham University Press, 2019.

Terada, Rei. "After the Critique of Lyric." *PMLA* 123, no. 1 (January 2008): 195–200.

———. "Looking at the Stars Forever." *Studies in Romanticism* 50, no. 2 (Summer 2011): 275–309.

———. *Looking Away: Phenomenality and Dissatisfaction, Kant to Adorno*. Cambridge, MA: Harvard University Press, 2009.

Thompson, Derek. "A World Without Work." *The Atlantic* (July/August 2015).

Thoreau, Henry David. *Collected Essays and Poems*. New York: Library of America, 2001.

Trump, Donald J. *Great Again: How to Fix our Crippled America*. New York: Threshold Editions, 2016.

Tyler, Andrea. *The Semantics of English Prepositions: Spatial Scenes, Embodied Meaning, and Cognition*. Cambridge, UK: Cambridge University Press, 2003.

Underwood, Ted. *Why Literary Periods Mattered: Historical Contrast and the Prestige of Literary Studies*. Palo Alto, CA: Stanford University Press, 2013.

Van Asbeck, Baron F. M., ed. *The Universal Declaration of Human Rights and Its Predecessors (1679–1948)*. Leiden, NL: E. J. Brill, 1949.

Vendler, Helen. *Coming of Age as a Poet: Milton, Keats, Eliot, Plath*. Cambridge, UK: Harvard University Press, 2003.

———. "The Experiential Beginnings of Keats's Odes." *Studies in Romanticism* 12, no. 3 (Summer 1973): 591–606.

Viswanathan, Gauri. *Masks of Conquest: Literary Study and British Rule in India*. New York: Columbia University Press, 1989.

Wang, Orrin N. C. *Fantastic Modernity: Dialectical Readings in Romanticism and Theory*. Baltimore, MD: Johns Hopkins University Press, 1996.

———. *Romantic Sobriety: Sensation, Revolution, Commodification, History*. Baltimore, MD: Johns Hopkins University Press, 2011.

———. *Techno-Magism: Media, Mediation, and the Cut of Romanticism*. New York: Fordham University Press, 2022.

Warren, Andrew. "'Incomprehensible Contextures': Laurence Sterne and David Hume on Entanglement" *Studies in English Literature* 59, no. 3 (Summer 2019): 581–603.

———. *The Orient and the Young Romantics*. Cambridge, UK: Cambridge University Press, 2014.

Washington, Chris. *Romantic Revelations: Visions of Post-Apocalyptic Life and Hope in the Anthropocene*. Toronto: University of Toronto Press, 2019.

Watkins, Daniel P. *Keats's Poetry and the Politics of the Imagination*. London and Toronto: Fairleigh Dickinson University Press, 1989.

Weheliye, Alexander G. *Habeas Viscus: Racializing Assemblages, Biopolitics, and Black Feminist Theories of the Human*. Durham, NC: Duke University Press, 2014.

Welberry, Karen. "Colonial and Postcolonial Deployment of 'Daffodils.'" *Kunapipi* 19, no. 1 (1997): 32–44.

Wendorf, Richard. *William Collins and Eighteenth-Century English Poetry*. Minneapolis, MN: University of Minnesota Press, 1981.

Weyman, Carl. "Studien über die Figur der Litotes." *Jahrbücher für classische Philologie*, fünfzehnter Supplementband (1887): 453–556.

White, Deborah Elise. *Romantic Returns: Superstition, Imagination, History*. Palo Alto, CA: Stanford University Press, 2000.

White, Hayden. *The Fiction of Narrative: Essays on History, Literature, and Theory, 1957–2007*. Baltimore, MD: Johns Hopkins University Press, 2010.

Wilde, Oscar. *The Artist as Critic: Critical Writings of Oscar Wilde*. Edited by Richard Ellmann. Chicago, IL: University of Chicago Press, 1982.

Wilner, Joshua. "'Self-Displacing Vision': Snowdon and the Dialectic of the Senses." *The Wordsworth Circle* 31, no. 1 (Winter 2006): 27–30.

Wolfson, Susan J., ed. "Keats and Politics." A special issue of *Studies in Romanticism* 25, no. 2 (Summer 1986).

Wolfson, Susan J. *The Questioning Presence: Wordsworth, Keats, and the Interrogative Mode in Romantic Poetry*. Ithaca, NY: Cornell University Press, 1986.

Wordsworth, William. *The Fenwick Notes of William Wordsworth*. Edited by Jared Curtis. London, UK: Bristol Classical Press, 1993.

———. *The Major Works including* The Prelude. Edited by Stephen Gill. Oxford, UK: Oxford University Press, 2008.

———. *The Poems*. Volume one. Edited by John O. Hayden. New York: Penguin Classics, 1977.

———. *The Poems*. Volume two. Edited by John O. Hayden. New Haven, CT: Yale University Press, 1977.

———. *The Prelude, 1799, 1805, 1850*. Edited by Jonathan Wordsworth, M. H. Abrams, and Stephen Gill. New York: W. W. Norton & Company, 1979.

Wright, Richard. "Between the World and Me." In *Against Forgetting: Twentieth-Century Poetry of Witness*, edited by Carolyn Forché, 633–34. New York: W. W. Norton & Company, 1993.

Young, Kevin. *For the Confederate Dead*. New York: Knopf, 2007.

Zelinsky-Wibbelt, C. *Semantics of Prepositions*. Berlin: Mouton de Gruyter, 1993.

Žižek, Slavoj. *Looking Awry: An Introduction to Jacques Lacan through Popular Culture*. Cambridge, MA: MIT Press, 1992.

Index

Brian McGrath is Associate Professor of English at Clemson University. He is the author of *The Poetics of Unremembered Acts: Reading, Lyric, Pedagogy.*

CPSIA information can be obtained
at www.ICGtesting.com
Printed in the USA
JSHW051005060522
25615JS00001B/13